THE WEST

CONTEMPORARY RECORDS
OF AMERICA'S EXPANSION
ACROSS THE CONTINENT:
1607-1890

Edited, with an Introduction, by

BAYRD STILL

PROFESSOR OF HISTORY, NEW YORK UNIVERSITY

CAPRICORN BOOKS *New York*

To the memory of
DEE
who loved the West

In the collection of materials for this book I am indebted to the staffs of the Boston Public Library, the Library Company of Philadelphia, the New York University Library, and the New York Public Library, especially to the personnel of the American History Room, whose helpfulness and interest are a real encouragement to research. In the preparation of the manuscript for the press I have enjoyed the efficient assistance of Constance Caruso, Sara Chesner, Judy Siegel, Ethel Stern, Alexa Barni, and especially Dorothy Burke and Stanley Wasserman, whose loyal and interested services are truly appreciated. For helpful suggestions I am grateful to my good friends Helen Sheehan and Ida Gershoy, as well as to Edmund L. Epstein, editor of Capricorn Books.

[NOTE ON STYLE: A conscientious effort has been made to adhere to the original style and spelling of the documents excerpted in this book. This will explain what on occasion appear to be misspelled words and inconsistencies in editorial style in the text.]

Library of Congress Catalog Card Number: 60-11839

TABLE OF CONTENTS

ILLUSTRATIONS

INTRODUCTION

In the development of the United States no factor has been of greater significance than the existence of the West. The frontier, the wide open spaces, the pioneer—these components of the West are conspicuous threads in the pattern of the American tradition. They symbolize the concept of the United States as a land of opportunity, of social regeneration, of progress—one of the most basic and enduring ingredients of the American point of view. The popular image of today's West is often a gaudy collage of interminable highways, mountain vacationlands, gamblers' oases in the desert, and jerry-built backgrounds for motion picture epics of the plains. But for by far the greater part of the American experience the West connoted, and in a sense guaranteed, the promise of America. It suggested an ever expanding area of abundance, rich in exploitable resources, which offered material and social betterment to enterprising individuals and increasing strength and security to the nation, as westward the course of settlement made its seemingly inevitable way.

For more than three centuries the locale of the American West moved continuously westward. Homeseekers who hesitantly ventured inland in the seventeenth century created America's first West in the back country of the seaboard colonies. By the mid-eighteenth century a newer West had taken shape in the upland region between the Appalachian barrier and the falls of the rivers which flowed eastward out of its timbered heights. Already the insatiable settler was exploring the natural highways leading to another West, this one in the valley of the westward-flowing Ohio. The achievement of independence from Britain, in 1783, attracted settlers to the "Old Northwest," a term then applied to the forested region between the Ohio River and the Great Lakes. Soon the demand for cotton was encouraging migration into the initial "Southwest"; and by 1830, the vanguard of farmer-pioneers had crossed the Mississippi into Missouri, Arkansas Territory, and Louisiana, to settle the lower valleys of the Missouri River, the Arkansas, and the Red. In the next half-century, west succeeded west as migrants, traversing the trails to Oregon and California, carved out a new "Far West" along the curve of the Pacific Coast, penetrated the mining regions of the mountainous inland area, and settled the ranch and farming country of the Great Plains. Not until 1890 did it appear that settlement of the continental United States was so general as to preclude the further existence of a "frontier" and the future development of additional wests.

The persistence of the westward march was in part the consequence of the nation's continuing acquisition of territory, which periodically opened new regions for pioneering. The Mississippi River constituted the western limits of the United States in 1783; but within seventy-five years, about twice the original area had been added by purchase, annexation, conquest, and diplomacy. With the purchase of Louisiana in 1803, the boundaries of the young nation were extended from the Mississippi to the distant Rockies. Undisputed claim to the Pacific Northwest was secured in 1846, when Britain and the United States settled a boundary controversy over Oregon; and the vast Southwest was acquired through the annexation of Texas (1845), the Mexican War (1846-1848), and the Gadsden Purchase (1853). By such territorial windfalls more than two million square miles of additional land surface became available to migrating America.

The nature of the Indian civilization, spread thinly over the continent, helps to explain the speed and thoroughness with which white settlement surged to the Pacific in these years. Despite the accomplishments of some of the Indian peoples, they were no match for the European invaders, either in mechanical and military skill or, ultimately, in numbers. The nomadic existence of many of them lessened their power to resist, as did their tribal organization, which made it possible to play one group against another. The encroachment of the farmer frontier upon the Indians' hunting grounds made tension inevitable; and this resulted in a growing conviction of incompatibility between the red man and the white which government policy did little to allay. As a result, the average frontiersman acted on the belief that the "only good Indian is a dead Indian," and frequently he had immediate excuse to do so. Yet despite the horrors of Indian forays along the frontier and on the plains, the "westward movement" of the Indian people in the face of the advancing Anglo-American frontier is a tragic story of futile resistance to superior numbers and organization. A long line of Indian leaders fought for their people's rights, but from Pontiac to Tecumseh and Red Cloud to Crazy Horse, they championed a losing cause.

The lure of the American West was compounded of many attractions, but first and foremost was the appeal of its virgin land. Daniel Denton, writing of New York in 1670, when the Atlantic seaboard was Europe's "West" in the New World, described grass as high as "a man's waste" and produce so abundant that one could "weary himself walking over his fields of corn." Here folk whom "Fortune hath frown'd upon in England" could procure "lands and possessions" of such quality and in such quantity as to defy belief. The abundance theme found continuous repetition in the next two centuries as reports of "beautiful meadows," "largest timber," "finest mould," "vast fields of golden grain," and "gigantic unbroken pasturelands" drew settlers to this "second paradise" in the American West. "You have no idea what nature has done here for man, and cannot unless you see it," wrote a New Hampshireman who cast his lot with Wisconsin in the late 1830's.

The opportunity to develop towns, as well as farms, figured significantly in the pull of the West throughout the nineteenth century. Towns were inevitable in the Western economy; but as early as the 1830's, newspaper editors in the West were deploring the prevailing tendency to project urban communities before there was a hinterland to support them. Speculators, however, saw faster profit in dealing in town lots than in farm property. As a result, in boom periods, the newest wests were overlaid with plats of potential cities, each of which was confidently promoted as the future "Queen City" of the area. Some, whose location made them centers for trade, industry, or administration, survived the excesses of their original promotion and remained to spearhead the westward advance, as well as to implement the cultural and economic development of the region. Many, however, never became more tangible than the paper on which their prospective futures were so glowingly described. In the trans-Missouri West, the cow towns, mining communities, and terminus cities of the advancing railroads constituted a kind of "mushroom" urbanism which, despite its often transient character, made a more lasting contribution to the lore of the American West than more permanent cities did.

Government land policy, during the years of settlement, contributed to the appeal of the West as a magnet for migration. In the seventeenth and eighteenth centuries, the Crown awarded vast tracts of wilderness America to companies and to individuals, who encouraged settlement on the basis of either rent or purchase. The colonial governments gave land bounties for military service and gifts of land to pioneers who would establish buffer communities on the remote frontier. The land law of the United States, once the nation was on its own, made the West progressively more attractive to land seeking settlers. In the early years under the Federal Constitution, pioneers could purchase land on a four-year installment plan, at $2.00 an acre. In 1820, the credit feature was abolished, but the price was reduced to a minimum of $1.25 an acre after the land had been offered at auction. In succeeding decades, Westerners won the right of preemption, which allowed actual settlers to buy at the minimum price; and the passage of the Homestead Act, in 1862, guaranteed 160 acres free of charge, except for a small filing fee, to settlers who would dwell on the land for five years and meet certain conditions regarding cultivation. Offsetting the advantage of this tardily achieved homestead privilege was the fact that much of the best land was now falling into the hands of speculators and of railroad companies as a result of the Government's policy of subsidizing railroad construction by grants of huge tracts of land from the public domain.

The envelopment of the exploitable West was in general

a continuing process, as the pressure of population and of soil exhaustion pushed settlers forward into the wilderness, more often than not in the latitude of their former homes and frequently not too far from them. On occasion, however, migration westward assumed epidemic proportions, and over-expansion and inflation ensued. This occurred in connection with the "Great Migration" into the Ohio Valley West following the close of the War of 1812 and again in the mid-1830's, mid-1850's, and mid-1880's, when home-seekers moved with fevered haste into newly opened farming country. In each instance, an economic crisis resulted; and in its wake the flood of newcomers momentarily abated.

The Ohio, Alabama, Wisconsin, and Oregon "fevers" aroused comment in the nation's press; but as items of news they could not hold a candle to the "gold fever" which drove hundreds of thousands to the Far West in the middle years of the nineteenth century. In two years alone, more than 80,000 persons, victims of this migratory virus, rushed to California, following the discovery of the alluring metal there in 1848. The pursuit of trade was another motive which pulled men westward; and the wide open spaces also had an understandable attraction for religious sects or social groups whose practices made them unwelcome in more settled parts. Less tangible, but no less compelling, was the appeal of the West as the embodiment of the ideal of freedom which informed American society in the mid-nineteenth century. "Fair freedom's star points to the sunset regions, boys," ran the refrain of a song heard frequently in Hamlin Garland's pioneering family; and Samuel Gompers recalled the wide-spread influence, among migrating Englishmen, of a popular ballad which began, "To the west, to the west, to the land of the free / Where the mighty Missouri rolls down to the sea."

Migrants from Europe participated in settling the American West from colonial times through the nineteenth century. Indeed, the existence of the West was a major attraction for the flood of European immigrants that swept toward the United States in ever increasing proportions between 1815 and 1890. The promotional activities of William Penn, as early as the 1680's, had induced the migration of non-English stocks to this "good and fruitful land." Many of them moved to the frontier; and by the mid-eighteenth century the colonies were flanked, to the westward, by a cordon of thrifty German farmers and vigorous Scotch-Irish pioneers. With the achievement of independence, the appeal of a democratic government augmented the pull of available land for potential settlers from across the sea. Between 1815 and 1860 more than four million immigrants cast their lot with the young United States; and by the latter date more than half of the foreign born in the nation's population were living west of the Alleghenies, most particularly in the upper Middle West. By the mid-century, and especially after the Civil War, steamship and railroad companies added their advertising efforts to the promotion implicit in the letters, travel books, and emigrant guides extolling the virtues of migration to the United States. The land-grant railroads advertised widely in Europe and, like many of the Western states, maintained agents at the ports of entry to induce immigrants to journey at once to the land of plenty. As a result, thousands of newcomers from central and northern Europe swelled the growth of Kansas, Nebraska, Minnesota, Dakota, and Texas, in the 1870's and 1880's, continuing the traditional contribution of Europe to the settlement of the New World.

Motion was the word for America during these years of settlement, especially after 1815, when to all appearances "Old America" seemed to be "breaking up and moving westward." From colonial times, the availability of an unoccupied West had kept Americans to some extent on the move; but by the nineteenth century "westering" seemed to have become a national habit, a state of mind. "Americans are undoubtedly the most mobile and roving people on earth," wrote a Finnish immigrant in the 1840's. "Even when they are very well off, they will pull up stakes, sell their possessions, and move west with a resolute courage one would expect only from those pressed by extreme want." The concourse of traffic on the roads and inland waterways pointed up the trend. In the boom years after 1815 the roads teemed with the vehicles of the migrating throng; and at times, in the 1840's, caravans of covered wagons, traveling the overland trails to the Far West, assumed the proportions of a parade. Many migrants made their way west as individuals, by foot or on horseback; but the family, with its barnyard accoutrements, and even its slaves, was the more customary unit in the westward trek. On occasion, organized groups joined forces to make the journey west, as in the case of the Mormon migrants, bound for their desert Zion, or the settlers who moved to Kansas, under the auspices of the New England Emigrant Aid Society, to make sure that this incipient state would become a bulwark of freedom in the developing contest between the North and the South.

A transportation revolution, which occurred between 1820 and 1870, contributed to the speed with which settlement overlaid the unoccupied West. The steamboat, plying the western waters by the turn of the 1820's, supplemented and in time replaced the barges, houseboats, and rafts originally used in riverborne migration. The completion of the Erie Canal, in 1825, shortened the journey from Albany to the Great Lakes and stimulated a generation of canal building which provided additional, though tedious, transportation facilities for the westward-moving horde. By the early 1850's, railroads, emanating from the seaboard cities, had made contact with the waterways west of the Appalachians; and by the eve of the Civil War, through rail connections were available between the East Coast and the Mississippi River. Already there was agitation for transcontinental lines that would link mid-America with the Pacific Coast. This monumental achievement was finally realized in 1869, with the driving of the golden spike that signalized the joining of two lines, the Central Pacific and the Union Pacific, the one built eastward from California, the other from Omaha, west. In a sense, the West itself was the resource that made many of these improvements in transportation possible. As early as 1827, the Federal Government authorized a gift of land from the public domain to subsidize the construction of a canal in Illinois; and between 1850 and 1871, millions of acres of public lands were awarded to states and private corporations to underwrite railroad building.

The extension of railroads west of the Missouri facilitated the exploitation and settlement of an area originally by-passed by the farmer-pioneer. This was the region lying between the 98th meridian and the Rocky Mountains. Explorers, venturing into this treeless, semi-arid country, in the early nineteenth century, labeled it the "Great American Desert." For several decades thereafter, it remained the undisturbed domain of the huge herds of buffalo and of the nomadic, warlike Indian tribes, such as the Sioux, the Cheyennes, the Comanches, and the Pawnees, who roamed its grassy wastes. On the presumption that it had no better use than as a permanent Indian country, tribes from east of the Mississippi were settled here between 1825 and the turn of the 1840's, in line with the Indian removal policy of the Federal Government.

Inevitably, however, the Plains, like their predecessor wests, fell within the orbit of interest of ever-moving America. By the 1830's and 1840's their vast expanse was bisected by the overland trails to Santa Fe, California, and Oregon; and by the later 1860's cattlemen were demonstrating the utility of the region as a grassy corridor through which great droves of steers could be moved from Texas to shipping points on the westward-moving railroads or farther north to the grazing lands of the open range. By the 1870's the potential of the Plains had become apparent for homesteading, as barbed wire provided a substitute for wooden fences, and windmills afforded a means of lifting water from beneath the timberless, arid soil. Improved farm machinery was now available to facilitate cultivation and the railroad, to export bonanza crops. To homeseekers of the post-Civil War period the boundless plains appeared to offer opportunities for farming that far exceeded the bounty of the forested frontier. Farmers and townmakers by the thousands, migrants from Europe as well as the United States, responded to the pull of this newest West. On came the sodbusting swarm, in spite of warnings of chinch-bugs, grasshoppers, over-extension, and drought, to settle the country's last frontier at railroad speed. Only when the inevitable reaction set in, in a social and economic climate increasingly different from that of pre-Civil War America, was the moving propensity of American society called into question. It was then that Hamlin Garland remembered his grandfather's comment, "It's the curse of our country—this constant moving, moving."

Motion, for good or ill, conditioned the culture of the pioneer West. In many ways, on each new frontier life reverted to the primitive. This was especially true of the trappers, in the vanguard of occupation, who frequently took on the habits and manners of the aborigines with whom they dealt. Even among the farmer pioneers, literacy usually declined during the first generation of settlement; for, as one observer put it, the frontiersman was less concerned with the cultivation of himself than of the soil. The "winning of the West" was a far less romantic or even exciting pursuit than it often has been pictured to be. Fevers, ague, loneliness, frustration, and back breaking toil characterized the greater, if hardly the better, part of life in the new settlements, whether in the backwoods or on the open plains. Schools, churches, and other institutions of a mature society, as well as homes and farms, had to be hewn from the wilderness, and by a people, in most instances, whose intellectual background, tastes, and skills equipped them less for cultural than for material achievement. Small wonder, then, that there was a strong tincture of the crude and the utilitarian in the attitudes, practices, and society of the frontier.

Chance, on occasion, permitted some intellectual enrichment of the Western community. Migrants from New England and from Germany often gave an impetus to education in areas where they settled that was not general throughout the West. Cities sometimes drew professional actors and now and then an artist or musician of some skill; and in view of the scarcity of libraries and museums the newspaper played a civilizing role. Benevolent societies in the East occasionally sent missionaries to "enlighten" the "benighted" West; but despite the contributions of these chance carriers of culture the prevailing emphasis in most frontiers was upon the practical and mundane rather than upon the intellectual or ideal. The schoolmaster, as often as not, only awaited the day when he could buy himself a farm; and the frontier minister was either a lay preacher or a meagerly trained circuit rider whose influence, like his contacts with the community, was intermittent at best. In an unspecialized society of this sort the practitioner of the professions and the arts was often an amateur and almost always, like the farmer himself, a "Jack of all trades." Physicians were dentists, druggists, and even veterinarians. Lawyers doubled as land speculators or commission merchants and frequently held public office. The Reverend Mr. Dickey of Indiana engaged in farming on a small scale, taught a singing class, wrote deeds, wills, and advertisements, surveyed land, and sometimes taught school. Mark Twain satirized this quality of frontier society in describing a factotum of the plains who in one person combined hotel keeper, postmaster, blacksmith, constable, city marshal, and mayor.

The fluid, open character of its society contributed to the prevalence of equalitarian and democratic attitudes in the West. The nature of the pioneering process drew to new settlements neither the very rich nor the very poor. This, together with the physical expansiveness of the environment, tended to induce an atmosphere of equality. The challenge to survival in a frontier setting put a premium upon self-reliance and self-sufficiency which fostered a belief in the worth of the individual and in his capacity to assume political responsibility, regardless of birth or breeding. The circumstance which often forced pioneers to frame their own rules of government, whether for Pilgrim existence in wilderness Massachusetts or for the duration of a journey over the Oregon trail, furthered the conviction that government was based upon popular consent. The vigor of political activity, which observers invariably noted in the West, owed much to the participation of persons who would have been inhibited, if not barred, from such activity in older communities. The opportunity to create new state governments, as frontier settlements matured into statehood, permitted the realization of constitutional innovations, democratic in character, which were less quickly achieved in the generally more conservative East. Despite its occasional subversion, at the hands of aggressive leaders, the "dogma of democracy" was a controlling force in the political life of the American West.

The economic and physical circumstances which underwrote democracy and equality in the West made for a society that was individualistic and expansive, as well. The abundance of natural resources, originally available to the small man as well as the big, connoted a promise of economic and social improvement for the individual that was generally taken for granted in the West. The average migrant, whether from the East or from Europe, cast his lot with the new country in the firm conviction that the move promised if not immediate, at least ultimate, progress and improvement for himself and his family. This expansiveness carried over to the aspirations which Westerners had for the cultural and institutional development of the region. Some of them thought of themselves as men of destiny who through their individual efforts were realizing the mission of America to achieve a more democratic world. Despite the endorsement of individualism, frontiersmen indulged in a good deal of associative effort when mutual assistance appeared to be expedient; but it was cooperation in the context of individual opportunity and achievement. Communitarian experiments rarely survived the realization of a secure environment, because of the ready availability of land. Participants in the Santa Fe trade submitted to rigid controls while the caravan was traversing hostile Indian country; they became rampant competitors, however, as the destination came into sight. The author of an emigrant guide published in 1832 described Westerners of his day as "almost without restraint, free as the mountain air"; and to an English visitor, as late as 1880, the independence, self-sufficiency, and freedom of the West recalled its "strong and wildly rushing rivers." Only when individualism overreached itself in the exploitative activities of railroad and range-cattle corporations in the post-Civil War years did the average Westerner propose more permanent associative effort, in the programs of the Grangers and the Populists, as a means of striking back.

Much has been written concerning the impact of the West

and the frontier experience upon the history of the United States and the personality of its people, especially since 1893, when Frederick Jackson Turner, addressing a meeting of American historians, asserted that up to that day American history and the American character had been shaped to a predominant degree by the availability of the open West and the nature of its settlement. As Turner expressed it, "The existence of an area of free land, its continuous recession, and the advance of civilization westward explain American development." He saw the evolution of society from the simple to the complex, recurring in each new West, as an experience which, through repetition, endowed the nation with the attitudes and characteristics which gave it its distinguishing flavor. These he identified as its composite nationality, its cohesiveness as a nation, its democratic institutions, its emphasis on individualism, and the inventiveness, materialism, even coarseness, characteristic of the popular mind. Recent scholarship has qualified some of Turner's generalizations and explained them in terms of the problems of the period in which he was writing, without seriously challenging the validity of his basic assumption concerning the significance of the West in American history.

Without question the West figured importantly in the play of politics and diplomacy during the greater part of the nation's history. For example, the aspirations of Americans with respect to the exploitable West contributed, in the colonial period, to the rising vision of American nationality; and policies of the British Government which appeared to thwart those aspirations were among the irritants which produced the War for American Independence. Similarly, the tensions that resulted in the Civil War can be seen to have arisen in part at least from the conflicting ambitions of a westward-moving North and a westward-moving South to gain advantage in the unsettled West. American diplomacy was conditioned by the pressure of an ever expanding frontier society. The purchase of Louisiana fits into this pattern as an expedient to acquire a highway for the exportation of Western produce by way of the Mississippi, as does the War of 1812, which was motivated in considerable measure by the hostility of Westerners to the activities of Britain and Spain on the young nation's western borders. In the 1840's, the theme of "manifest destiny," as an overtone of the advancing pioneer society, served to rationalize the contest with Mexico that led to the acquisition of California and the vast Southwest.

It would be difficult, moreover, to overestimate the importance of the resources of the West—its cotton, its grain, its timber, its livestock, as well as its precious metal—in underwriting the prosperity that attended the evolution of the United States to powerful nationhood, or, indeed, the bearing of the West upon the dislocations of the economy which periodically followed the unrestrained assault upon the West and its resources. The existence of the West was a powerful attraction to the waves of European migrants whose advent bolstered the economic growth of the nation in the nineteenth century. Whether life on the frontier shaped the foreign born to an American pattern more speedily than did other experiences in the United States has been a matter of controversy; but certainly they, as much as the American born, were responsible for developing the reputation of the West as a symbol of American opportunity. It has been asserted that the West, by drawing off urban workers in time of depression, served as a "safety-valve" against the development of radical labor philosophy in the East. The facts seem to show, however, that few factory workers moved west, either because of the costs involved or because of lack of interest in or aptitude for farming. Moreover, migration dwindled rather than increased in times of economic crisis. This is not to deny the possibility that the pull of the agrarian West, especially in prosperous times, attracted farmers from the East who otherwise might have moved into cities, glutting the labor market and possibly causing discontent.

One can only speculate upon the extent of the impact of the West and the frontier experience upon the American point of view. Traditionally, the United States, like the nineteenth-century West, is prevailingly democratic, individualistic, and concerned with material considerations. It is still basically nationalistic in its thinking and expansive in its outlook upon life. Its behavior still reflects a sympathy for change and innovation and an expectation of progress which are in the idiom of a people traditionally optimistic and on the move. Access as well as success is still a controlling force in American thought. These attitudes are undoubtedly the heritage in part of experiences connected with the opening of the West. As one of the most perceptive interpreters of westward expansion has written, "Rugged individualism did not originate on the frontier any more than did democracy, but each concept was deepened and popularized by conditions that existed there." Other forces exerted a strong, perhaps a comparable influence: the heritage of the European tradition and continued contact with European thought, transmitted through a stream of visitors as well as immigrants; life in factory and town, which has become the lot of increasing numbers of Americans; and a communication revolution, which has involved the United States increasingly with the rest of the world. To quote another distinguished historian of the West: "The frontier no doubt had much to do with making us the kind of people we are, and with making our individualistic democracy what it is, but other ingredients also entered into the process."

Nonetheless, the existence of the West and the exploitation of its potential have figured in an inextricable way in the growth of the American tradition. The story of the westward movement is still the great American epic; and its *dramatis personae* include the most traditionally American types. In this respect, the cowboy, the Indian, the miner, the lumberman, and the fur trader have had somewhat more attention than they deserve. The real heroes of the saga are the farmer-pioneers, the settler-homesteaders, who laid the foundations of civilization in the wilderness, and the frontier wives and mothers, whose heroism was reflected in lives of almost unrelieved privation and toil. Less heroic but more omnipresent than is generally realized were the speculators, the land agents and townsite promoters, who induced and negotiated the individual acquisition of much of the West. Every settler was in a sense a speculator, gambling on the promise of the soil; but professional land agents were more continuously in the picture than is usually supposed. Even after the passage of the Homestead Act of 1862, for every settler who obtained a grant from the Government six or seven purchased their farms from jobbers or agents of railroad and speculative companies. Nor should one overlook the presence of the soldiers, surveyors, territorial officials, commission merchants, lawyers, physicians, newspaper editors, circuit riders, teachers, boatmen, and stagecoach drivers who added their contribution to the life as well as the lore of the West as they serviced the frontier scene.

The voice of the West found expression in the journals of explorers and Indian agents, the letters and diaries of the settlers, and the promotional output of newspaper editors, townsite speculators, and authors of emigrant guides. It was heard, too, in the speeches of representatives of the West, not only in Congress, but in local assemblies such as farmers' picnics, Fourth of July celebrations, and local political campaigns. In time, professional writers, travelers, newspaper correspondents, and publicists added their description and interpretation to the comments of the less literary, if sometimes more oratorical, participants in the westward march. A portion of this record of the evolving West is reproduced in the ensuing pages.

The United States still has its wide open spaces and, in Hawaii and Alaska, its outposts of settlement; but their accessibility by jet aircraft removes the remoteness that was a characteristic feature of the traditional American West. Today, the West has become a more or less static place, more a geographical location in the nation than a dynamic stage in its developing society. But although the West, today, is geographically localized to a degree not true of America's past, its popularity as a theme for novels, motion picture plots, television fare, and even controversies among historians reveals its prevailing vitality; and the continuing reference to "new frontiers" in many aspects of the political and social scene shows how deeply this concept is engrained in American life and thought and how real a force the West has been, and still is, in the American tradition.

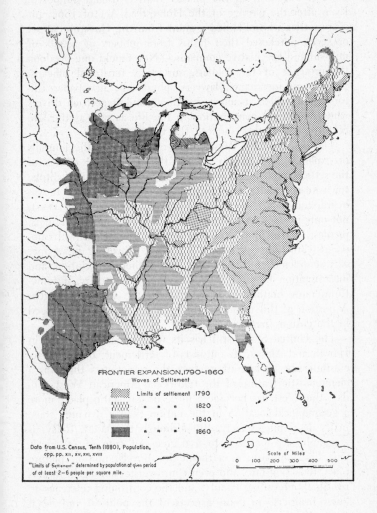

FRONTIER EXPANSION, 1790-1860
Waves of Settlement

	Limits of settlement 1790
	" " " 1820
	" " " 1840
	" " " 1860

Data from U.S. Census, Tenth (1880), Population,
opp. pp. xii, xv, xvi, xviii,

"Limits of Settlement" determined by population at given period
of at least 2-6 people per square mile.

Scale of Miles
0   100   200   300   400   500

PART I

EUROPE'S FRONTIER IN THE NEW WORLD

"Paradice it self seem'd to be there, in its first Native Lustre." (*Robert Beverley*)

East was "West" when the march of settlement across the Continent began. During most of the seventeenth century the Atlantic Coast was Europe's frontier in the New World. Here seaboard settlements backed up against the wilderness; and the nation's first trans-oceanic pioneers—adventurers, traders, and home-seeking settlers—laid the foundations of a society which in less than two and a half centuries their successors were to carry as far as the Pacific Coast. The abundance of the land was the quality of this initial West which earned it the early residents' and adventurers' most frequent acclaim. Their published accounts of the new country, and many of their letters describing it, glowed with praise of the natural riches of the region, the sweetness of the air, the phenomenal fertility of the soil, and even the friendliness of the Indian population. Less often did they record the loneliness and fear which many experienced as they turned their backs upon Europe and faced an unknown West.

Typical of the enthusiasm with which Englishmen of the late sixteenth century reported upon this new frontier are the reactions of two sea captains who in 1584 were sent out by Sir Walter Raleigh in connection with his efforts to exploit the opportunities of the New World. Their responses are described by Robert Beverley, public servant and historian, who was in an equally laudatory mood when he wrote his History and Present State of Virginia, *published in 1705.*

The Learned and Valiant Sir *Walter Raleigh.* . . . having laid together the many Stories then in *Europe* concerning *America;* the Native Beauty, Riches, and Value of this Part of the World; and the immense Profits the *Spaniards* drew from a small Settlement or two thereon made; resolv'd upon an Adventure for further Discoveries.

According to this Purpose, in the Year of our Lord, 1583,

He got several Men of great Value and Estate to join with him in an Expedition of this Nature: And for their Incouragement obtain'd Letters Patents from Queen *Elizabeth*, bearing date the 25th of *March*, 1584, for turning their Discoveries to their own Advantage. . . .

In *April* following they set out Two small Vessels under the Command of Capt. *Philip Amidas*, and Capt. *Arthur Barlow*; who, after a prosperous Voyage, anchor'd at the Inlet by *Roenoke*. . . . They made good Profit of the *Indian* Truck, which they bought for Things of much inferior Value, and return'd. Being over-pleased with their Profits, and finding all Things there entirely new, and surprizing; they gave a very advantageous Account of Matters; by representing the Country so delightful, and desirable; so pleasant, and plentiful; the Climate, and Air, so temperate, sweet, and wholsome; the Woods, and Soil, so charming, and fruitful; and all other Things so agreeable, that Paradice it self seem'd to be there, in its first Native Lustre.

They gave particular Accounts of the Variety of good Fruits, and some whereof they had never seen the Like before; but above all, that there were Grapes in such abundance, as was never known in the World: Stately tall large Oaks, and other Timber; Red Cedar, Cypress, Pines, and other Evergreens, and Sweetwoods; for tallness and largeness exceeding all they had ever heard of: Wild Fowl, Fish, Deer, and other Game in such Plenty, and Variety; that no Epicure could desire more than this New World did seem naturally to afford.

And, to make it yet more desirable, they reported the Native *Indians* (which were then the only Inhabitants) so affable, kind, and good-natur'd; so uncultivated in Learning, Trades, and Fashions; so innocent, and ignorant of all manner of Politicks, Tricks, and Cunning; and so desirous of the Company of the *English:* That they seem'd rather to be like soft Wax, ready to take any Impression, than any ways likely to oppose the Settling of the *English* near them. . . .

Her Majesty . . . being so well pleased with the Account given, that as the greatest Mark of Honour she could do the Discovery, she call'd the Country by the Name of *Virginia*;

as well, for that it was first discover'd in her Reign, a Virgin Queen; as that it did still seem to retain the Virgin Purity and Plenty of the first Creation.

* * *

Printed descriptions of the New World, designed for English readers, praised conditions in Europe's "New West" and provided information to encourage migration. This was true of Daniel Denton's A Brief Description of New York, *published in 1670, six years after the former Dutch colony had fallen into English hands. Written while Denton was in London on a business trip, it appears to be the first separate description of New York published in English. It is also a forerunner in a long line of emigrant guides to the New World West, for it included "Some Directions and Advice to such as shall go thither: . . . what Commodities they shall take with them; The Profit and Pleasure that may accrew to them thereby."*

I may say, and say truly, that if there be any terrestrial happiness to be had by people of all ranks, especially of an inferior rank, it must certainly be here: here any one may furnish himself with land, and live rent-free, yea, with such a quantity of land, that he may weary himself with walking over his fields of Corn, and all sorts of Grain: and let his stock of Cattel amount to some hundreds, he needs not fear their want of pasture in the Summer, or Fodder in the Winter, the Woods affording sufficient supply. For the Summer-season, where you have grass as high as a mans knees, nay, as high as his waste, interlaced with Pea-vines and other weeds that Cattel much delight in, as much as a man can press thorough; and these woods also every mile or half-mile are furnished with fresh ponds, brooks, or rivers, . . . : Here those which Fortune hath frown'd upon in *England*, to deny them an inheritance amongst their Brethren, or such as by their utmost labors can scarcely procure a living, I say such may procure here inheritances of lands and possessions, stock themselves with all sorts of Cattel, enjoy the benefit of them whilst they live, and leave them to the benefit of their children when they die: Here you need no[t] trouble the Shambles for meat, nor Bakers and Brewers for Beer and

Bread, nor run to a Linnen-Draper for a supply, every one making their own Linnen, and a great part of their woollen-cloth for their ordinary wearing: And how prodigal, if I may so say, hath Nature been to furnish the Countrey with all sorts of wilde Beasts and Fowle, which every one hath an interest in, and may hunt at his pleasure; where besides the pleasure in hunting, he may furnish his house with excellent fat Venison, Turkies, Geese, Heath-Hens, Cranes, Swans, Ducks, Pidgeons, and the like: and wearied with that, he may go a Fishing, where the Rivers are so furnished, that he may supply himself with Fish before he can leave off the Recreation: where you may travel . . . from one end of the Countrey to another, with as much security as if you were lockt within your own Chamber; And if you chance to meet with an *Indian*-Town, they shall give you the best entertainment they have, and upon your desire, direct you on your way: But that which adds happiness to all the rest, is the Healthfulness of the place, where many people in twenty years time never know what sickness is: . . . where besides the sweetness of the Air, the Countrey it self sends forth such a fragrant smell, that it may be perceived at Sea before they can make the Land: where no evil fog or vapour doth no sooner appear, but a North-west or Westerly winde doth immediately dissolve it, and drive it away: What shall I say more? you shall scarce see a house, but the South side is begirt with Hives of Bees, which increase after an incredible manner: That I must needs say, that if there be any terrestrial *Canaan*, 'tis surely here, where the land floweth with milk and honey.

*   *   *

In marked contrast to Denton's effervescent description of conditions in the New World was the initial reaction of William Bradford to the Massachusetts frontier, where he and his Pilgrim compatriots landed, after a stormy voyage, in November of 1620. Here in his account of the beginnings of the Plymouth settlement are expressed the forlornness, apprehension, and anxiety with which many a migrant, ill equipped for coping with the wilderness, must have viewed his commitment to life on the American frontier.

Being thus arrived in a good harbor and brought safe to
land, they fell upon their knees and blessed the God of
Heaven who had brought them over the vast and furious
ocean and delivered them from all the perils and miseries
thereof, again to set their feet on the firm and stable earth,
their proper element.

But here I cannot but stay and make a pause, and stand
half amazed at this poor people's present condition. . . .
Being thus past the vast ocean and a sea of troubles before in
their preparation, . . . they had now no friends to welcome
them, nor inns to entertain or refresh their weatherbeaten
bodies, no houses or much less towns to repair to, to seek
for succor. . . . And for the season, it was winter, and they
that know the winters of that country know them to be
sharp and violent, and subject to cruel and fierce storms,
dangerous to travel to known places, much more to search
an unknown coast. Besides, what could they see but a hideous
and desolate wilderness, full of wild beasts and wild men?
And what multitudes there might be of them they knew
not. . . .

For summer being done, all things stand upon them with
a weatherbeaten face; and the whole country, full of woods
and thickets, represented a wild and savage hue. If they
looked behind them, there was the mighty ocean which they
had passed, and was now as a main bar and gulf to separate
them from all the civil parts of the world. . . . May not and
ought not the children of these fathers rightly say: "Our
fathers were Englishmen which came over this great ocean,
and were ready to perish in this wilderness; but they cried
unto the Lord, and he heard their voice, and looked on their
adversity."

*   *   *

*While England was consolidating its Atlantic Coast frontier,
Frenchmen were pressing rapidly into the heart of the Continent. Here they staked a claim that was to stand in the way
of the Anglo-American advance until 1763. Fur traders, missionaries, and agents of the Crown carried the flag of France
into the wilderness of North America. As early as 1634, Jean
Nicolet, a protégé of Champlain, ventured westward by way*

of the St. Lawrence, the Ottawa River, and the upper Great Lakes and touched what is now Wisconsin; in 1673, Marquette and Joliet pushed still further west to enter the Mississippi. Their accomplishments were soon eclipsed by the large-scale, empire-building endeavors of Robert Cavelier, Sieur de la Salle. Before 1680, La Salle and his friend Tonty were exploring the Illinois country and projecting a center of French influence in the West. In the Winter and Spring of 1681-1682, they journeyed southward from Lake Michigan to the mouth of the Mississippi, claiming the valley of the great river and all its tributaries in the name of Louis XIV, King of France. The pageantry attending the acquisition of this great inland domain is recorded in the official account of La Salle's exploration, written by the notary, Jacques de La Metairie. (The translation and editing of the excerpt follow the edition by B. F. French (1875).)

On the 27th of December, 1681, M. *de la Salle* departed on foot to join M. *de Tonty,* who had preceded him with his followers and all his equipage forty leagues into the *Miamis* country [at the south end of Lake Michigan], where the ice on the river Chicagou, in the country of the *Mascoutens,* had arrested his progress, and where, when the ice became stronger, they used sledges to drag the baggage, the canoes, and a wounded Frenchman through the whole length of this river, and on the *Illinois,* a distance of seventy leagues.

At length, all the *French* being together, on the 25th of January, 1682, we came to Pimiteoui [Peoria, on the Illinois River]. From that place, the river being frozen only in some parts, we continued our route to the River Colbert (Mississippi), sixty leagues or thereabouts from Pimiteoui. . . . We reached the banks of the River Colbert on the 6th of February, and remained there until the 13th, waiting for the Indians, whose progress had been impeded by the ice. On the 13th, all having assembled, we renewed our voyage, being twenty-two Frenchmen, carrying arms, accompanied by the Reverend Father Zenobe Membré and one of the Recollect missionaries, and followed by eighteen New England savages and several women, Algonquins, Otchepóse, and Hurons. . . .

On the 3d of April, at about ten o'clock in the morning, we saw, among the canes, thirteen or fourteen canoes. M. de la Salle landed, with several of his people. Footprints were seen, and also savages, a little lower down, who were fishing, and who fled precipitately as soon as they discovered us. Others of our party then went ashore on the borders of a marsh formed by the inundations of the river. M. de la Salle sent two Frenchmen, and then two savages, to reconnoiter, who reported that there was a village (Quinipisas) not far off, but that the whole of this marsh, covered with canes, must be crossed to reach it; that they had been assailed with a shower of arrows by the inhabitants of the town, who had not dared to engage with them in the marsh, but who had then withdrawn, although neither the French nor the savages with them had fired on account of the orders they had received not to fire, unless in pressing danger. Presently, we heard a drum beat in the village, and the cries and howlings with which these barbarians are accustomed to make attacks. We waited three or four hours, and as we could not encamp in this marsh, and seeing no one, and no longer hearing anything, we embarked. . . . We continued our voyage until the 6th, when we discovered three channels, by which the River Colbert discharges itself into the sea. We landed on the bank of the most western channel, about three leagues from its mouth. On the 7th, M. de la Salle went to reconnoiter the shores of the neighboring sea (Gulf of Mexico), and M. de Tonty likewise examined the great middle channel. They found these three outlets beautiful, large, and deep.

On the 8th we reascended the river, a little above its confluence with the sea, to find a dry place beyond the reach of inundation. . . . Here we prepared a column and a cross, and to the said column were affixed the arms of France with this inscription:

LOUIS LE GRAND, ROI DE FRANCE ET DE
NAVARRE, RÈGNE; LE NEUVIÈME
AVRIL, 1682.

The whole party under arms chanted the *Te Deum*, the *Exaudiat*, the *Domine Salvum fac Regem*; and then, after a salute of fire-arms and cries of *Vive le Roi*, the column was erected by M. de la Salle, who, standing near it, said with a loud voice, in French: 'In the name of the most high, mighty, invincible, and victorious Prince, LOUIS THE GREAT, by the grace of God, King of France and Navarre, fourteenth of that name, this ninth day of April, one thousand six hundred and eighty-two, I, in virtue of the commission of his Majesty (Louis XIV.) which I hold in my hand, and which may be seen by all whom it may concern, have taken, and do now take in the name of his Majesty and of his successors to the crown, possession of this country of Louisiana, the seas, harbors, ports, bays, adjacent straits; and all the nations, people, provinces, cities, towns, villages, mines, minerals, fisheries, streams, and rivers comprised in the extent of Louisiana, from the mouth of the great River St. Louis on the eastern side, otherwise called Ohio, Alighinsipou (Alleghany), or Chickagoua, and this with the consent of the Chouanons (Shawanoes), Chicachas (Chickasaws), and other people dwelling therein, with whom we have made alliance; as also along the River Colbert or Mississippi, and rivers which discharge themselves therein, from its source; beyond the country of the Kious (*Sioux*) or Nadouessions, and this with their consent, and with the consent of the Motantees, Illinois, Mesigameas (Metchigamias), Akansas, Natches, and Koroas, which are the most considerable nations dwelling therein, with whom also we have made alliance either by ourselves or by others in our behalf; as far as the mouth at the sea or Gulf of Mexico, about the 27th degree of the elevation of the north pole, and also to the mouth of the river of Palms (Rio de Palmas); upon the assurance which we have received from all these nations that we are the first Europeans who have descended or ascended the River Colbert, hereby protesting against all those who may in future undertake to invade any or all of these countries, people, or lands above described to the prejudice of the right of his Majesty acquired by the consent of the nations herein named, of which and all that can be needed, I hereby take to witness those who hear me, and demand an act of the notary as required by law.'

To which the whole assembly responded with shouts of *Vive le Roi* and with salutes of fire-arms. Moreover, the said Sieur de la Salle caused to be buried at the foot of the tree to which the cross was attached a leaden plate, on one side of which were engraved the arms of France and the following Latin inscription:

LVDOVICVS MAGNVS REGNAT.

NONO APRILIS CIƆ IƆC LXXXII.

ROBERTVS CAVELIER, CVM DOMINO DE TONTY, LEGATO
R. P. ZENOBIO MEMBRÈ, RECOLLECTO, ET VIGINTI GALLIS,
PRIMVS HOC FLVMEN, INDE AB ILINEORVM PAGO, ENAVIGAVIT,
EJVSQVE OSTIVM FECIT PERVIVM, NONO APRILIS ANNI
CIƆ IƆC LXXXII.

After which the Sieur de la Salle said that his Majesty, as eldest Son of the Church, would annex no country to his crown without making it his chief care to establish the Christian religion therein, and that its symbol must now be planted, which was accordingly done at once by erecting a cross, before which the *Vexilla* and the *Domine Salvum fac Regem* were sung, whereupon the ceremony was concluded with cries of *Vive le Roi*.

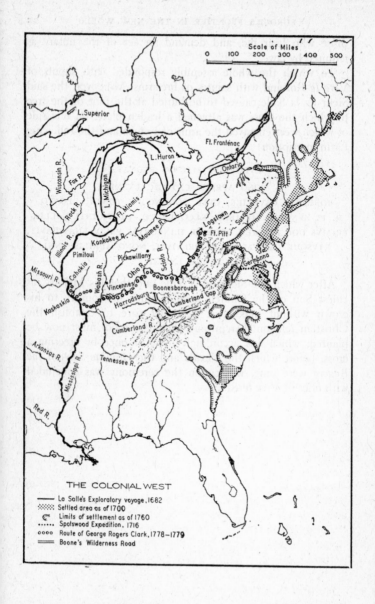

THE COLONIAL WEST

—— La Salle's Exploratory voyage, 1682
∷∷∷∷ Settled area as of 1700
ℭ Limits of settlement as of 1760
········ Spotswood Expedition, 1716
ooooo Route of George Rogers Clark, 1778–1779
═══ Boone's Wilderness Road

Part II

BREACHING THE APPALACHIAN BARRIER

"I . . . gained the summit of a commanding ridge, . . .
beheld the ample plains, the beauteous tracts below."
(*Daniel Boone*)

*By 1700, settlement had spread inland along the rivers that
flowed eastward from the Alleghenies to the Atlantic Coast.
The seaboard was filling up; and British America looked to a
new West that lay within the ridges of the Appalachians and
beyond. The policies of Alexander Spotswood, lieutenant
governor of Virginia from 1710 to 1722, encouraged interest
in this newly developing West. In 1714 he planted a colony
of Germans in the Virginia piedmont as part of a scheme of
frontier defense; and in 1716 he led a company of Virginia
gentlemen, rangers, servants, and Indians over the Blue Ridge
and into the Shenandoah Valley. By following the headwaters
of the James, the governor and his convivial party found a
passage through a major ridge, from which rivers ran both
east and west—an occasion which they celebrated by copious
toasts to the royal health. Upon their return, the Governor
presented each of his companions with a golden horseshoe to
"encourage gentlemen to venture backwards and make discoveries and new settlements." John Fontaine, a young British
officer who sojourned in the colonies from 1715 to 1719,
recorded in his journal the eventful details of this high-spirited
pathfinding expedition.*

[August] 29*th*. [1716]—In the morning we got all things
in readiness, and about one we left the German-town to set
out on our intended journey. At five in the afternoon, the
Governor gave orders to encamp near a small river, three miles
from Germanna, which we called Expedition Run, and here
we lay all night. . . . We made great fires, and supped, and
drank good punch. . . .

30*th*.—In the morning about seven of the clock, the
trumpet sounded to awake all the company, and we got

up. . . . At nine in the morning, we sent our servants and baggage forward, and we remained, because two of the Governor's horses had strayed. At half past two we got the horses, at three we mounted, and at half an hour after four, we came up with our baggage at a small river, three miles on the way. . . . We made about three miles more, and came to another small river, which is at the foot of a small mountain, so we encamped here and called it Mountain Run. . . . We had good pasturage for our horses, and venison in abundance for ourselves, which we roasted before the fire upon wooden forks, and so we went to bed in our tents. . . .

31st.—At eight in the morning, we set out from Mountain Run, and after going five miles we came upon the upper part of Rappahannoc River. . . . About five miles further we crossed the same river again, and two miles further we met with a large bear, which one of our company shot, and I got the skin. We killed several deer, and about two miles from the place where we killed the bear, we encamped upon Rappahannoc River. From our encampment we could see the Appalachian Hills very plain. We made large fires, pitched our tents, and cut boughs to lie upon, had good liquor, and at ten we went to sleep. . . .

1st. September.—At eight we mounted our horses, and made the first five miles of our way through a very pleasant plain, which lies where Rappahannoc River forks. I saw there the largest timber, the finest and deepest mould, and the best grass that I ever did see. . . .

2d.—At nine we were all on horseback, and after riding about five miles we crossed Rappahannoc River, almost at the head, where it is very small. We had a rugged way. . . . Several of our company were dismounted, some were down with their horses, others under their horses, and some thrown off. We saw a bear running down a tree, but it being Sunday, we did not endeavor to kill any thing. . . .

3d.—About eight we were on horseback, and about ten we came to a thicket, so tightly laced together, that we had a great deal of trouble to get through; our baggage was injured, our clothes torn all to rags, and the saddles and holsters also torn. About five of the clock we encamped almost at the head of James River, just below the great mountains. . . .

4th.— . . . The sides of the mountains were so full of vines and briers, that we were forced to clear most of the way before us. . . . We made about four miles, and so came to the side of James River, where a man may jump over it, and there we pitched our tents. . . .

5th.—A fair day. At nine we were mounted; we were obliged to have axe-men to clear the way in some places. We followed the windings of James River, observing that it came from the very top of the mountains. . . . In some places it was very steep, in others, it was so that we could ride up. About one of the clock we got to the top of the mountain; . . . and we came to the very head spring of James River, where it runs no bigger than a man's arm, from under a large stone. We drank King George's health, and all the Royal Family's, at the very top of the Appalachian mountains. About a musket-shot from the spring there is another, which rises and runs down on the other side; it goes westward, and we thought we could go down that way, but we met with such prodigious precipices, that we were obliged to return to the top again. We found some trees which had been formerly marked, I suppose, by the Northern Indians, and following these trees, we found a good, safe descent. Several of the company were for returning; but the Governor persuaded them to continue on. About five, we were down on the other side, and continued our way for about seven miles further, until we came to a large river, by the side of which we encamped. . . .

6th.—We crossed the river, which we called Euphrates. It is very deep; the main course of the water is north; it is fourscore yards wide in the narrowest part. We drank some healths on the other side, and returned; after which I went a swimming in it. . . . the Governor buried a bottle with a paper inclosed, on which he writ that he took possession of this place in the name and for King George the First of England. We had a good dinner, and after it we got the men together, and loaded all their arms, and we drank the

King's health in Champagne, and fired a volley—the Princess's health in Burgundy, and fired a volley, and all the rest of the Royal Family in claret, and a volley. We drank the Governor's health and fired another volley. We had several sorts of liquors, viz., Virginia red wine and white wine, Irish usquebaugh, brandy, shrub, two sorts of rum, champagne, canary, cherry, punch, water, cider, &c. . . .

7th.—At seven in the morning we mounted our horses, and parted with the rangers, who were to go farther on, and we returned homewards.

*   *   *

Fur traders, emissaries to the Indians, and scouts of speculative land companies crossed the Alleghenies into the Ohio Valley in advance of the farmer pioneer. This area, claimed by both France and England, was the home of numerous Indian nations, whose loyalties shifted with the changing strength of the two rival European powers. The fur trading activities of George Croghan, extending from western Pennsylvania to the Miami country in what is now western Ohio, put him in a position to woo the allegiance of tribes traditionally friendly to the French. In the Spring of 1748, the Pennsylvania and Virginia authorities commissioned Croghan to carry presents to the Indians; and in August they sent out Conrad Weiser, Pennsylvania's official Indian negotiant, to treat with the tribes. Weiser's journal recounts the details of this first official embassy to the Indians who lived beyond the Alleghenies. It reflects the bearing of the fur trade (and its alcoholic lubricant) upon the relations of the colonies with the Indians, and also the role of the Indian nations as counterweights in the contest between England and France for control of the trans-Allegheny West. It exhibits, too, the elementary idiom invariably employed by the Americans in their negotiations with the Indian tribes.

[August 27, 1748] . . . arrived . . . at Logs Town [on the upper Ohio River, in what is now western Pennsylvania] & Saluted the Town [by firing off 4 pair of pistols] . . . ; the Indians returned about One hundred Guns. . . .
[September] 3d. Set up the Union Flagg on a long Pole.

Treated all the Company with a Dram of Rum; The King's Health was drank by Indians & white men. . . .

[September] 8th. Had a Council with the Chiefs of the Wondats [Wyandots]; . . . they inform'd me their coming away from the French was because of the hard Usage they received from them; That they wou'd always get their Young Men to go to War against their Enemies, and wou'd use them as their own People, that is like Slaves, & their Goods were so dear that they, the Indians, cou'd not buy them; . . . that they had a very good Correspondence with the Six Nations many Years, & were one People with them, that they cou'd wish the Six Nations wou'd act more brisker against the French; That above fifty Years ago they made a Treaty of Friendship with the Governor of New York at Albany, & shewed me a large Belt of Wampum they received there from the said Governor as from the King of Great Britain; the Belt was 25 Grains wide & 265 long, very Curiously wrought, there were seven Images of Men holding one another by the Hand, the 1st signifying the Governor of New York (or rather, as they said, the King of Great Britain), the 2d the Mohawks, the 3d the Oneidos, the 4th the Cajugas, the 5th the Onondagers, the 6th the Senekas, the 7th the Owandaets [Wyandots], the two Rows of black Wampum under their feet thro' the whole length of the Belt to signify the Road from Albany thro' the 5 Nations to the Owendaets; That 6 Years ago, they had sent Deputies with the same Belt to Albany to renew the Friendship.

I treated them with a quart of Whiskey & a Roll of Tobacco; they expressed their good Wishes to King George & all his People, & were mightily pleas'd that I look'd upon them as Brethren of the English. . . .

[September] 17th. . . . the Deputies of the several Nations met in Council & I delivered them what I had to say from the President & Council of Pennsylvania by [the interpreter] Andrew Montour. . . .

"Brethren: Some of You have been in Philadelphia last Fall & acquainted us that You had taken up the English Hatchet [taken sides with the English], and that You had already made use of it against the French, & that the French had very hard heads, & your Country afforded nothing but Sticks & Hickerys which was not sufficient to break them. You desir'd your Brethren wou'd assist You with some Weapons sufficient to do it. Your Brethren the Presid^t. & Council [of Pennsylvania] promis'd you then to send something to You. . . . [They now] have sent You this Present to serve to strengthen the Chain of Friendship between us the English & the several Nations of Indians to which You belong. A French Peace is a very uncertain One, they keep it no longer than their Interest permits, then they break it without provocation given them. The French King's People have been almost starv'd in old France for want of Provision, which made them wish & seek for Peace; but our wise People are of opinion that after their Bellies are full they will quarrel again & raise a War. All nations in Europe know that their Friendship is mix'd with Poison, & many that trusted too much on their Friendship have been ruin'd. . . .

"Brethren: You have of late settled the River of Ohio for the sake of Hunting, & our Traders followed you for the sake of Hunting also. You have invited them yourselves. Your Brethren, the President & Council, desire You will look upon them as your Brethren & see that they have justice done. Some of your Young Men have robbed our Traders, but you will be so honest as to compel them to make Satisfaction. . . .

"Brethren: You have of late made frequent Complaints against the Traders bringing so much Rum to your Towns, & desir'd it might be stop't; & . . . the President & Council made an Act accordingly & put a stop to it, & no Trader was to bring any Rum or strong Liquor to your Towns. . . . But it seems it is out of [Pennsylvania's] Power to stop it entirely. You send down your own Skins by the Traders to buy Rum for you. You go yourselves & fetch Horse loads of strong Liquor. But the other Day an Indian came to this Town out of Maryland with 3 Horse loads of Liquor, so that it appears you love it so well that you cannot be without it. You know very well that the Country near the endless Mountain affords strong Liquor, & the moment the Traders buy it they are gone out of the Inhabitants & are travelling to this Place without being discover'd; besides this, you never agree about it—one will have it, the other won't (tho' very few), a third says we will have it cheaper; this last we believe is spoken from your Hearts (here they Laughed). Your Brethren, therefore, have order'd that every cask of Whiskey shall be sold to You for 5 Bucks in your Town, & if a Trader offers to sell Whiskey to You and will not let you have it at that Price, you may take it from him & drink it for nothing."

*   *   *

By the mid-eighteenth century, land company agents and farmer-hunters and traders from the backwoods of Virginia and North Carolina had penetrated the lower Appalachians, reached the headwaters of the Cumberland and Tennessee, and ventured into the Kentucky country beyond. This was the scene of the exploits of that prototype of pathmaking pioneers—Daniel Boone. In 1769, Boone and a number of companions set out on a long hunting trip which took them, by way of Cumberland Gap, into central Kentucky. Here Boone remained for two years, during part of which, because of the return or loss of his associates, he was alone in the wilderness. He was already casually committed, as a land scout, to the speculator Judge Richard Henderson; and in 1775, at Henderson's request, he and a company of axmen cut a road from the Holston River through the Cumberland Gap to the Kentucky River where Henderson intended to plant a settlement. Unhappily, we are dependent on a "ghost writer" for the narrative of Boone's early adventures. In 1783, he told his story to John Filson, a Kentucky schoolmaster, who couched it in an elegant prose that hardly suggests the robust if untutored personality of this most famous of American pioneers.

It was on the first of May, in the year 1769, that I resigned my domestic happiness for a time, . . . to wander through the wilderness of America, in quest of the country of Kentucke, in company with John Finley, John Stewart, Joseph Holden, James Monay, and William Cool. . . . After a long and fatiguing journey through a mountainous wilderness, we found ourselves on Red-River, where John Finley had formerly been trading with the Indians, and, from the top of an eminence, saw with pleasure the beautiful level of Kentucke. . . . We found every where abundance of wild beasts of all sorts, through this vast forest. The buffaloes were more frequent than I have seen cattle in the settlements, browsing on the leaves of the cane, or croping the herbage on those extensive plains. . . . Sometimes we saw hundreds in a drove, and the numbers about the salt springs were amazing. In this forest, . . . we practised hunting with great success until the twenty-second day of December following.

This day John Stewart and I had a pleasing ramble, but fortune changed the scene in the close of it. . . . In the decline of the day, near Kentucke river, as we ascended the brow of a small hill, a number of Indians rushed out of a thick cane-brake upon us, and made us prisoners. . . . The Indians plundered us of what we had, and kept us in confinement seven days, treating us with common savage usage. During this time we discovered no uneasiness or desire to escape, which made them less suspicious of us; but in the dead of night, as we lay in a thick cane brake by a large fire, when sleep had locked up their senses, . . . I touched my companion and gently awoke him. We . . . speedily directed our course towards our old camp, but found it plundered, and the company dispersed and gone home. About this time my brother, Squire Boon, with another adventurer, who came to explore the country shortly after us, was wandering through the forest, determined to find me, if possible, and accidentally found our camp. . . .

Soon after this, my companion in captivity, John Stewart, was killed by the savages, and the man that came with my brother returned home by-himself. We were then in a dangerous, helpless situation, exposed daily to perils and death amongst savages and wild beasts, not a white man in the country but ourselves. . . .

We . . . hunted every day, and prepared a little cottage to defend us from the Winter storms. We remained there undisturbed during the Winter; and on the first day of May, 1770, my brother returned home to the settlement by himself, for a new recruit of horses and ammunition, leaving me by myself, without bread, salt or sugar, without company of my fellow creatures, or even a horse or dog. . . .

One day I undertook a tour through the country, and the

diversity and beauties of nature I met with in this charming season, expelled every gloomy and vexatious thought. . . . I had gained the summit of a commanding ridge, and, looking round with astonishing delight, beheld the ample plains, the beauteous tracts below. On the other hand, I surveyed the famous river Ohio that rolled in silent dignity, marking the western boundary of Kentucke with inconceivable grandeur. At a vast distance I beheld the mountains lift their venerable brows, and penetrate the clouds. All things were still. I kindled a fire near a fountain of sweet water, and feasted on the loin of a buck, which a few hours before I had killed. . . . I continued this tour, and in a few days explored a considerable part of the country, each day equally pleased as the first. I returned again to my old camp, which was not disturbed in my absence. I did not confine my lodging to it, but often reposed in thick cane-brakes, to avoid the savages, who, I believe, often visited my camp, but fortunately for me, in my absence. . . .

Thus, . . . I spent the time until the 27th day of July following, when my brother to my great felicity, met me, according to appointment, at our old camp. Shortly after, we left this place, not thinking it safe to stay there longer, and proceeded to Cumberland river, reconnoitring that part of the country until March, 1771, and giving names to the different waters.

Soon after, I returned home to my family with a determination to bring them as soon as possible to live in Kentucke, which I esteemed a second paradise, at the risk of my life and fortune. . . .

I sold my farm on the Yadkin, and what goods we could not carry with us; and on the twenty-fifth day of September, 1773, bade a farewell to our friends, and proceeded on our journey to Kentucke, in company with five families more, and forty men that joined us in Powel's Valley, which is one hundred and fifty miles from the now settled parts of Kentucke. This promising beginning was soon overcast with a cloud of adversity; for upon the tenth day of October, the rear of our company was attacked by a number of Indians, who killed six, and wounded one man. Of these my eldest son was one that fell in the action. Though we defended ourselves, and repulsed the enemy, yet this unhappy affair scattered our cattle, brought us into extreme difficulty, and so discouraged the whole company, that we retreated forty miles, to the settlement on Clench river. [The Clinch is a tributary of the westward-flowing Tennessee.] We had passed over two mountains, viz. Powel s and Walden's, and were approaching Cumberland mountain when this adverse fortune overtook us. These mountains are in the wilderness, as we pass from the old settlements in Virginia to Kentucke, are ranged in a S. west and N. east direction, are of a great length and breadth, and not far distant from each other. Over these, nature hath formed passes, that are less difficult than might be expected from a view of such huge piles. The aspect of these cliffs is so wild and horrid, that it is impossible to behold them without terror. . . .

I remained with my family on Clench until the sixth of June, 1774, when I and one Michael Stoner were solicited by Governor Dunmore, of Virginia, to go to the Falls of the Ohio, to conduct into the settlement a number of surveyors that had been sent thither by him some months before; this country having about this time drawn the attention of many adventurers. We immediately complied with the Governor's request, and conducted in the surveyors, compleating a tour of eight hundred miles, through many difficulties, in sixty-two days.

* * *

The routes of the hunters, fur traders, and land agents were soon being traversed by farmer-pioneers. By the mid-1750's thousands of homeseekers had crossed the mountains to settle in southwestern Pennsylvania, only to be forced back to safer ground, during the Anglo-French conflict of 1755 to 1763 and the Indian uprising led by the Ottawa chieftain Pontiac, which followed it. Once the transmontane frontier was cleared of organized opposition from both the French and the Indians, migration flowed anew. Pioneers from the piedmont and valley sections of Virginia, Maryland, and Pennsylvania poured into southwestern Pennsylvania in the 1760's; the population of the area numbered 40,000 by 1774. To the southward, clusters of cabins appeared, during the late 1760's

and early 1770's, on the headwaters of the Tennessee River;
and by the mid-1770's settlers, moving along Boone's Wilder-
ness Road, were making their way into central Kentucky. Life
was insecure in these outposts of settlement in trans-Ap-
palachia, as the Indians contested possession of their hunt-
ing grounds with the oncoming farmer flood. A boyhood
spent amid Indian alarms acquainted Joseph Doddridge with
the hazards of life on the western Pennsylvania frontier in
the 1770's and the methods by which the pioneers adjusted
to them. These he later recalled in his Notes on the Settlement and Indian Wars, *which he wrote in 1824. His* Notes
also suggest the extent to which settlers were reduced to the
primitive in wearing apparel and standard of living in these
stockade days on the trans-Allegheny frontier.

The settlements on . . . [the western] side of the mountains commenced along the Monongahela, and between that
river and the Laurel Ridge, in the year 1772. In the succeeding
year they reached the Ohio river. . . . Land was the object
which invited the greater number of these people to cross the
mountain, for as the saying then was, "it was to be had here
for taking up." . . . There was, at an early period of our
settlements, an inferior kind of land title denominated a
tomahawk right, which was made by deadening a few trees
near the head of a spring, and marking the bark of some one,
or more of them with the initials of the name of the person
who made the improvement.

Some of the early settlers took the precaution to come over
the mountains in the spring, leaving their families behind to
raise a crop of corn, and then return and bring them out in
the fall. . . . Others, especially those whose families were
small, brought them with them in the spring. . . .

The necessary labors of the farms along the frontiers, were
performed with every danger and difficulty imaginable. The
whole population of the frontiers . . . huddled together in
their little forts, left the country with every appearance of a
deserted region; and such would have been the opinion of a
traveler concerning it, if he had not seen, here and there,
some small fields of corn or other grain in a growing state.

The fort consisted of cabins, blockhouses, and stockades. A

range of cabins, commonly formed one side, at least, of the fort. Divisions or partitions of logs separated the cabins from each other. The walls on the outside were ten or twelve feet high, the slope of the roof being turned wholly inward. A very few of these cabins had puncheon floors, the greater part were earthen. The blockades were built at the angles of the fort. They projected about two feet beyond the outer walls of the cabins and stockades. The upper stories were about eighteen inches every way larger than the under one. . . . A large folding gate made of thick slabs, nearest the spring, closed the fort. . . .

The families belonging to these forts were so attached to their own cabins on their farms, that they seldom moved into their fort in the spring until compelled by some alarm, as they called it; that is, when it was announced by some murder that the Indians were in the settlement. . . .

I well remember that, when a little boy, the family were sometimes waked up in the dead of night, by an express with a report that the Indians were at hand. The express came softly to the door, or back window, and by a gentle tapping waked the family. This was easily done, as an habitual fear made us ever watchful and sensible to the slightest alarm. The whole family were instantly in motion. My father seized his gun and other implements of war. My stepmother waked up and dressed the children as well as she could. . . . Besides the little children, we caught up what articles of clothing and provision we could get hold of in the dark, for we durst not light a candle or even stir the fire. All this was done with the utmost dispatch and the silence of death. The greatest care was taken not to awaken the youngest child. To the rest it was enough to say *Indian* and not a whimper was heard afterwards. Thus it often happened that the whole number of families belonging to a fort who were in the evening at their homes, were all in their little fortress before the dawn of the next morning. In the course of the succeeding day, their household furniture was brought in by parties of men under arms. . . .

The furniture for the table, for several years after the settlement of this country, consisted of a few pewter dishes, plates, and spoons; but mostly of wooden bowls, trenchers, and noggins. If these last were scarce, gourds and hard shelled squashes made up the deficiency. The iron pots, knives, and forks, were brought from the east side of the mountains along with salt and iron on pack horses. These articles of furniture corresponded very well with the articles of diet on which they were employed. "Hog and hominy" were proverbial for the dish of which they were the component parts. Johnny cake and pone were at the outset of the settlements of the country, the only forms of bread in use for breakfast and dinner. At supper, milk and mush was the standard dish. When milk was not plenty, which was often the case, owing to the scarcity of cattle, or the want of proper pasture for them, the substantial dish of hominy had to supply the place of them; mush was frequently eaten with sweetened water, molasses, bear's oil, or the gravy of fried meat.

Every family, besides a little garden for a few vegetables which they cultivated, had another small enclosure containing from half an acre to an acre, which they called a *truck patch*, in which they raised corn, for roasting ears, pumpkins, squashes, beans, and potatoes. These, in the latter part of the summer and fall, were cooked with their pork, venison, and bear meat for dinner, and made very wholesome and well tasted dishes. The standard dish for every log rolling, house raising, and harvest day was a pot pie. . . . This, besides answering for dinner, served for a part of the supper also. The remainder of it from dinner, being eaten with milk in the evening, after the conclusion of the labor of the day. . . .

On the frontiers, and particularly amongst those who were much in the habit of hunting, and going on scouts and campaigns, the dress of the men was partly Indian, and partly that of civilized nations.

The hunting shirt was universally worn. This was a kind of loose frock, reaching half way down the thighs, with large sleeves, open before, and so wide as to lap over a foot or more when belted. The cape was large, and sometimes handsomely fringed with a ravelled piece of cloth of a different color from that of the hunting shirt itself. The bosom of this dress served as a wallet to hold a chunk of bread, cakes, jerk, tow for wiping the barrel of the rifle, or any other necessary for the hunter or warrior. The belt which was always tied behind, answered several purposes, besides that of holding the dress together. In cold weather the mittens, and sometimes the bullet-bag, occupied the front part of it. To the right side was suspended the tomahawk and to the left the scalping knife in its leathern sheath. The hunting shirt was generally made of linsey, sometimes of coarse linen, and a few of dressed deer skins. These last were very cold and uncomfortable in wet weather. The shirt and jacket were of the common fashion. A pair of drawers or breeches and leggins, were the dress of the thighs and legs; a pair of moccasons answered for the feet much better than shoes. These were made of dressed deer skin. . . .

In cold weather the mocassons were well stuffed with deer's hair, or dry leaves, so as to keep the feet comfortably warm; but in wet weather it was usually said that wearing them was "a decent way of going barefooted;" and such was the fact, owing to the spongy texture of the leather of which they were made. . . .

The linsey petticoat and bed gown . . . were the universal dress of our women. . . .

They went barefooted in warm weather, and in cold, their feet were covered with moccasons, coarse shoes, or shoepacks.

*　　*　　*

The western settlements became even more vulnerable to Indian attack during the period of the American Revolution. Now the British found it expedient to encourage the red man's efforts to stem the farmer advance. No frontier dwelling was safe from Indian firebrand, tomahawk, or scalping knife. The Americans' only defense appeared to be to take the fight to the British outposts from which the Indian strength arose. This a young Virginian, George Rogers Clark, resolved to do. He led a party of less than two hundred men into the Illinois country, in 1778, and there effected a surprise attack on Kaskaskia, which won for the Americans the respect of the French inhabitants, as well as the Indians, in the area. Then with his miniature army he moved, under the most gruelling conditions, to Vincennes on the Wabash, where—again employing surprise—he forced the surrender of Colonel Henry

Hamilton, the British commandant in the West. Clark's narrative of his expedition reveals the nature of frontier warfare during the American Revolution and reflects the courage, ingenuity, and forthright manner of this hero of the war in the West, whose exploits had significant morale and propaganda value for the Patriot cause.

On the evening of July fourth [1778] we arrived within a few miles of . . . [Kaskaskia], where we threw out scouts in advance and lay until nearly dark. We then resumed our march and took possession of a house on the bank of the Kaskaskia River, about three-quarters of a mile above the town, occupied by a large family. . . . We obtained from the man boats enough to convey us across the river, where I formed my force in three divisions. I felt confident the inhabitants could not now obtain knowledge of our approach in time to enable them to make any resistance. . . . I set out for the fort with one division, ordering the other two to proceed to different quarters of the town. If I met with no resistance, at a certain signal a general shout was to be given and a certain part of the town was to be seized immediately, while men from each detachment who were able to talk French were to run through the streets proclaiming what had happened and informing the townsmen to remain in their houses on pain of being shot down.

These arrangements produced the desired effect, and within a very short time we were in complete possession of the place. . . .

The neighboring villages followed the examples set by Kaskaskia and Cahokia, and since we made no strict inquiry concerning those who had been engaged in encouraging the Indians to war, within a few days the country appeared to be in a state of perfect harmony. . . .

Being now in position to procure all the information I desired, I was astonished at perceiving the pains and expense the British had incurred in inciting the Indians. They had sent emissaries to every tribe throughout that vast country, even bringing the denizens of Lake Superior by water to Detroit and there outfitting them for war. The sound of war was universal, there being scarcely a nation among them but what had declared and received the bloody belt and hatchet. . . .

In a short time large numbers of Indians belonging to tribes inhabiting the Illinois country, came to Cahokia to make peace with us. . . .

The treaties we made . . . were negotiated in a different fashion, probably, than any others in America prior to that time. I had always been convinced that our general conduct of Indian affairs was wrong. Inviting them to treaties was considered by them in a different manner than we realized; they imputed it to fear on our part, and the giving of valuable presents confirmed them in this opinion. I resolved, therefore, to guard against this. . . . After the ceremonies commonly employed at the commencement of Indian treaties, they [the Indians] as the petitioning party, made the opening speech. They laid the entire blame for their taking up the bloody hatchet to the deception of the English, acknowledging their error and making many protestations that they would guard in future against those bad birds (alluding to the British emissaries sent among them) flying through the land. They concluded by expressing the hope that . . . they might be received as our friends, and that peace might take the place of the bloody belt, at the same time throwing down and stamping on the implements of war such as flags and red belts of wampum, which they had received from the British. I told them I had given attention to what they said, and that I would give them an answer the next day. . . . I then dismissed them, not suffering any of our people to shake hands with them as peace was not yet concluded. . . .

On the following day I delivered this speech:

Men and warriors, pay attention. . . . I am a man and a warrior, not a councilor. I carry War in my right hand and in my left Peace. I was sent by the great council fire of the Big Knives [the United States] and their friends to take control of all the towns the English possess in this country, and to remain here watching the conduct of the red men. . . .

The Big Knives are very much like the red men; they do not know well how to make blankets, powder and cloth;

they buy these things from the English (from whom they formerly descended) and live chiefly by raising corn, hunting and trading, as you and your neighbors, the French, do. . . . the English became angry and stationed strong garrisons through all our country (as you see they have done among you on the lakes and among the French) and would not let our women spin nor the men make powder, nor let us trade with anybody else. They said we must buy everything from them, and since we had become saucy they would make us give them two bucks for a blanket that we used to get for one. They said we must do as they pleased, and they killed some of us to make the rest afraid. . . .

Thus the war began, and the English were driven from one place to another, until they became weak and hired you red men to fight for them, and help them. The Great Spirit became angry at this, and caused your Old Father, the French king, and other great nations to join the Big Knives and fight with them against all their enemies, so that the English have become like deer in the woods. From this you may see that it is the Great Spirit that caused your waters to be troubled, because you fought for the people he was angry with, and if your women and children should cry you must blame yourselves for it, and not the Big Knives.

You can now judge who is in the right. I have already told you who I am. Here is a bloody belt and a white one. Take whichever you please. Behave like men. . . .

. . . on their return the next day, . . . they said that we were in the right, . . . and that they, the red men, ought to help us. They had taken up the belt of peace with a sincere heart, and . . . were determined to hold it fast. . . . They would call in all their warriors, and cast the tomahawk into the river where it could never be found again. . . .

This is the substance of their answer to me. The pipe was again kindled and presented to all the spirits to be witnesses, and with smoking and shaking of hands this grand piece of business was concluded, with as much dignity and importance in their eyes, I suppose, as was the treaty between France and America in ours.

Part III

THE OHIO VALLEY THRUST

"We . . . now . . . find ourselves in the very stream of emigration. Old America seems to be breaking up and moving westward." (*Morris Birkbeck*)

With the achievement of independence, the young United States was confirmed in its possession of the trans-Allegheny West. The boundaries of the new republic stretched westward to the Mississippi, from the Great Lakes on the north to Spain's Gulf Coast holdings on the south. The Ohio River, cutting through this vast territory from east to west, dictated the course of the westward advance for the ensuing forty years. By 1820, eleven states had been added to the original thirteen, and more than two million people—close to a third of the total population of the United States—were residing west of the mountains. Pressed by prospective purchasers—speculators, veterans, and farm-seeking settlers, the government of the new nation worked out a plan for administering its transmontane domain. This was the justly famous Ordinance of 1787 for the government of the Northwest Territory, which set the pattern by which the United States was to evolve from a nation of thirteen states to one of fifty. Of major importance was the provision that after a period of territorial status, during which the Federal Government would exert the chief control, eligible portions of the West could achieve statehood on the basis of equality with the existing states. Its assurance of eventual statehood, together with its guarantees on the subject of religion, education, equality in property descent, and freedom from human bondage, make the Ordinance of 1787 the most significant single piece of legislation dealing with the development of the American West.

An Ordinance for the government of the territory of the United States northwest of the river Ohio.

Sec. 3. *Be it ordained* . . . That there shall be appointed . . . , by Congress, a governor, whose commission shall continue in force for the term of three years . . . ; he shall reside in the district, and have a freehold estate therein in one thousand acres of land, while in the exercise of his office.

Sec. 4. There shall be appointed . . . , by Congress, a secretary, whose commission shall continue in force for four years . . . ; he shall reside in the district, and have a freehold estate therein, in five hundred acres of land, while in the exercise of his office. . . . There shall also be appointed a court, to consist of three judges, any two of whom to form a court, who shall have a common-law jurisdiction, and reside in the district, and have each therein a freehold estate, in five hundred acres of land, while in the exercise of their offices. . . .

Sec. 5. The governor and judges, or a majority of them, shall adopt and publish in the district such laws of the original States, criminal and civil, as may be necessary, and best suited to the circumstances of the district, . . . which laws shall be in force . . . until the organization of the general assembly therein, unless disapproved of by Congress; but afterwards the legislature shall have authority to alter them as they shall think fit. . . .

Sec. 9. So soon as there shall be five thousand free male inhabitants, of full age, in the district, . . . they shall receive authority . . . to elect representatives from their counties or townships, to represent them in the general assembly: . . . *Provided*, That no person be eligible or qualified to act as a representative, unless he shall have been a citizen of one of the United States three years, and be a resident in the district, or unless he shall have resided in the district three years; and, in either case, shall likewise hold in his own right, in fee-simple, two hundred acres of land within the same: *Provided, also*, That a freehold in fifty acres of land in the district, having been a citizen of one of the States, and being resident in the district, or the like freehold and two years' residence in the district, shall be necessary to qualify a man as an elector of a representative. . . .

Sec. 11. The general assembly, or legislature, shall consist of the governor, legislative council, and a house of representatives. The legislative council shall consist of five members, to continue in office five years; . . . and the members of the council shall be . . . appointed in the following manner, to wit: As soon as representatives shall be elected . . . they shall nominate ten persons, residents in the district, and each possessed of a freehold in five hundred acres of land, . . . five of whom Congress shall . . . commission to serve as aforesaid. . . . And the governor, legislative council, and house of representatives shall have authority to make laws in all cases. . . . And all bills, having passed by a majority in the house, and by a majority in the council, shall be referred to the governor for his assent; but no bill . . . shall be of any force without his assent. . . .

Sec. 12. . . . As soon as a legislature shall be formed in the district, the council and house assembled, in one room, shall have authority, by joint ballot, to elect a delegate to Congress who shall have a seat in Congress, with a right of debating, but not of voting, during this temporary government. . . .

Sec. 14. It is hereby ordained . . . that the following articles shall be considered as articles of compact, between the original States and the people and States in the said territory, and forever remain unalterable, unless by common consent, to wit:

Article I.

No person, demeaning himself in a peaceable and orderly manner, shall ever be molested on account of his mode of worship.

Article II.

The inhabitants . . . shall always be entitled to the benefits of the writ of *habeas corpus,* and of the trial by jury; of a proportionate representation of the people in the legislature, and of judicial proceedings according to the course of common law. . . .

Article III.

Religion, morality, and knowledge being necessary to good government and the happiness of mankind, schools and the means of education shall forever be encouraged. The utmost good faith shall always be observed towards the Indians. . . .

Article IV.

The said territory, and the States which may be formed therein, shall forever remain a part of . . . the United States of America. . . .

Article V.

. . . whenever any of the said States shall have sixty thousand free inhabitants therein, such State shall be admitted, by its delegates, into the Congress of the United States, on an equal footing with the original States, in all respects whatever; and shall be at liberty to form a permanent constitution and State government: *Provided*, The constitution and government, so to be formed, shall be republican. . . .

Article VI.

There shall be neither slavery nor involuntary servitude in the said territory. . . .

*   *   *

Organized companies were among the original purchasers of the land which the Federal Government had for sale in the Northwest Territory. One of these was the Ohio Company of Associates, made up of Massachusetts veterans of the Revolutionary War. In the Spring of 1788 they founded Marietta, at the point where the Muskingum River joins the Ohio. The first settlers arrived on a flatboat appropriately called the "May-Flower," and, under the benevolent auspices of the Company, shortly established a comfortable New England community. Less fortunate was a body of French migrants located farther down the Ohio at Gallipolis. This settlement was the product of the shady operations of the Scioto Company, a group of Congressmen and their friends who, through a political deal, obtained an option on a vast tract along the river. The promotional efforts of the Company's agents, one of whom was the poet Joel Barlow, induced some 600 Frenchmen, most of them unsuited to pioneering, to buy land and come to America. Upon their arrival, in the early 1790's, they found the Ohio wilderness less like the Garden of Eden than they had been led to believe. Their plight was described by their compatriot, the French philosophical writer and politician Constantin François Chasseboeuf, later the Count of Volney, who visited the settlement in 1796.

A certain association, called the Scioto Company, proposed, at Paris, in 1790, with much parade, the sale of some lands in the best part of the United States, at 120 cents an acre. They dealt out the most liberal promises and charming prospects, such as people are generally accustomed to offer on these occasions. "A climate wholesome and delightful, frost, even in winter, almost entirely unknown, and a river called, by way of eminence, the *beautiful,* and abounding in excellent fish, of a vast size. Noble forests, consisting of trees that spontaneously produce sugar . . . and a plant that yields ready made candles. . . . Venison in plenty, the pursuit of which is uninterrupted by wolves, foxes, lions, or tygers. A couple of swine will multiply themselves a hundred fold in two or three years, without taking any care of them. No taxes to pay, no military services to be performed."

These munificent promisers forgot to say, that these forests must be cut down before corn could be raised; that for a year at least they must bring their daily bread from a great distance; that hunting and fishing are agreeable amusements, when pursued for the sake of amusement, but are widely different when followed for the sake of subsistence: and they quite forgot to mention, that though there be no bears or tygers in the neighbourhood, there are wild beasts infinitely more cunning and ferocious, in the shape of men, who were at that time at open and cruel war with the whites.

In truth, the market value of these lands, at that time, in America, was no more than six or seven cents an acre. In France, in Paris, the imagination was too heated to admit of doubt or suspicion, and people were too ignorant and uninformed to perceive where the picture was defective, and its colours too glaring. . . .

On my arrival in America, in October, 1795, I made some enquiry after these people, but could only hear a vague story that they were buried somewhere in the western wilds, and had not prospered. Next summer I shaped my course through

Virginia, and after travelling . . . to the Ohio, I . . . reached . . . Gallipolis; by this splendid appellation (which means *French city*) the emigrants denominated their settlement. . . .

I could perceive nothing but a double row of small white houses, built on the flat top of the bank of the Ohio, which here laves the foot of a cliff fifty feet high. . . .

Next day I took a view of the place, and was struck with its forlorn appearance; with the thin pale faces, sickly looks, and anxious air of its inhabitants. They were shy of conversing with me. Their dwellings, though made externally cheerful by whitewash, were only log huts, patched with clay, and roofed with shingles, consequently damp, unwholesome, and uncomfortable. The village forms an oblong quadrangle of two rows of contiguous buildings, which a spark would consume altogether. . . . Adjoining these huts are gardens, fenced with thorn, destitute of trees, but well stocked with useful vegetables. . . . I collected from several persons the following history of their disastrous expedition.

About five hundred mechanics, artists, and tradesmen, in easy circumstances, and of good morals, arrived, in 1791 and 1792, at New York, Philadelphia, and Baltimore, from France. Each paid twenty or twenty-four guineas passage money, and their journies by land, in both hemispheres, cost them an equal sum. Thus dispersed, without any common plan of operations, they made, separately, their way towards Pittsburg and the Ohio, where their new home was situated. After many mistakes on the road, and a great waste of time and money, they reached a point, marked out upon a map, where the company had erected barracks for their accommodation. This company soon after became bankrupt, failing in its payments to the Ohio company, the original proprietors. . . . The United States were at war with the Indians, who disputed the right of the former to this very district. After the defeat of St. Clair, the savages blockaded the poor Frenchmen in their settlement, made captives of four, and scalped a fifth, who survived this dreadful operation.

Despondency overwhelmed them: some of them forsook the fatal spot, and withdrew into the country better peopled, or passed into Louisiana. At last, after four years of dangers, hardships, and vexations, the poor remnant obtained a tract of 912 acres, for a new advance of 1100 dollars. This *boon* they owed to a son of General Putnam, who benefited them in a still more signal and disinterested manner, by refusing 1200 dollars offered by two Frenchmen, with a view of getting the whole into their own hands, and then extorting an exorbitant price from their companions.

They were again fortunate in receiving, from the Congress of 1795, a gratuitous present of 20,000 acres, opposite Sandy Creek. . . .

When I paid my visit, only a year had elapsed since this arrangement had been made, and the settlement had already begun to revive and prosper, in such a manner as showed that great things would have been effected, had not its progress been checked by such heavy misfortunes. Still the situation of the colonists was far from being agreeable. All the labours of clearing and tillage were imposed on the family itself of the proprietor, laborers not being to be hired but at enormous prices. It may easily be imagined how severe a hardship it was, on men brought up in the ease and indolence of Paris, to chop trees, to plough, to sow, to reap, to labor in the field or the barn, in a heat of 85 or 95 degrees. . . .

Such is the condition of the Scioto colony, which does not altogether realize the pictures of the inland paradise given by American farmers.

*   *   *

To the Indians of the Old Northwest, the continuing stream of farmer settlement caused renewed alarm. Defeats suffered at the hands of "Mad" Anthony Wayne in the mid-1790's had quieted the natives for a time; but by 1810 they were again in a mood to resist. At this juncture the Shawnee states-man Tecumseh and his brother the Prophet were the champions of the Indian cause. Their antagonist was William Henry Harrison, governor of Indiana Territory, which had been carved out of the Northwest Territory in 1800. Unity of the Indian nations, both north and south, was the Indian leaders' goal, but Harrison's skill in dealing with the individual tribes made this hard to achieve. The conflict came to a head

*in the Fall of 1811, in connection with American attempts
to survey a tract of land along the Wabash, which had been
ceded through controversial Indian negotiations in 1809.
Harrison's efforts to disperse the Indians at Prophet's Town
led to the defeat of the outnumbered natives, in the so-called
Battle of Tippecanoe, on November 7, 1811. Signs of British
assistance to the Indians, detected on this occasion, heightened
the antagonism of the West toward England and, along with
other causes, helped to precipitate the War of 1812. John M.
Oskison's account of negotiations between Harrison and
Tecumseh in 1810 concerning the disputed cession drama-
tizes the difficulty of resolving the impasse which inevitably
existed between the advancing white and resisting Indian
civilizations.*

The time was now July of 1810. Time for another letter to
the Indians at Tippecanoe. Addressing the Prophet . . . ,
Harrison charged: "You are an enemy to the Seventeen Fires
[United States], and you have used the greatest exertions with
other tribes to lead them astray. In this you have been in
some measure successful, as I am told they are ready to raise
the tomahawk against their father." . . .

He spoke of the bright chain of friendship that had long
linked the Great Father's white and red children together,
and hoped it would not be broken. But the red children must
know that the Seventeen Fires had many more warriors than
all the Indians together could muster. "Do not think that the
redcoats can protect you; they are not able to protect themselves. They do not think of going to war with us. If they did,
you would in a few moons see our flag wave over all the forts
of Canada." . . .

The Prophet sent a messenger to say that the Indians' answer would be carried to Harrison by Tecumseh in a few
weeks. Harrison replied that he would be glad to receive
Tecumseh, but that he must not bring more than a small
delegation with him.

To that stipulation Tecumseh paid no attention. On the
twelfth of August, he appeared on the river opposite Fort
Knox with 400 followers in 80 canoes. . . .

If Tecumseh meant to impress the Governor with his

strength by bringing so many painted, armed, and well-dressed warriors, Harrison also prepared a show. He gathered at Grouseland the judges of the Supreme Court of the Territory, a contingent of army officers, posted a guard of twelve soldiers in charge of a sergeant, and for a considerable number of ladies and gentlemen of Vincennes placed seats on the portico of his mansion. . . .

Tecumseh spoke at length, after saying that his talk would be a repetition of what he had told the whites often but which they seemed unable to understand:

"Brothers: Since the peace was made, you have killed some of the Shawnees, Winnebagoes, Delawares, and Miamis, and you have taken our land from us; and I do not see how we can remain at peace if you continue to do so. You try to force the red people to do some injury; it is you who are pushing them on to do mischief. You try to keep the tribes apart, and make distinctions among them. You wish to prevent the Indians from uniting and looking upon their lands as common property. You take tribes aside, and advise them not to come into this union. But until they do, and we have accomplished our design to unite them, we do not wish to accept your offer to send us to see the President. . . .

"Brothers: You ought to realize what you are doing with the Indians. It is a very bad thing, and we do not like it. Since I have lived at Tippecanoe, we have tried to do away with all tribal distinctions, and take away power from the town chiefs who have done us mischief by signing away our land; it is they who have sold it to the Americans; and it is our wish that our affairs shall be managed by the warriors.

"Brothers: This land was sold, and the goods received for it went only to a few. . . . In the future we are prepared to punish those chiefs who may come forward to propose selling the land. If you continue to purchase it from them, it will cause war among the different tribes; and in the end I do not know what will be the consequences for the white people."

Addressing Harrison, Tecumseh said:

"Brother: I was glad to hear you say that if we could show that the land was sold by people who had no right to sell, you would restore it. Those tribes that sold did not own it. They set up a claim, but the tribes with me will not agree to those claims. If the land is not restored to us you will see, when we return to our homes, how it will be settled. We shall have a great council, at which all the tribes will be present, when we shall show to those who sold that they had no right to the claims they set up. You will see what will be done to those chiefs who did sell the land to you.

"I am not alone in this; it is the determination of all the warriors and red people who listen to me. I now wish you to listen to me. If you do not, it will appear that you wished me to kill all the chiefs who sold you the land. I tell you so because I am authorised by all the tribes to do so. I am head of them all; I am a warrior; and all the warriors will meet together in two or three moons from this one; then I shall call for those chiefs who sold you the land, and shall know what to do with them."

*   *   *

The close of the War of 1812 unloosed a flood of migration into the lower Ohio Valley and the Gulf Coast South. With the cessation of hostilities, by 1815, the threat of further British interference was removed; and treaties, soon forced upon the Indians, opened most of their lands in the Old Northwest. Spain's former possessions, Louisiana and West Florida, were already in American hands. Veterans were eager to return to fertile areas they had spied while on military duty in the West; and a now peaceful Atlantic Ocean facilitated migration from Europe, especially from the British Isles. The United States, in general, was on the move; and much of this movement was to the West. Roads and rivers teemed with the migrating throng. Some journeyed overland, by horse-back, stage coach, or private vehicle, along the few dependable roads into the West; the Cumberland Road was completed to Wheeling by 1818. Others preferred to travel the water highways, by flatboat or ark; and steamboats were available on the Ohio after 1811. The English reformer Morris Birkbeck elected to go by land (sometimes it meant walking), as he and eight others journeyed westward, in the late Spring of 1817, to found a settlement for English immigrants in the prospective State of Illinois. He described this experience in his Notes on a Journey in America from the Coast of Virginia to the Territory of Illinois.

So here we are [at McConnel's Town, Pennsylvania], nine in number, one hundred and thirty miles of mountain country between us and Pittsburg. We learn that the stages which pass daily from Philadelphia and Baltimore are generally full, and that there are now many persons at Baltimore waiting for places. No vehicles of any kind are to be hired, and here we must either stay or *walk* off: the latter we prefer; and separating each our bundle from the little that we have of travelling stores, we are about to undertake our mountain pilgrimage; accepting the alternative most cheerfully, after the dreadful shaking of the last hundred miles by stage. . . .

We have now fairly turned our backs on the old world and find ourselves in the very stream of emigration. Old America seems to be breaking up and moving westward. We are seldom out of sight, as we travel on this grand track towards the Ohio, of family groups, behind and before us, some with a view to a particular spot; close to a brother perhaps, or a friend, who has gone before, and reported well of the country. Many, like ourselves, when they arrive in the wilderness, will find no lodge prepared for them.

A small wagon (so light that you might almost carry it, yet strong enough to bear a good load of bedding, utensils, and provisions, and a swarm of young citizens,—and to sustain marvellous shocks in its passage over these rocky heights), with two small horses; sometimes a cow or two, comprises their all; excepting a little store of hard-earned cash for the land office of the district; where they may obtain a title for as many acres as they possess half-dollars, being one-fourth of the purchase money. The waggon has a tilt, or cover, made of a sheet, or perhaps a blanket. The family are seen before, behind or within the vehicle, according to the road or weather, or perhaps the spirits of the party. . . .

June 4. [Having reached Pittsburgh we] purchased horses for our party at fifty to sixty dollars, and are making preparations for proceeding through the state of Ohio, to Cincinnati. [They travelled via Wheeling, Zanesville, Chillicothe, Cincinnati, Madison, and Vincennes.]

It is more usual for a party, or even for individuals, who have no business on land, to pass down the Ohio. "Arks," of which hundreds are on the river, are procured of a size suitable for the number. They are long floating rooms, built on a flat bottom, with rough boards, and arranged within for sleeping and other accommodations. You hire boatmen and lay in provisions, and, on your arrival at the destined port, sell your vessel as well as you can, possibly at half cost. On the whole, when the navigation is good, this is pleasant and cheap travelling.

But we, putting health and information against ease and saving of expence, have unanimously given the preference to horse-back.

*   *   *

Migrants from the seaboard South, who were destined for the West, sometimes traveled by way of the Ohio River, especially Virginians bound for Kentucky, Missouri, or sections of the Old Northwest; but for those moving into the lower South the overland route was obviously more expedient. Cotton lands were the magnet that pulled many Southerners westward, now that the cotton gin made production for a world market practical; and slaveholding was no impediment to pioneering, for the Negro slave was often as effective in clearing the wilderness as was the white frontiersman who opened up the West. Massachusetts-born Timothy Flint had a chance to observe the slave-implemented caravans of migrating Southerners during his ten-year residence in the Mississippi Valley. He came West in 1815, after his graduation from Harvard University, and spent the next ten years in missionary activity in Ohio, Missouri, and Louisiana. Here he was able to observe the ways in which the techniques of migration in the South differed from those in the North. He described these in his History and Geography of the Mississippi Valley (1832), *an expanded version of his* A Condensed Geography and History of the Western States, *published in Cincinnati in 1828.*

Immigrants from Virginia, the two Carolinas and Georgia . . . still immigrate, after the ancient fashion, in the southern wagon. This is a vehicle almost unknown at the north, strong, comfortable, commodious, containing not only a movable kitchen, but provisions and beds. Drawn by four or six horses, it subserves all the various intentions of house, shelter and transport; and is, in fact, the southern ship of the forests and prairies. The horses, that convey the wagon, are large and powerful animals, followed by servants, cattle, sheep, swine, dogs, the whole forming a primitive caravan not unworthy of ancient days. The procession moves on with power in its dust, putting to shame and uncomfortable feelings of comparison the northern family with their slight wagon, jaded horses and subdued, though jealous countenances. Their vehicle stops; and they scan the strong southern hulk, with its chimes of bells, its fat black drivers and its long train of concomitants, until they have swept by. . . .

Ten wagons are often seen in company. It is a fair allowance, that a hundred cattle, beside swine, horses and sheep, and six negroes accompany each. The train, with the tinkling of an hundred bells, and the negroes, wearing the delighted expression of a holiday suspension from labor in their countenances, forming one group, and the family slowly moving forward, forming another, as the whole is seen advancing along the plains, it presents a pleasing and picturesque spectacle.

They make arrangements at night fall to halt at a spring, where there is wood and water, and a green sward for encampment. The dogs raise their accustomed domestic baying. The teams are unharnessed, and the cattle and horses turned loose into the grass. The blacks are busy in spreading the cheerful table in the wilderness, and preparing the supper, to which the appetite of fatigue gives zest. They talk over the incidents of the past day, and anticipate those of the morrow. If wolves and owls are heard in the distance, these desert sounds serve to render the contrast of their society and security more sensible. In this order they plunge deeper and deeper into the forest or prairie, until they have found the place of their rest.

* * *

The appeal of the Ohio Valley West for migrants from the British Isles, following the close of the War of 1812, is suggested in the chronicle of George Flower, who was associated with Morris Birkbeck in his efforts to establish an English settlement in Illinois. Flower returned to England in the Fall of 1817 to publicize their wilderness enterprise, recruit funds, and bring back additional settlers. He described these colo-

nizing activities in his History of the English Settlement in Edwards County, Illinois, founded in 1817 and 1818 by Morris Birkbeck and George Flower.

The publication in England of our travels, my return, and personal communication with a host of individuals, had given a wide-spread knowledge of what we had done and what we intended to do. Our call had received a response from the farmers of England, the miners of Cornwall, the drovers of Wales, the mechanics of Scotland, the West-India planter, the inhabitants of the Channel Isles, and the "gentleman of no particular business" of the Emerald Isle. All were moving or preparing to move to join us in another hemisphere. The cockneys of London had decided on the reversal of their city habits, to breathe the fresh air of the prairies. Parties were moving, or preparing to move, in all directions. . . .

The Lawrence-and-Trimmer party [which sailed from Bristol] landed safely at Philadelphia early in June [1819]. They made their way some in wagons some on horseback, over the mountains to Pittsburgh, then descending the Ohio in flatboats to Shawneetown, in August, proceeded without delay on foot, in wagons and on horseback, to Mr. Birkbeck's cabin on Boltenhouse Prairie. . . .

It is a noticeable fact that emigrants bound for the English Settlement in Illinois, landed at every port from the St. Lawrence to the Gulf of Mexico. This arises from the fact that the laborers and small-farmers of England are very imperfectly acquainted with the geography of America. Indeed, among all classes in England there is a very inadequate idea of the extent of the United States. . . . As various as their ports of debarkation, were the routes they took, and the modes of conveyance they adopted.

Some came in wagons and light carriages, overland; some on horseback; some in arks; some in skiffs; and some by steamboat, by New Orleans. One Welshman landed at Charleston, S.C. "How did you get here?" I asked. "Oh," he innocently replied, "I just bought me a horse, sir, and inquired the way." It seems our Settlement was then known at the plantations in Carolina and in the mountains of Tennessee. The great variety found among our people, coming as they did from almost every county in the kingdom, in complexion, stature, and dialect, was in the early days of our Settlement very remarkable. . . .

Individuals and families were frequently arriving, and occasionally a party of thirty and forty. A fresh cause induced this tide of emigration. It arose from the private correspondence of the first poor men who came. Having done well themselves, and by a few years of hard labor acquired more wealth than they ever expected to obtain they wrote home to friend or relative an account of their success. These letters handed round in the remote villages of England, in which many of them lived, reached individuals in a class to whom information in book form was wholly inaccessible. Each letter had its scores of readers, and, passing from hand to hand, traversed its scores of miles. The writer, known at home as a poor man, earning perhaps a scanty subsistence by his daily labor, telling of the wages he received, his bountiful living, of his own farm and the number of his live-stock, produced a greater impression in the limited circle of its readers than a printed publication had the power of doing. His fellow-laborer who heard these accounts, and feeling that he was no better off than when his fellow-laborer left him for America, now exerted every nerve to come and do likewise.

*   *   *

A letter written by Samuel Crabtree to his brother in England, in April, 1818, is typical of the promotion through correspondence to which George Flower referred. His praise of the agricultural abundance of the Ohio country, though expressed in humble terms, is nevertheless in the idiom of the original, seventeenth-century eulogies to the plenitude of the New World, and reflects the appeal which, more than any other, drew Europeans as well as Americans to the West. Crabtree seems to have expected that his letter might be put into print. Later in the year it appeared in a pamphlet published by John Knight, in Manchester, England, entitled Important Extracts from Original and Recent Letters, written by Englishmen, in the United States of America to their Friends in England. Knight was also the author of a brochure

which came out in the same year: The Emigrants Best Instructor, or, the most Recent and Important Information
respecting the United States of America, Selected from the
Works of the latest Travellers in that Country. . . .

. . . this is the country for a man to enjoy himself: . . .
Ohio, Indiana, and the Missouri Territory; where you may see
prairies 60 miles long and ten broad, not a stick nor a stone
in them, at two dollars an acre, that will produce from seventy
to one hundred bushels of Indian corn per acre: too rich for
wheat or any other kind of grain. I measured Indian corn in
Ohio State, last September more than fifteen feet high, and
some of the ears had from four to seven hundred grains. I
believe I saw more peaches and apples rotting on the ground
than would sink the British fleet. I was at many plantations in
Ohio where they no more knew the number of their hogs
than myself. . . . and they have such flocks of turkeis, geese,
ducks, and hens, as would surprise you: they live principally
upon fowls and eggs: and in summer upon apple and peach
pies. The poorest family has a cow or two and some sheep:
and in the fall can gather as many apples and peaches as
serves the year round. Good rye whiskey; apple and peach
brandy, at forty cents per gallon, which I think equal to rum.
Excellent cider at three dollars per barrel of thirty-three gal-
lons, barrel included.

There is enough to spare of everything a person can desire;
have not heard either man or woman speak a word against the
government or the price of provisions.

The poorest families adorn the table three times a day like
a wedding dinner—tea, coffee, beef, fowls, pies, eggs, pickles,
good bread; and their favorite beverage is whiskey or peach
brandy. Say, is it so in England? . . .

If you knew the difference between this country and England you would need no persuading to leave it and come
hither. It abounds with game and deer; I often see ten or
fifteen together; turkeis in abundance, weighing from eighteen
to twenty-four pounds. The rivers abound with ducks and
fish. There are some elks and bears. We have no hares, but
swarms of rabbits: the woods are full of turtle doves, and eight

or nine kinds of wood peckers. Robin red-breast about the size of your pigeon.

*   *   *

Between 1810 and 1820, more than half a million new-comers poured into Kentucky, Tennessee, Alabama, Mississippi, and Louisiana, while at the same time Ohio, Indiana, Illinois, and Missouri experienced an almost identical increase. Testimony to the magnitude of the migration westward after 1815 was the publication of counter-propaganda designed to satirize and presumably to offset the influence of the glowing accounts written by land speculators, town-site promoters, inspirited settlers, and enthusiastic authors of emigrant guides. One example is the pamphlet entitled Western Emigration, *which Henry Trumbull published in Boston in 1819. It purported to be the journal of "Dr. Jeremiah Simpleton's Tour to Ohio," supplying the "unvarnished truth" concerning the "numerous difficulties, Hair-breadth Escapes, Mortifications and Privations, which the Doctor and his family experienced on their Journey from Maine, to the 'Land of Promise,' and during a residence of three years in that highly extolled country." This disclosure of Dr. Simpleton's alleged hardships apparently dissuaded few Yankees from undertaking the journey west.*

Now, friend Scruple, . . . I hope . . . you will listen to a piece of my mind which I mean to give you, and which I intend to apply to all those in our parts, who are filled with the desire of emigrating to the westward—I would seriously advise you to 'face to the right about,' and re-establish yourself in the place from whence you came, among your neighbors and friends, if you have the smallest regard for the welfare of yourself and family.

In Maine, we have, or can procure with industry, every thing we want for food, clothing, and all the other conveniences of life, at a moderate rate. We have plenty of beef, pork, mutton, poultry and wild fowl, as well as fish of all sorts; here are mills to grind our corn, and factories to manufacture our cloth—we have mechanics of all sorts to make our shoes, hats, furniture, and everything else; and all these comforts can be obtained almost at our doors—our land is well cultivated and we have good houses to live in.—I swaggers! I think people are downright fools, to think of leaving their good homes in such numbers, and run on a wild goose chace in a dreary wilderness, where they are liable to endure every hardship that can befall man, as I have done, only because they are not satisfied with their condition. They hearken too readily to the idle tales of the peskit Ohio speculators, who with great parade tell us that that land is a perfect Paradise—that there, civil and military commissions pour down from the clouds in torrents—that provisions abound in such profusion, that geese, turkeys, oppossums, bears, raccoons and rabbits may be seen running in the woods in droves, ready cooked, with knives and forks stuck in their flanks, crying out to the newly arrived emigrant, 'come eat me.'—The reverse of this, friend Scruple, is the case, as you may perceive by my account of the mishaps and disasters that I met with. You will, on your arrival there, be obliged to sleep in a hollow tree, or build yourself a log hut, for here are no carpenters—kill and dress your own game, for here are no butchers—clothe yourself in skins, when your stock of apparel is worn out, for here are no factories, shoemakers, tailors, hatters, or tanners—and pound your own corn, for you may travel in this wild wilderness fifty miles, without discovering the sign of a mill—in short, nothing can be obtained here without costing more for the transportation than the original price of any article you may want. As to *society*, if you wish to converse in any human language out of your family, you must go twenty or thirty miles to your next door neighbor, with your axe instead of staff—for you must cut your way thither, for want of roads—and perhaps, after all, find him almost as hoggish as the 'swines in your pens' or the more numerous class of the inhabitants of Ohio, the wild-cat, panther, etc. who frequently associate with our tame animals to their sorrow, and sometimes with young children, to *our* mourning;—and, fags, I'd rather be a hog-reeve in good New-England, than hold any office in this back woods country, where the inhabitants walk on all fours, with the exception of a few double headed fools. Take my advice, therefore, Scruple, and put off your journey, till you think a little further on the subject.

PART IV

FRONTIER SOCIETY

"The first business is to clear away the trees from the spot where the house is to stand. . . . The people are . . . too much occupied in making farms and speculations, to think of literature." (*Timothy Flint*)

Trees shaped the appearance of the society that developed as pioneers pushed across the Alleghenies and into the Ohio and Mississippi valleys before 1830. North of the Ohio, the timber covering was interrupted in places by oak openings and by the grassy prairies of western Indiana and central Illinois; and in the South a treeless, fertile black belt varied the monotony of the pines. But elsewhere, generally, the forest prevailed. It was a wooden world, made habitable only by the axe. For the earliest settlers, trees supplied the material for fences, for sheltering livestock, and for the log cabin and its crude furniture and utensils. At the same time, the trees were impediments to the agricultural development on which the frontier economy primarily depended; and usually the first crop of corn—the staple of the frontier—was planted amid trunks that had been girdled but left standing; and the settlers' livestock had to forage in the woods. Timothy Flint's ten years' residence in the Ohio and Missouri country equipped him to provide a detailed description of the first stages of farm-making in this part of the forested frontier. It is included in his History and Geography of the Mississippi Valley, *written at the turn of the 1830's, not without, presumably, the interest of prospective settlers in mind.*

The first business is to clear away the trees from the spot where the house is to stand. . . . Straight trees are felled of a size, that a common team can draw, or as the phrase is 'snake,' them to the intended spot. . . . The logs, of which [the cabin] is composed, are notched on to one another, in the form of a square. The roof is covered with thin splits of oak, not unlike staves. Sometimes they are made of ash, and in the lower country of cypress, and they are called clap boards.

Instead of being nailed, they are generally confined in their place by heavy timbers, laid at right angles across them. This gives the roof of a log house an unique and shaggy appearance. But if the clap boards have been carefully prepared from good timber they form a roof sufficiently impervious to common rains. The floors are made from short and thick plank, split from yellow poplar, cotton wood, black walnut, and sometimes oak. They are confined with wooden pins, and are technically called 'puncheons.'

The southern people, and generally the more wealthy immigrants advance in the first instance to the luxury of having the logs hewed on the inside, and the puncheon floor hewed, and planed, in which case it becomes a very comfortable and neat floor. The next step is to build the chimney. . . . The hearth is made with clay mortar, or, where it can be found, sand stones, as the common lime stone does not stand the fire. The interstices of the logs in the room are first 'chincked;' that is to say, small blocks and pieces of wood in regular forms are driven between the intervals, made by laying the logs over each other, so as to form a kind of a coarse lathing to hold the mortar.

The doors are made of plank, split in the manner mentioned before, from fresh cut timber; and they are hung after an ingenious fashion on large wooden hinges, and fastened with a substantial wooden latch. The windows are square apertures, cut through the logs, and are closed during the cooler nights and the inclement weather by wooden shutters. . . .

The field, in which the cabin is built, is generally a square or oblong enclosure, of which the buildings are the centre, if the owner be from the south; or in the centre of one side of the square, if from the north. . . . Nine tenths of the habitations in the upper western states are placed near springs, which supply the family with water. The settlers on the prairies, for the most part, fix their habitations in the edges of the wood, that skirts the prairie, and generally obtain their water from wells. The inhabitants of the lower country, on the contrary, except in the state of Mississippi, where springs are common, chiefly supply themselves with water from cisterns filled by rain. . . . the trees are carefully cleared away, by cutting them down near the ground. That part of the timber, which cannot be used either for rails, or the construction of the buildings, is burned, and a clearing is thus made for a considerable space round the cabin. In the remaining portion of the field, the trees undergo an operation, called by the northern people 'girdling,' and by the southern 'deadening.' That is, a circle is cut, two or three feet from the ground, quite through the bark of the tree, so as completely to divide the vessels which carry on the progress of circulation. . . . The smaller trees are all cut down; and the accumulated spoils of vegetable decay are burned together; and the ashes contribute to the great fertility of the virgin soil. If the field contain timber for rails, the object is to cut as much as possible on the clearing; thus advancing the double purpose of clearing away the trees, and preparing the rails, so as to require the least possible distance of removal. An experienced hand will split from an hundred to an hundred and fifty rails in a day. Such is the convenience of finding them on the ground to be fenced, that Kentucky planters and the southern people generally prefer timbered land to prairie; notwithstanding the circumstance, so unsightly and inconvenient to a northern man, of dead trees, stumps, and roots, which, strewed in every direction over his field, even the southern planter finds a great preliminary impediment in the way of cultivation. The northern people prefer to settle on the prairie land, where it can be had in convenient positions.

The rails are laid zigzag, one length running nearly at right angles to the other. This in west country phrase, is 'worm fence,' and in the northern dialect 'Virginia fence.' The rails are large and heavy, and to turn the wild cattle and horses of the country, require to be laid ten rails or six feet in height. The smaller roots and the underbrush are cleared from the ground by a sharp hoe, known by the name 'grubbing hoe.' This implement, with a cross cut saw, a whip saw, a hand saw, axes, a broad axe, an adze, an auger, a hammer, nails, and an iron tool to split clap boards, constitute the indispensable apparatus for a backwoodsman. The smoke house, spring house, and other common appendages of such an establishment it is unnecessary to describe; for they are the same as in the establishment of the farmers in the middle and southern Atlantic states.

A peach orchard is generally the first object in raising fruit; because it is easily made, and begins to bear the second or third year. Apple orchards with all good farmers are early objects of attention. . . . Maize is planted the first year without ploughing. Afterwards the plough becomes necessary. Turnips, sweet potatoes, pumpkins and melons flourish remarkably on the virgin soil. It is a pleasant spectacle, to see with what luxuriance the apple tree advances, South of 33° the fig tree is substituted for the apple tree. If the log buildings were made of good and durable materials, they remain comfortable dwellings seven or eight years. By this time in the ordinary progress of successful farming, the owner replaces them by a house of stone, brick, or frame work; and the object is to have the second house as large, and showy, as the first was rustic and rude.

* * *

Although self-sufficiency was the prevailing characteristic of frontier society in these years, numerous activities involved associative effort. A house-raising often enlisted the volunteer services of a settler's neighbors, as did butchering, flax scutching, corn husking, or household pursuits such as fulling and quilting. These cooperative endeavors, which combined an element of both work and play, provided utilitarian excuses for socializing on the inevitably lonely rural frontier. John Knight's emigrants guide, published in England in 1818, assured prospective settlers of this quality in the residents of the Ohio Valley West.

. . . In the settlement of a country, there are many things to be done, which require the united strength of many; this money cannot purchase: but that kind and generous feeling, which men (not rendered callous by wealth or poverty) have for each other, comes to their relief. The neighbors, (even unsolicited) appoint a day, when as a frolic, they shall (for instance,) build the new settler a house.—On the morning appointed, they assemble; and divide themselves into parties: one party cut down the trees; another lops them and cuts them into proper lengths; a third, (with horses or oxen) drag them to the intended spot; another party make shingles for the roof; and at night all the materials are on the spot: and the night of the next day, the family sleep in their new habitation.—No payment is expected, nor would be received: it is considered a duty; and lays him under obligation, to assist the next settler. But this cooperation of labour is not confined to new settlers; it occurs frequently, in the course of a year, amongst the old settlers with whom it is a bond of amity and social intercourse: and in no part of the world, is good neighbourship, in greater perfection, than in America.

*   *   *

The self-sufficiency of the farm unit was one of the attributes of frontier society which impressed Gottfried Duden, an educated German who spent four years (1824-1827) in the young State of Missouri. His account of his residence there was so approving of the West as to attract thousands of his countrymen to settle in Missouri and neighboring Illinois.

Until his domestic animals are sufficient to supply the settler with meat, hunting keeps him in provisions. . . . There are so many deer, stag, turkeys, hens, pigeons, pheasants, snipes, and other game that without much exertion a good hunter can provide for the needs of a large family. . . .

Buffalo are no longer seen in these parts. They have moved farther to the west and north. One occasionally sees a bear, and I hear wolves howling almost every night. Yet the sheep need no shepherd, and the farmer suffers no more from wild animals than from robbers or thieves. . . .

In the American West corn is the farmer's main crop. It might be called the nurse of the growing population. It supplies food for all the domestic animals. Meal is made of it, which, when cooked with milk, offers a very nourishing, wholesome, and palatable food. When it is kneaded with the boiled pulp of the pumpkin, a kind of bread can be made of it which is preferable to wheat bread, especially if the dough has been allowed to ferment for twelve hours. Meal mixed with water or milk and baked without other ingredients makes a kind of dry bread which is edible when consumed with fatty vegetables. The baking is done in covered, iron pots, which are placed beside the fire and completely covered with burning coals. . . .

Peas and beans flourish beyond all expectation. . . . The beans are sown in the corn fields where the high cornstalks serve the rows of beans as a support. In the same fields are also sown pumpkins, lettuce, and many other things. . . .

In the second year cotton is also raised, although north of Missouri only for family needs. The American farmer aims to provide his food, drink, and clothing, except for special finery, without having to pay money for them. Thus, flax and hemp are raised and a small flock of sheep is maintained. Flax, hemp, and wool are entirely worked up in the household. Everyone has a spinning wheel; and if there is no loom in the house, the housewife or one of her daughters goes now and then to a neighbor who has one of these implements. Just as most of the men practise shoemaking, so most women make not only their own but their husband's clothing. . . .

Once the household is organized and the first necessities are supplied, the family lives happily without a single piece of ready money. . . . Only for taxes is ready money needed. But these are so slight that one rarely thinks of them. Land acquired from the government is completely tax free for the first five years. . . .

There is an overabundance of food at hand. Beer can be easily brewed since hops are in adequate supply in the woods. Apple and peach orchards, which no farm is without, provide the makings of cider and brandy. A very good brandy is made from corn, but the brandy from apples and peaches is preferred. I have bought old corn brandy at 30 cents a gallon which equaled the best French brandy. . . . the farmer lives in a situation which is far superior to that of a German farmer with the same holdings.

The soil is so productive that the corn crop demands nothing but a mere breaking of the soil, a single ploughing.

* * *

The self-sufficiency of this frontier society extended, in the early days, to the point where the settler was obliged even to assume responsibility for marketing his crops, once he began to produce a surplus. For this and other reasons towns appeared on the traditionally agrarian frontier. Some were the creation of townsite promoters who, in the interest of speculative profits, often attempted to establish urban communities before there was a hinterland to support them. Others were the natural entrepôts of the maturing frontier economy. The beginnings of trade and the emergence of towns are described in George Flower's account of the English settlement which he and Morris Birkbeck founded in 1817 and 1818 on the southern Illinois frontier.

In about three years [after the original foundation of the settlement], a surplus of corn, pork, and beef was obtained, but no market. Before they could derive any benefit from the sale of their surplus produce, the farmers themselves had to quit their farms and open the channels of commerce, and convey their produce along until they found a market. At first there were no produce-buyers, and the first attempts at mercantile adventures were almost failures. In the rising towns, a few buyers began to appear, but with too small a capital to pay money, even at the low price produce then was. They generally bought on credit, to pay on their return from New Orleans. In this way, the farmers were at disadvantage; if the markets were good, the merchant made a handsome profit. If bad, they often had not enough to pay the farmer. Then the farmers began to build their own flat-boats, load them with the produce of their own growth, and navigate them by their own hands. They traded down the Mississippi to New Orleans, and often on the coast beyond. Thus were the channels of trade opened, and in this way was the chief trade of the country carried on for many years. . . .

One evening . . . we discussed the measures that should be taken to form some village or town, as a centre for those useful arts necessary to agriculture. Every person wanted the services of a carpenter and blacksmith. But every farmer could not build workshops at his own door. . . . Thus the spot for our town as a central situation was decided upon. Now for a name. . . . At last we did what almost all emigrants do, pitched on a name that had its association with the land of our birth. Albion was then and there located, built, and peopled in imagination. . . .

We met the next day in the woods according to appointment. The spot seemed suitable. . . . "Here shall be the centre of our town," we said. . . . Mr. Fordham . . . forthwith went to work, and completed the survey and the plat. One of our number went to Shawneetown, and entered the section of six hundred and forty acres, which was laid off in town lots. The public square was in the middle. . . .

The first double-cabin built, was designated for a tavern, and a single one for its stable. . . . Another and second double and single cabin were occupied as dwelling and shop by a blacksmith. I had brought bellows, anvils, tools, and appliances for three or four blacksmith-shops, from the City of Birmingham, England. There were three brothers that came with Mr. Charles Trimmer, all excellent mechanics. . . . Jacob, the blacksmith, was immediately installed, and went to work. There stood Albion, no longer a myth, but a reality, a fixed fact. A log-tavern and a blacksmith-shop.

Two germs of civilization were now planted—one of the useful arts, the other a necessary institution of present civilization. Any man could now get his horse shod and get drunk in Albion, privileges which were soon enjoyed, the latter especially. . . .

The town-proprietors, at first four, afterwards increased to eight (each share five hundred dollars), went to work vigorously. They put up cabin after cabin, which were occupied as soon as put up, by emigrants coming in. The builders of these were the backwoodsmen, some from twenty to thirty miles distant. Attracted by our good money and good whisky, these new gathered in.

*   *   *

A number of bona-fide cities existed in the trans-Allegheny West by 1830. By that date, Pittsburgh could claim 15,369 residents, and Cincinnati, 24,831. Louisville and Lexington totalled 10,341 and 6,026 respectively, and St. Louis across the Mississippi already had close to 5,000. The population of New Orleans, gulf port metropolis of the West, stood at

46,082. *It was mainly commerce that underwrote this urban growth, although, as early as 1815, manufacturing had made substantial beginnings in Pittsburgh, Cincinnati, and Louisville. Visitors commented upon the wide streets and handsome houses which could be found in these urban communities of the new West and noted the specialized and sometimes refined society, the hotels and boarding houses, newspapers, schools, libraries, museums, and theaters, which gave them most of the attributes of the other American cities of their day. But above all, travelers were impressed with the fact of "towns springing into importance within the memory of comparatively young men." All these qualities were observed in Cincinnati by Mrs. Frances Trollope, who resided there from February, 1828 to March, 1830. This somewhat patronizing English visitor was probably a bit hard on the "Queen City," as she was on most of the United States; but her comments, as published in her* Domestic Manners of the Americans, *serve to offset the exaggerated praise with which "puffing" promoters often described Western cities in these years.*

We had heard so much of Cincinnati, its beauty, wealth, and unequalled prosperity, that when we left Memphis to go thither, we almost felt the delight of Rousseau's novice, "un voyage à faire, et Paris au bout!"—As soon, therefore, as our little domestic arrangements were completed, we set forth to view this "wonder of the west," this "prophet's gourd of magic growth,"—this "infant Hercules." . . . I hardly know what I expected to find in this city, fresh risen from the bosom of the wilderness, but certainly it was but a little town, about the size of Salisbury, without even an attempt at beauty in any of its edifices, and with only just enough of the air of a city to make it noisy and bustling. The population is greater than the appearance of the town would lead one to expect. This is partly owing to the number of free Negroes who herd together in an obscure part of the city, called little Africa; and partly to the density of the population round the paper-mills and other manufactories. I believe the number of inhabitants exceeds twenty thousand.

We arrived in Cincinnati in February, 1828, and I speak of the town as it was then; several small churches have been built since, whose towers agreeably relieve its uninteresting mass of buildings. At that time I think Main-street, which is the principal avenue (and runs through the whole town, answering to the High-street of our old cities), was the only one entirely paved. The *trottoir* is of brick, tolerably well laid, but it is inundated by every shower, as Cincinnati has no drains whatever. . . .

Though I do not quite sympathize with those who consider Cincinnati as one of the wonders of the earth, I certainly think it a city of extraordinary size and importance, when it is remembered that thirty years ago the aboriginal forest occupied the ground where it stands; and every month appears to extend its limits and its wealth.

Some of the native political economists assert, that this rapid conversion of a bear-brake into a prosperous city is the result of free political institutions; not being very deep in such matters, a more obvious cause suggested itself to me, in the unceasing goad which necessity applies to industry in this country, and in the absence of all resource for the idle. During nearly two years that I resided in Cincinnati, or its neighbourhood, I neither saw a beggar, nor a man of sufficient fortune to permit his ceasing his efforts to increase it; thus every bee in the hive is actively employed in search of that honey of Hybla, vulgarly called money; neither art, science, learning, nor pleasure, can seduce them from its pursuit. . . .

Cincinnati has not many lions to boast, but among them are two museums of natural history; both of these contain many respectable specimens, particularly that of Mr. Dorfeuille, who has, moreover, some highly interesting Indian antiquities. He is a man of taste and science, but a collection formed strictly according to their dictates would by no means satisfy the western metropolis. The people have a most extravagant passion for wax figures, and the two museums vie with each other in displaying specimens of this barbarous branch of art. . . .

There is also a picture-gallery at Cincinnati, and this was a circumstance of much interest to us, as our friend Mr. H., who had accompanied Miss Wright to America, in the expectation of finding a good opening in the line of historical painting, intended commencing his experiment at Cincinnati. It would be invidious to describe the picture gallery; I have no doubt, that some years hence it will present a very different appearance. Mr. H. was very kindly received by many of the gentlemen of the city, and though the state of the fine arts there gave him but little hope that he should meet with much success, he immediately occupied himself in painting a noble historical picture of the landing of General Lafayette at Cincinnati. . . .

I heard another anecdote that will help to show the state of art at this time in the west. Mr. Bullock was showing to some gentlemen of the first standing, the very *élite* of Cincinnati, his beautiful collection of engravings, when one among them exclaimed, "Have you really done all these since you came here! How hard you must have worked!"

I was also told of a gentleman of high Cincinnati *ton*, and critical in his taste for the fine arts, who, having a drawing put into his hands, representing Hebe and the bird umquhile sacred to Jupiter, demanded in a satirical tone, "What is this?" "Hebe," replied the alarmed collector. "Hebe," sneered the man of taste, "What the devil has Hebe to do with the American eagle?" . . .

I never saw any people who appeared to live so much without amusement as the Cincinnatians. . . . They have no public balls, excepting, I think, six, during the Christmas holidays. They have no concerts. They have no dinner parties.

They have a theatre, which is, in fact, the only public amusement of this triste little town; but they seem to care little about it, and either from economy or distaste, it is very poorly attended. Ladies are rarely seen there, and by far the larger proportion of females deem it an offence against religion to witness the representation of a play. It is in the churches and chapels of the town that the ladies are to be seen in full costume: and I am tempted to believe that a stranger from the continent of Europe would be inclined, on first reconnoitering the city, to suppose that the places of worship were the theatres and cafés of the place.

*   *   *

No development was more important to the growth of cities on this frontier than the introduction of the steamboat, which revolutionized the utility of the western rivers as highways of travel and commerce. The first steamboat to ply the western waters was launched at Pittsburgh in 1811; and five years later the Enterprise *steamed from New Orleans to Louisville in twenty-five days, a trip that a keel boat would have needed more than three months to accomplish. By 1830, steamboats had monopolized passenger traffic and were handling most upstream freight, as well. Because movement was so much the essence of the West in these years, the activity on the river highways mirrored the society of the region as well as the nature of its economy. Timothy Flint, who came west by way of the Ohio in 1815, was impressed with the variety of craft that comprised the Western marine and with the prevalence of river-borne merchandising in the economy of the West. He included a description of this aspect of Western society in his* Recollections of the Last Ten Years, *published in 1826.*

The first thing that strikes a stranger . . . arrived at the boat-landing [at Pittsburgh] is the . . . spectacle, of the varieties of water-craft, of all shapes and structures. There is the stately barge, of the size of a large Atlantic schooner, with its raised and outlandish looking deck. This kind of craft, however, which required twenty-five hands to work it up stream, is almost gone into disuse, and though so common ten years ago, is now scarcely seen. Next there is the keel-boat, of a long, slender, and elegant form, and generally carrying from fifteen to thirty tons. This boat is . . . easily propelled over shallow waters in the summer season, and in low stages of the water is still much used, and runs on waters not yet frequented by steam-boats. Next in order are the Kentucky flats, or in the vernacular phrase, "broad-horns," a species of ark, very nearly resembling a New England pig-stye. They are fifteen feet wide, and from forty to one hundred feet in length, and carry from twenty to seventy tons. Some of them, that are called family-boats, and used by families in descending the river, are very large and roomy, and have comfortable and separate apartments, fitted up with chairs, beds, tables and stoves. It is no uncommon spectacle to see a large family, old and young, servants, cattle, hogs, horses, sheep, fowls, and animals of all kinds, bringing to recollection the cargo of the ancient ark, all embarked, and floating down on the same bottom. Then there are what the people call "covered sleds," or ferry-flats, and Allegany-skiffs, carrying from eight to twelve tons. In another place are pirogues of from two to four tons burthen, hollowed sometimes from one prodigious tree, or from the trunks of two trees united, and a plank-rim fitted to the upper part. There are common skiffs, and other small craft, named, from the manner of making them, "dug-outs," and canoes hollowed from smaller trees. . . . You can scarcely imagine an abstract form in which a boat can be built, that in some part of the Ohio or Mississippi you will not see, actually in motion. . . .

The terms of the navigation are as novel as are the forms of the boats. You hear of the danger of "riffles," meaning probably, ripples, and planters, and sawyers, and points, and bends, and shoots, a corruption, I suppose, of the French "chute." You hear the boatmen extolling their prowess in pushing a pole, and you learn . . . that a "Kentuck" is the best man at a pole, and a Frenchman at the oar. A firm push of the iron-pointed pole on a fixed log, is termed a "reverend" set. You are told when you embark, to bring your "plunder" aboard, and you hear about moving "fernenst" the stream; and you gradually become acquainted with a copious vocabulary of this sort. The manners of the boatmen are as strange as their language. Their peculiar way of life has given origin not only to an appropriate dialect, but to new modes of enjoyment, riot and fighting. Almost every boat, while it lies in the harbour has one or more fiddles scraping continually aboard, to which you often see the boatmen dancing. There is no wonder that the way of life which the boatmen lead, in turn extremely indolent, and extremely laborious; for days together requiring little or no effort, and attended with no danger, and then on a sudden, laborious and hazardous, beyond Atlantic navigation; generally plentiful as it respects food, and always so as it regards whiskey, should always have seductions that prove irresistible to the young people that live near the banks of the river. . . .

In the spring, one hundred boats have been numbered, that landed in one day at the mouth of the Bayan, at New Madrid [a Mississippi port south of St. Louis]. I have . . . seen them arriving in fleets. . . . You can name no point from the numerous rivers of the Ohio and the Mississippi, from which some of these boats have not come. In one place there are boats loaded with planks, from the pine forests of the southwest of New York. In another quarter there are the Yankee notions of Ohio. From Kentucky, pork, flour, whiskey, hemp, tobacco, bagging, and bale-rope. From Tennessee there are the same articles, together with great quantities of cotton. From Missouri and Illinois, cattle and horses, the same articles generally as from Ohio, together with peltry and lead from Missouri. Some boats are loaded with corn in the ear and in bulk; others with barrels of apples and potatoes. Some have loads of cider, and what they call "cider royal," or cider that has been strengthened by boiling or freezing. There are dried fruits, every kind of spirits manufactured in these regions, and in short, the products of the ingenuity and agriculture of the whole upper country of the west. They have come from regions, thousands of miles apart. They have floated to a common point of union. The surfaces of the boats cover some acres. Dunghill fowls are fluttering over the roofs, as an invariable appendage. The chanticleer raises his piercing note. The swine utter their cries. The cattle low. The horses trample, as in their stables. There are boats fitted on purpose, and loaded entirely with turkeys, that, having little else to do, gobble most furiously. The hands travel about from boat to boat, make inquiries, and acquaintances, and form alliances to yield mutual assistance to each other, on their descent from this to New Orleans. After an hour or two passed in this way, they spring on shore to raise the wind in town. It is well for the people of the village, if they do not become riotous in the course of the evening; in which case I have often seen the most summary and strong measures taken. About midnight the uproar is all hushed. The fleet unites once more at Natchez, or New Orleans, and, although they live on the same river, they may, perhaps, never meet each other again on the earth.

Next morning at the first dawn, the bugles sound. Every thing in and about the boats, that has life, is in motion. The boats, in half an hour, are all under way. In a little while they have all disappeared, and nothing is seen, as before they came, but the regular current of the river. In passing down the Mississippi, we often see a number of boats lashed and floating together. I was once on board a fleet of eight, that were in this way moving on together. It was a considerable walk, to travel over the roofs of this floating town. . . . These confederacies often commence in a frolic, and end in a quarrel, in which case the aggrieved party dissolves the partnership by unlashing, and managing his own boat in his own way. . . .

While I was at New Madrid, a large tinner's establishment floated there in a boat. In it all the different articles of tinware were manufactured and sold by wholesale and retail. . . . When they had mended all the tin, and vended all that they could sell in one place, they floated on to another. . . . I have frequently seen in this region a dry goods shop in a boat, with its articles very handsomely arranged on shelves. Nor would the delicate hands of the vender have disgraced the spruce clerk behind our city counters. . . .

St. Louis is a kind of central point, in this immense valley. From this point, outfits are constantly making to the military posts, and to the remotest regions by the hunters for furs. Boats are also constantly ascending to the lead-mine districts, on the upper Mississippi. From our boat, as we lay in the harbour of St. Louis, we could see "The Mandan," as the name of a boat bound far up the Missouri. Another was up for "Prairie du Chien," and the Falls of St. Anthony; another for the highest points of the Illinois; another for the Arkansas; and "The Gumbo," for Natchez and New Orleans. . . .

To feel what an invention [the steamboat] is for these regions, one must have seen and felt . . . the difficulty and danger of forcing a boat against the current of these mighty rivers, on which a progress of ten miles in a day, is a good one. Indeed those huge and unwieldy boats, the barges in which a great proportion of the articles from New Orleans used to be transported to the upper country, required twenty or thirty hands to work them. I have seen them day after day, on the lower portions of the Mississippi, where there was no other way of working them up, than carrying out a cable half a mile in length, in advance of the barge, and fastening it to a tree. The hands on board then draw it up to the tree. While this is transacting, another yawl, still in advance of that, has ascended to a higher tree, and made another cable fast to it, to be ready to be drawn upon, as soon as the first is coiled. This is the most dangerous and fatiguing way of all, and six miles advance in a day, is good progress.

It is now refreshing . . . to see the large and beautiful steam-boats scudding up the eddies, as though on the wing; and when they have run out the eddy, strike the current. The foam bursts in a sheet quite over the deck. She quivers for a moment with the concussion; and then, as though she had collected her energy, and vanquished her enemy, she resumes her stately march, and mounts against the current, five or six miles an hour. I have travelled in this way for days together, more than a hundred miles in a day, against the current of the Mississippi. The difficulty of ascending, used to be the only circumstance of a voyage that was dreaded in the anticipation. This difficulty now disappears.

*   *   *

The advantages of steamboat travel, as well as the details of life aboard, were described by Robert Baird, a Presbyterian clergyman, in his View of the Valley of the Mississippi: or the Emigrant's and Traveller's Guide to the West. *The Rev. Mr. Baird wrote from first-hand experience, since his duties in the service of the American Sunday School Union, from 1829 to 1834, took him to many parts of the country, including the West. Like Timothy Flint he was impressed with the transportation revolution that followed the introduction of the steamboat on western waters.*

The facilities for *travelling* which steam boats furnish in the West, are inconceivable to . . . any one who did not travel

here in the "olden time." *Then* it was a journey, on horseback, of several months to go up from New Orleans to Pittsburg; *now* it can be done with ease in *three weeks*, in almost
any steam boat, and allow much time for stopping at the
intermediate places. When steam-boats first began to run,
$125 and even $150 were cheerfully paid for a passage from
New Orleans to Louisville! And when the charges were so
diminished as to be only $100, from New Orleans to Pitts-
burg, which is 650 miles further, and in all more than 2000
miles, it was thought truly astonishing. But now one can
go from New-Orleans to Pittsburg as a cabin passenger, for
from $35 to $45, and fare sumptuously every day! And if he
chooses to go as a deck passenger he can do it for perhaps
$10 or $12! Consequently astonishing facilities are afforded
to families removing to distant parts of the entire Valley.
The passengers are denominated either "cabin" or "deck"
passengers from the different parts of the boat which they
occupy. Those in the cabin pay a much higher price, and have
every thing furnished. The deck passengers occupy either the
upper deck or the one immediately astern of, the machinery
. . . , and find their own provisions. Their part of the boat
is not generally finished with much particularity, and is
indeed rather an uncomfortable place in cold weather.

Although the steam-boats of the West are generally designed for carrying freight as well as passengers, yet it is
astonishing what a number of persons one of them can carry.
Even a boat of 100 tons often carries 50 cabin passengers;
as many more, or perhaps twice as many, on deck; and withal
75 or 80 tons of freight! And a boat of 500 tons, such as the
Uncle Sam, or the Red Rover, or Belfast, has often carried
100 passengers in the cabin, 500 on deck, and 400 tons of
freight, and withal marched up the mighty Mississippi at the
rate of six or eight miles an hour! Immense numbers of
passengers are carried from one part of the Valley to another
by these boats. Those boats which come up from New
Orleans bring, besides merchants and other inhabitants or
strangers, who occupy the cabin, hundreds of Germans, Irish,
and other foreign emigrants who land at that port, and are
seeking a home in the interior of the Valley of the Mississippi.

On the other hand those which descend from Pittsburg carry hundreds of travellers and emigrants from the east, as well as from foreign lands.

One of these large boats, filled with passengers, is almost a *world* in miniature. In the cabin you will find ladies and gentlemen of various claims to merit; on the forward part of the boat are the sailors, deck hands, and those *sons of Vulcan* —the firemen—possessing striking traits of character, and full of noise, and song, and too often of *whiskey*; whilst *above*, in the deck cabin, there is every thing that may be called *human*,—all sorts of men and women, of all trades, from all parts of the world, of all possible manners and habits. There is the half-horse and half-alligator Kentucky boatman, swaggering, and boasting of his prowess, his rifle, his horse, and his wife. One is sawing away on his wretched old fiddle all day long; another is grinding a knife or razor; here is a party *playing cards*; and in yonder corner is a *dance* to the sound of the Jew's harp; whilst a few are trying to demean themselves soberly, by sitting in silence or reading a book. But it is almost impossible—the wondrous tale and horrible Indian story are telling; the bottle and the jug are freely circulating; and the boisterous and deafening laugh is incessantly raised, sufficient to banish every vestige of seriousness, and thought, and sense. A friend of mine, some time ago, went down from Cincinnati to New Orleans on board the steam boat—, which carried fifty cabin passengers, one or two hundred deck passengers; one negro-driver with his gang of negroes; a part of a company of soldiers; a menagerie of wild beasts; a whole circus; and a company of play actors!

When a traveller from the East enters a crowded steamboat at Pittsburg or Cincinnati, and takes his passage for New Orleans, he very soon perceives a manifest contrast between western and eastern manners, and western and eastern steam-boats. He soon discovers that the western people have much more equality in their intercourse; are remarkably sociable, unceremonious, and independent. He will be very likely to consider them too forward and indifferent to the opinions of others. But he will find upon better acquaintance with them, that their apparent rudeness and incivility of manners soon disappear, and that they are truly courteous, respectful, and kind to those who display similar traits of character. They are candid and independent, and but little disposed to yield arrogated deference to any persons.

*   *   *

Since the West of the early nineteenth century was a society in motion, the church that could move most easily with the frontier seemed best suited to its religious needs. This was the aspect of the Methodist Church which gave it especial appeal in the West. Its itinerant preachers, riding their wilderness circuits, often showed up in frontier communities while log cabins were still rising; and its willingness to allow farmer-preachers to conduct services was a practical expedient in line with the equalitarian philosophy of the frontier. In the camp meeting, which was employed by other denominations as well, it found a technique for religious services which ministered to the social as well as the emotional needs of settlers subject to the loneliness of frontier life. Both the nature of the camp meeting and the practices of the frontier circuit rider are described in the Autobiography of Peter Cartwright, *an itinerant Methodist preacher, who became almost a legendary folk character in the West. Cartwright grew up on the Kentucky frontier. In 1802, at the age of 17, he was commissioned to create a new circuit to the westward. From then on, for many years, he rode circuits in Kentucky, Tennessee, Indiana, Ohio, and Illinois.*

From 1801 for years a . . . revival of religion spread through almost the entire inhabited parts of the West. . . . The Presbyterians and Methodists in a great measure united in this work, met together, prayed together, and preached together.

In this revival originated our camp-meetings, and in both these denominations they were held every year. . . . They would erect their camps with logs or frame them, and cover them with clapboards or shingles. They would also erect a shed, sufficiently large to protect five thousand people from wind and rain, and cover it with boards or shingles; build a large stand, seat the shed, and here they would collect together from forty to fifty miles around, sometimes further than that.

Ten, twenty and sometimes thirty ministers, of different denominations, would come together and preach night and day, four or five days together; and, indeed, I have known these camp-meetings to last three or four weeks, and great good resulted from them. I have seen more than a hundred sinners fall like dead men under one powerful sermon, and I have seen and heard more than five hundred Christians all shouting aloud the high praises of God at once. . . .

Just in the midst of our controversies on the subject of the powerful exercises among the people under preaching, a new exercise broke out among us, called the *jerks*, which was overwhelming in its effects upon the bodies and minds of the people. No matter whether they were saints or sinners, they would be taken under a warm song or sermon, and seized with a convulsive jerking all over, which they could not by any possibility avoid, and the more they resisted the more they jerked. . . . I have seen more than five hundred persons jerking at one time in my large congregations. Most usually persons taken with the jerks, to obtain relief, as they said, would rise up and dance. Some would run, but could not get away. Some would resist; on such the jerks were generally very severe.

To see those proud young gentlemen and young ladies, dressed in their silks, jewelry, and prunella, from top to toe, take the *jerks*, would often excite my risibilities. The first jerk or so, you would see their fine bonnets, caps, and combs fly; and so sudden would be the jerking of the head that their long loose hair would crack almost as loud as a wagoner's whip. . . .

There were many other strange and wild exercises into which the subjects of this revival fell; such, for instance, as what was called the running, jumping, barking exercise. The Methodist preachers generally preached against this extravagant wildness. . . .

In traveling the Christian Circuit [during 1816 and 1817], which crossed the Tennessee State line and lay partly in Tennessee, and partly in Kentucky, in one of my exploring routes, hunting up new ground and new appointments to preach at, late one evening, in or near the Cumberland River

Bottom, I called at a gentleman's gate, and asked the privilege of staying all night. The gentleman very readily granted my request. He was a wealthy farmer, the owner of several slaves. . . . I soon found they had very little preaching of any kind. I told the gentleman my business was to preach any where I could get peaceable and orderly hearers, and asked him if I might not leave an appointment to preach at his house. He pleasantly said, if he had heard me preach and liked my preaching, he could better determine whether to grant me the privilege to leave an appointment or not. I told him . . . I would preach to [his family], and he could the better judge how he liked my preaching. . . . I sung and prayed, took my text, and preached to them about an hour as best I could. The colored people wept; the white people wept; the man of the house wept, and when I closed, he said, "Do leave another appointment, and come and preach to us, for we are sinners, and greatly need preaching.". . .

When I came to my appointment there was a large congregation; the house and porch were literally crowded. I preached to them with great freedom, and almost the whole congregation were melted into tears. . . . I opened the doors of the Church for the reception of members, and some ten persons joined. . . . This was the first fruits of a gracious revival, and a large society in this neighborhood; and while I lived in that country we held a sacramental meeting at this place every year.

*   *   *

By 1830, as a result of half a century of growth, the trans-Allegheny West had developed a definable personality. Since the close of the War of 1812, the authors of travel accounts and emigrant guides had been describing an identifiable West, blessed with a special abundance, and possessed of a population whose experience with pioneering had made it different, in degree at least, from the rest of the nation. At the turn of the 1830's, these characteristics were summed up and systematized by the Reverend Robert Baird, in his View of the Valley of the Mississippi: or the Emigrant's and Traveller's Guide to the West.

The peculiarities . . . of character, which may be said to distinguish the population of the West, are all created by the peculiar circumstances in which the people have been placed in that new world. They are,

1. A *spirit of adventurous enterprise:* a willingness to go through any hardship or danger to accomplish an object. It was the spirit of enterprise which led to the settlement of that country. The western people think nothing of making a long journey, of encountering fatigue, and of enduring every species of hardship. The great highways of the west—its long rivers—are familiar to very many of them, who have been led by trade to visit remote parts of the valley.

2. *Independence of thought and action.*—They have felt the influence of this principle from their childhood. Men who can endure any thing: that have lived almost without restraint, free as the mountain air, or as the deer and the buffalo of their forests—and who know that they are Americans all—will act out this principle during the whole of life. I do not mean that they have such an amount of it as to render them *really* regardless alike of the opinions and the feelings of everyone else. But I have seen many who have the virtue of independence greatly perverted or degenerated. . . .

3. *An apparent roughness,* which some would deem *rudeness of manners.*

These traits characterize, especially, the agricultural portions of the country, and also in some degree the new towns and villages. They are not so much the offspring of ignorance and barbarism, (as some would suppose), as the results of the circumstances of a people thrown together in a new country, often for a long time in sparse settlements; where, of course, acquaintances for many miles around are soon, of necessity, made and valued from few adventitious causes. Where there is perfect equality in a neighbourhood of people who know but little about each other's previous history or ancestry—but where each is lord of the soil which he cultivates. Where a log cabin is all that the best of families can expect to have for years, and of course can possess few of the external decorations which have so much influence in creating a diversity of rank in society. These circumstances have laid the foundation for that equality of intercourse, simplicity of manners, want of deference, want of reserve, great readiness to make acquaintances, freedom of speech, indisposition to brook real or imaginary insults, which one witnesses among the people of the west.

The character and manners of the traders and merchants who inhabit the principal cities and towns of the West, do not differ greatly from those of the same class in the Atlantic states.

*　　*　　*

One further quality of Western society—the vigor of local political activity—struck a Yankee visitor to Frankfort, Kentucky, when he visited this Western capital in 1834. His description of a political barbecue, which took place on the Fourth of July, was published in the Western Monthly Magazine, *a few months later. The election of the Tennesseean Andrew Jackson to the Presidency, in 1828, had already testified to the growing influence of the West in the national political scene.*

Friday evening, July 4th.—I have just returned from the barbecue, much amused and much fatigued with the day's excursion. . . . You wonder at the multitude of people—I suppose there are three or four thousand. You notice that enclosure, with a crowd of anxious-looking men around it— that is the *bar*, and within are several hogsheads of that famous beverage, called *mint julep*. This is made by mixing, in proper proportions, sugar, water, ice, mint, and old whisky. . . . You see that old man who stands by himself, smiling and scowling by turns, as he drinks his julep, or looks upon the crowd—he is of the opposite party of politics, but could not, for that cause, forego the pleasure of a free barbecue, and its appendages.

But now the crowd, having quenched their thirst, gather about the stand, and a call is made for a speech. As might be expected, that call is for J. J. Crittenden. He is a favorite, . . . and he possesses that peculiar power in oratory, which can charm the learned and ignorant at the same time. His voice, though commanding, is rich and mellow in its tones, and a multitude would stand by the hour, gazing on his glowing countenance, and hanging with breathless silence on the words, as they leap apparently unbidden from his lips. . . .

Now comes the signal for dinner, and every man forgets his politics for the time being. The mode of cooking at barbecues is peculiar. A trench is dug, and the bottom covered with live coals; over these the smaller kinds of meat, such as pigs, lambs, &c. are placed whole, supported by skewers passed through them and stuck in the sides of the trench. The beef is cooked in the same way, except that it is cut into pieces of convenient size. . . .

After dinner was over . . . the multitude gathered once more around the stand, to hear toasts and speeches, which were accompanied at intervals, with appropriate music and shouts of applause. . . . The people of this state are remarkable for their enthusiasm in politics. None are so ignorant, but they can talk fluently on this subject. The greatest clown from the knobs can tell you what he 'reckons,' on the subject of state and national policy, as well as HENRY CLAY. This proceeds from the fact, that candidates are obliged to be constantly among the people, delivering stump speeches, harangues, &c. Indeed, a candidate would be politically damned, if he did not mingle with the people, from the time he offers until the close of the polls; and it frequently happens, that during the election, he must suffer himself to be placed astride, upon the shoulders of some Hercules, and thus exhibited for the plaudits of the crowd.

I shall close this anomalous epistle by an anecdote, illustrative of what I have just said. A deaf mute, in the southern part of this state, wishing to make the son of a congressman understand, that he was acquainted with his father, commenced the motion of bowing and shaking hands, apparently with a number of persons in quick succession; as much as to say, a candidate shakes hands with all the people. This was satisfactory evidence to the son that the mute knew his father.

*   *   *

*In the opinion of John Mason Peck, author of one of the most
widely read emigrant guides, the independence of thought
and feeling which characterized the Western mind was a
product of the plenty which God and nature had bestowed
upon the interior of the Continent. It was a product, too, of
the pattern of migration which resulted as successive waves
of settlers exploited the abundance of the West. Peck, a
native of Connecticut, resided in the West after 1817. Baptist
missionary, farmer, editor of religious periodicals, and author
of emigrant guides, Peck exerted a significant influence on the
colonization and cultural development of the Middle West.
His* Guide for Emigrants, *first published in 1831, was expanded in 1836 and 1837, with the growth of interest in the
great Valley. With each new edition Peck became more
eloquent concerning the progress and promise of the Mississippi Valley West.*

The rough, sturdy habits of the backwoodsmen, living in
that plenty which depends on God and nature, have laid
the foundation of independent thought and feeling deep in
the minds of western people.

Generally, in all the western settlements, three classes, like
the waves of the ocean, have rolled one after the other. First,
comes the pioneer, who depends for the subsistence of his
family upon the natural growth of vegetation, called the
"range," and the proceeds of hunting. His implements of
agriculture are rude, chiefly of his own make, and his efforts
directed mainly to a crop of corn, and a "truck patch." The
last is a rude garden for growing cabbage, beans, corn for
roasting ears, cucumbers and potatoes. A log cabin, and,
occasionally, a stable and corn-crib, and a field of a dozen
acres, the timber girdled or "deadened," and fenced, are
enough for his occupancy. It is quite immaterial whether he
ever become the owner of the soil. He is the occupant for
the time being, pays no rent, and feels as independent as the
"lord of the manor." With a horse, cow, and one or two
breeders of swine, he strikes into the woods with his family,
and becomes the founder of a new county, or perhaps State.
He builds his cabin, gathers around him a few other families
of similar taste and habits, and occupies till the range is

somewhat subdued, and hunting a little precarious, or, which is more frequently the case, till neighbors crowd around, roads, bridges and fields annoy him, and he lacks elbow room. The preemption law enables him to dispose of his cabin and corn-field to the next class of emigrants, and, to employ his own figures, he "breaks for the high timber," "clears out for the New Purchase," or migrates to Arkansas, or Texas, to work the same process over.

The next class of emigrants purchase the lands, add field to field, clear out the roads, throw rough bridges over the streams, put up hewn log houses, with glass windows, and brick or stone chimneys, occasionally plant orchards, build mills, school-houses, court-houses, &c., and exhibit the picture and forms of plain, frugal, civilized life.

Another wave rolls on. The men of capital and enterprise come. The "settler" is ready to sell out, and take advantage of the rise of property,—push farther into the interior, and become himself, a man of capital and enterprise in turn. The small village rises to a spacious town or city; substantial edi-fices of brick, extensive fields, orchards, gardens, colleges and churches are seen. Broadcloths, silks, leghorns, crapes, and all the refinements, luxuries, elegancies, frivolities and fashions, are in vogue. Thus wave after wave is rolling west-ward:—the real *el dorado* is still farther on.

A portion of the two first classes remain stationary amidst the general movement, improve their habits and condition, and rise in the scale of society. . . .

Migration has become almost a habit in the West. Hun-dreds of men can be found, not fifty years of age, who have settled for the fourth, fifth, or sixth time on a new spot. To sell out, and remove only a few hundred miles, makes up a portion of the variety of backwoods life and manners.

PART V

WIDENING THE PERIMETER
OF THE "GREAT WEST"

"The West is a young empire of mind, and power, and
wealth, and free institutions, rushing up to giant manhood
with a rapidity and power never before witnessed below
the sun." (*Lyman Beecher*)

*Between 1830 and 1860, settlement pushed the farmer
frontier into the first column of states west of the Mississippi
and, in places, even beyond. On the eve of the Civil War, the
arc of settlement ran through southeastern Minnesota, central
Iowa, the eastern parts of what are now Nebraska and Kansas,
western Arkansas, and the lowlands of Texas. By 1860, four
times as many people were living in the Mississippi Valley as
had done so thirty years before; and the great interior section of the Continent now contained nearly half the population of the nation. Improvements in transportation speeded
this growth; and the sources of population were greatly
augmented by a flood of Europeans, now migrating to the
United States in unprecedented numbers. The Erie Canal
directed the flow of settlers into northern Ohio, Michigan,
and Wisconsin, often by way of the Great Lakes. For a
generation after 1825, when the "great ditch" first reached
Buffalo, it was the major highway by which Yankees, Yorkers,
and European newcomers made their way westward. The
experience of a Scandinavian pioneer in 1841 reveals the
details of migration by this route into the West. Arriving in
New York, in mid-September, 1841, after a three-months'
voyage from Sweden, Finnish-born Gustav Unonius and his
wife set out, via the Hudson River, for the West. The trip
from Albany to Buffalo, by way of the Erie, consumed eight
days; and six more were spent on the lakes from Buffalo to
Milwaukee, Wisconsin. This newcomer's account describes
not only the prevailing facilities for western travel but also
the hazards to which European immigrants were subjected
along the way.*

An immigrant . . . who is on his way to the West, can hardly avoid doing business with [the agents of the transportation companies]. . . . But he will do well to take care lest he be duped by the ridiculously low price quoted for the transportation of himself and his belongings. . . . Either the ticket he sells does not take the passenger beyond Albany or Buffalo, even if the agreement calls for the entire distance to Milwaukee or Chicago, or else somewhere along the way, at some change of canal—or steamboat, some mistake will be discovered through which the immigrant will be compelled to make additional payments. . . . These demands he will be obliged to meet or be detained at some completely strange place where he would be subjected to still greater expense.

We finally contracted with a transportation company to take us to Chicago for twelve dollars a person. This seemed like a real bargain. . . .

On our arrival in Albany we found proof of the unreliable nature of the agreements of the transportation company. "One dollar," "two dollars," "three dollars" were the words repeated again and again as our trunks were brought to the gangplank, across which we were not permitted to carry them until we had paid to the ship's clerk a fee that seemed entirely arbitrary. The transportation of our goods . . . was to have been made without extra charge—at least for this part of our trip; for the agent had insisted that he had made special arrangement with the commanding officer of the steamer to that effect. Our protests, registered in broken English, were all in vain. . . . For every piece of luggage that was brought ashore we had to open our purse, and with the calmest air in the world, but also with a trace of malice, the ship's clerk pocketed one dollar after another. Thus far we had traveled only 149 miles, and we reasoned that if this were to happen at every stopping place, there would not be much left for purchasing cattle and farming equipment.

From Albany we were to continue our journey on the Erie Canal to Buffalo. . . . We were immediately brought on board one of those queer-looking Noah's ark boats on which freight and passengers are pulled along through the country from one end of the state to the other. . . .

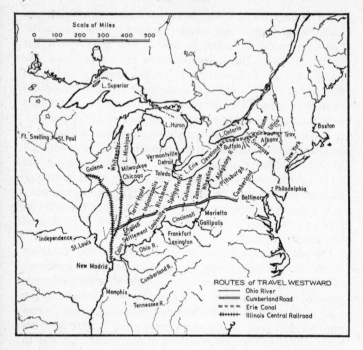

Scale of Miles
0 100 200 300 400 500

ROUTES of TRAVEL WESTWARD
——— Ohio River
——— Cumberland Road
= = = Erie Canal
+++++ Illinois Central Railroad

These canalboats are of various kinds. Some of them, both decked and open, are used only for freight shipments; others are furnished both for passenger service and freight; while still a third kind, somewhat better looking than the rest, is used exclusively for passenger traffic. The last are known as packets and are drawn by three horses, which are frequently changed, so that in them one can sometimes make as much as six miles an hour. They are completely decked, with a narrow stairway aft leading to the saloon. Another leads to the kitchen, which is so small that no one but the cook can find room to move in it. The saloon takes up the entire length of the boat, probably eighty or ninety feet. It is generally divided into two parts, of which one is used at night as sleeping quarters for women, the other for men. In the daytime it is used by all passengers as a lounge and dining room.

In the wall are low windows, through which passengers sitting on the sofas arranged about the walls can watch the landscape as the boat moves along. The room is high enough to permit a man to stand upright unless he is too tall or insists on keeping his hat on. In the daytime this floating retreat did not appear to me so very uncomfortable, but how all these people were to pass the night was a complete puzzle. No sign of bed or bedstead could I see.

I was not permitted to spend very much time examining the packet boat, for I was soon informed that it did not fall to our lot this time to get any closer acquaintance with its conveniences or lack of them. All of us, along with our baggage, were stowed in one of the second-class boats—one of those provided for immigrants or for people who like ourselves had elected to travel cheaply. . . .

The boat on which we and all our possessions were stowed had a saloon only half as big as that of the packet boat. Even so, this boat seemed clean and neat, with tiny red curtains in front of the windows, a long wood-stained table in the middle of the floor, and on either side of it a rather comfortable sofa covered with red damask. . . . So we had not, after all, thanks to our transportation company, been relegated to one of the real immigration boats, which are nothing but freight scows with a big, dark room below deck and with walls, floors, and furnishings like the empty hold of a coastal freighter.

On the packet boats meals are always included in the price of the ticket, and on the kind of boat we were traveling on it was also possible at an additional price to enjoy this privilege. This was not included in our bargain, however. We thought we might save a little by providing our own meals, knowing as we did that there were cities, villages, and inns all along the canal line where we could augment our food supply at any time. In great haste we supplied ourselves with some bread and other provisions, for the captain informed us that the boat was ready to leave at any time. . . . Little did we know about the traffic on the Erie Canal, or about the length of time the skipper might decide to delay the departure!

These boats do not leave at certain hours like the packet boats, but wait like omnibuses until enough places have been engaged to pay to make the run. They keep stopping incessantly, now here, now there, to take on and unload freight and passengers, and everywhere they take their time. . . .

The sun, however, set on our day in Albany, and our canalboat was still moored to the same spot. That it was soon to start we gathered from the two horses waiting on the shore, by the mass of freight that almost filled the hold, and by the number of passengers that had crowded themselves into the small cabin. A curtain now cut off one end of the cabin, making a separate room for the women; through further scene shifting, the entire room had been changed into the strangest and most compendious sleeping quarters for no less than twenty-four persons, not to speak of the number that might be accommodated on chairs and tables. On both sides of the walls half a dozen shelves, bunks, or whatever they may be called, were hung. The steward, as if by magic, extracted these from the aforesaid sofas. As they were hung up, each of them was supplied with a thin mattress, or pad, on which sheet, pillow, and blanket were spread—everything as smooth and pressed as if it had been tacked to the shelf, which proved wide enough to serve as a bed for an ordinary man not accustomed to sleeping on his back. As already said, these bed-shelves were now hooked on the wall, in two rows, one above the other, with the sofas serving as the third and longest row. On one side they were attached by hooks to the wall, on the other by ropes to the ceiling. The contraption really looked very fragile and altogether risky, especially for those who were to occupy the lower beds. The places were given out by lots, and I was unfortunate enough to draw mine in the second tier, where I was unable to lift my head more than a few inches above the pillow without pushing the person above me. During the night the crowded condition also made me frequently aware of the stirring of my neighbor on the sofa beneath. . . .

The closer we came to Buffalo, the denser grew the crowd of passengers. . . . On this last leg of the trip we were unfortunate enough to add to our company a few Irish people.

These are unpleasant enough as neighbors ashore, but having them on board made us wish they might depart for *Blåkulla*, a more suitable destination for them and one I suspect most of them will eventually, willy-nilly, reach. A genuine Paddy had seated himself at the table with us. In his entire person he reflected something of that rag-bag bully which generally characterizes the Irishman, especially after he has come to America and been enfranchised as an American citizen. One can readily see by looking at him that he feels his citizenship entitles him to any public office just as his membership in the "only true Church" entitles him to a place in heaven by the side of St. Patrick and St. Columcille. With a clay pipe in his vest pocket and a whiskey bottle in his coat, he is fully prepared for a fist fight with anybody who dares dispute his right in either of these respects. By his side is his better half, whose dress is somewhat better than her husband's. This suggests that they have been in America for some time and have managed to get a fair start in life. In her arms she carries a child, some two or three years of age, a dirty and squalling brat. The Irishman pulls out his whiskey bottle, and his wife a small teacup from her handbag, where along with some bits of toast it has been wrapped up in a linen article used to complete the toilet of a child. The husband first takes a drink and wishes to treat all around, both ladies and gentlemen, but we, at least, are unable to avail ourselves of his well-intentioned courtesy. Finally he fills the cup for his wife. After she has drunk part of it she dips some pieces of toast in the remainder and gives them to her little boy, who swallows them greedily, accustomed already to the diet. . . .

The trip on Lake Erie, during which we enjoyed calm weather and a bright sky, would have been a real pleasure excursion had it not been for the inconvenience of traveling in steerage. . . .

But though we did not have admittance to everything, we were still able to get a general view of the variegated and in many respects interesting life on board the big steamer.

Here we saw proof of a statement for which we later had still more evidence, that Americans are undoubtedly the most mobile and roving people on earth. Even when they are very well off, living in the northern, central, or southern states, they will pull up stakes, sell their possessions, and move west with a resolute courage one would expect only from those pressed by extreme want. Passengers in first class are for the most part either people that have lived for some time in the West, and having acquired wealth are now returning from a business or pleasure trip to the eastern states, or they are capitalists or speculators who are going out to reconnoiter. Probably there is also in the company some bankrupt business man who is now retiring to a new territory with a nest egg kept from his creditors, ready to try his luck again and after a few years become as rich as a nabob in the new neighborhood. Some are planning to purchase a piece of fertile soil and become farmers. They are not yet inured to the hardships of pioneer life, look down with an air of superiority on the rough and patched working clothes of their fellow mortals, and as long as they can, they lead a gentleman's life, keep the silk lining in their coats, the panama hats on their heads, and a chief place in the cabin.

Among the second-class passengers we find all kinds of folk. We ourselves are the only representatives of the Scandinavian peninsula, but the foredeck and lower decks are crowded with Yankees, English, Irish, Germans, etc. They all have their heads full of plans for the future and how to establish themselves in a region of which they have only the slight knowledge to be derived from rather unreliable newspaper propaganda and guidebooks or the even less reliable and highly colored descriptions given by fly-by-night land agents. . . .

It was reported that we were about to arrive in Milwaukee, a city in Wisconsin, one of the new territories of the United States. In New York we had heard of neither one nor the other. But during our trip through the canal we had met several, both Americans and Europeans, who had spoken of Wisconsin as one of the most attractive and fertile districts in the great West, and under present conditions the most favorable to immigrants. On the lake steamer we had heard similar reports, and most of the other immigrants were preparing to disembark in Milwaukee that evening. We really had no good reason for continuing to Illinois, where most of the land, according to reports, already had got into the hands of individual speculators. Besides, we were tired of traveling and were anxious as soon as possible to exchange our place in steerage for a plain log house. One state, we felt, was probably as good as another. We really knew as much or as little of Illinois as of Wisconsin. Perhaps it might be just as well for us to look around in this region since everybody seemed to be going there and since, besides, it was right on our way. So after some consultation with each other we made our decision and notified the captain that we too wanted to leave the ship in Milwaukee.

*   *   *

The migration of New Englanders, by the canal and lake route, threatened to depopulate whole areas of Vermont, western Massachusetts, and western Connecticut, as ambitious Yankees abandoned the stony fields of northern New England for the fertile oak openings of Michigan, Wisconsin, and the upper Mississippi Valley. New England youth was attracted, too, by the opportunities the new country offered in the professions and in business. The exodus to the prairie states from New England and New York grew to flood proportions in the decade preceding the Civil War. A typical Yankee migrant was Joseph V. Quarles, a native of eastern New Hampshire, who cast his lot with Wisconsin in the late 1830's and whose Wisconsin-born son ultimately represented Wisconsin in the United States Senate. Quarles' letters, written in 1838 and 1839, from Southport (now Kenosha) in the southeastern corner of the young Territory, reveal the enthusiasm with which migrants from New England viewed the abundance of the West, and the extent to which the individual pioneer promoted westward migration.

I suppose a description of this part of the world will be interesting to you and my friends generally. . . . The country is level that is there are no hills—the land . . . rises gradually [*sic*] in swells and what is termed rolling prairie. . . . the soil is very rich and produces abundantly and will grow grain or corn vastly better than N[ew] H[ampshire] lands. Another part of the lands are called oak openings—on which are scattering oaks and occationally [sic] bunches of them the ground covered with grass is fine land— We cut out the smaller trees girdle the larger and plow and plant or sow among them—other sections are covered thickly with timber. . . . It is about three years since the first settler came in and the land is mostly taken up . . . to the Mississippi— . . . The corn is heavy and is nearly as high as I can reach when horse back— One man wished me to ride into his wheat to see how it was— I objected that it would injure it— O says he we have . . . enough of it we don't mind such little things. . . . No man can do better than invest his money here. . . . Rest assured speculators will not be allowed to purchase or even bid on a settlers lot it would be death for him. . . . We have considerable of a vilage [sic] here 4 stores other building and one Lawyer and not very smart— I think you would do well here. . . . The Indians are all gone west from here. not one have I seen this side of Milwaukee

The state of the society here is good a large portion of them are N Englanders. . . . very inteligent [sic] and polite. . . .

You say Jeffersons wife does not believe all I say of the country— I have stated nothing but truth and I think not so strong as the country will bear— You have no idea what nature has done here for man and cannot unless you see it. I had rather have 160 acres land here in the state of nature to live on than the best farm in righteous Ossipee [eastern New Hampshire]. You say to J. H. Y. that there is one tailor in this place and he has $10 for making a coat Say to T. G. his business is good here or if he choose . . . he can farm it for a livelihood. If he could forward me 200$ I could make him a claim of 160 acres and carry it through land sale or for 100$ 80 acres or for 200$ I can pay for a quarter section well located with some improvements and have 80 acres of it and land too free from stone & a rich black soil that will bear any crop without dressing and on which he can cut next year 80 tons hay if he choose— I intend to have me a farm here and put a family on it and reserve a part for myself to work on when I feel like it and [have] no other a better business to attend to— And we do not work for nothing in this country A man here to make cart wheels and carts could mak [*sic*] 3$ a day I have no doubt.— . . . Emigrants are coming here from N. Y. Mass. Vermont & from Connecticut river in N H from Michigan &c &c—but from the eastern part of N. H. although it is obviously the last place that was made there are none As to Mrs. Youngs recommendation in relation to a wife I am unprepared to say positively but if you will bring me out a wife and one that suits I will either marry her myself or see that she is well provided for. . . .

There has been some cases of fever & ague and billious fiver in this place . . .

A large proportion of the emigrants & settlers here are from N. Y. but few from N. H. . . . how is this?— You will admit there is no effect without a cause—the cause?— I can think of but one solution—the land is so poor & hard that if a man should cease laboring long enough for an idea in relation to emigration to shoot across his brain his whole family would perish with hunger—& the naked fact of my being a bachelor saved my bacon.

*   *   *

In general, New England and New York moved west by individual families; but on occasion an area was settled by a land company or a "colony," which had many of the characteristics of the migrating New England towns of colonial days. Such was the history of Vermontville in southern Michigan, which was the creation of the Union Colony, composed of migrants from western Vermont. Its leader was a Congregational minister, and its formal constitution, adopted by the members before their departure, was designed to ensure the reproduction in the West of the kind of Yankee Puritan society they had known in New England. Recalling the Biblical precedent, "And Moses sent them to spy out the land of Canaan," three members were dispatched in advance to locate and purchase the land. The tract was laid out in the pattern of a New England town, with the farm lots surrounding the village to facilitate contact with church and school. Among the members who followed, in addition to their clergyman leader, were a blacksmith, a wheelwright, a cooper, a cabinet maker, a machinist, a printer, a merchant, a physician, a surveyor, and at least ten farmers. With its emphasis on church, school, Sabbath observance, and the prohibition of "ardent spirits," as well as its concern for "temporal" advantage, Vermontville was typical of many communities that developed in the wake of the expansion of New England into the Mississippi Valley West. The record of the genesis of the Union Colony was kept by Edward W. Barber, a son of one of the original Vermontville pioneers.

In the fall of 1835 Rev. Sylvester Cochrane, a Congregational minister of East Poultney, Vermont, came to Michigan with a view to making a permanent location. . . . Mr. Cochrane found settlements so few and the inhabitants so widely scattered that it was impossible for them, except when gathered in villages, to have schools and enjoy religious privileges. . . . He returned to Vermont, thought out the plan of a colony and began preparations for the execution of his project. The prevalence of the "Michigan fever," easily increased by accounts of the great lakes in the heart of the continent, the oak openings, the beautiful prairies and the vast wilderness of the wonderful peninsula, . . . made it an easy matter to arouse the . . . tendency . . . to move westward among enterprising Vermonters. . . . Early in the winter of 1835-6 a meeting was held in East Poultney, which was attended by a number of persons who had caught the western fever. . . . Subsequent meetings were held in Castleton, Vermont, and on the 27th day of March, 1836, the constitution of "The Union Colony" was formally adopted. . . .

RULES AND REGULATIONS OF UNION COLONY:

"WHEREAS, The enjoyment of the ordinances and institutions of the Gospel is in a great measure unknown in many parts of the western country; and

"WHEREAS, We believe that a pious and devoted emigration is to be one of the most efficient means, in the hands of God, in removing the moral darkness which hangs over a great portion of the valley of the Mississippi; and

"WHEREAS, We believe that a removal to the west may be a means of promoting our temporal interest, and we trust be made subservient to the advancement of Christ's kingdom;

"*We do therefore,* Form ourselves into an association or colony with the design of removing into some parts of the western country which shall hereafter be designated, and agree to bind ourselves to observe the following rules:

"1. The association or colony shall be known by the appellation or name of 'The Union Colony.'

"2. The Colony shall consist of those only who shall be admitted through a committee appointed for that purpose, and will subscribe their names to the articles and compact adopted by the colony.

"3. We hereby agree to make our arrangements for a removal as soon as our circumstances will permit—if possible, some time during the summer or fall of the present year, 1836.

"4. We agree, when we have arrived in the western country, to locate ourselves, if possible, in the same neighborhood with each other, and to form ourselves into such a community as will enable us to enjoy the same social and religious privileges which we leave behind.

"5. In order to accomplish this object, we solemnly pledge ourselves to do all that is in our power to carry with us the institutions of the Gospel, to support them with the means which God has given us, and to hand them down to our children.

"6. We do also agree that, for the benefit of our children and the rising generation, we will endeavor, so far as possible, to carry with and perpetuate among us the same literary privileges that we are permitted here to enjoy.

"7. We do also pledge ourselves that we will strictly and rigidly observe the holy Sabbath, neither laboring ourselves, nor permitting our children, or workmen, or beasts to desecrate this day of rest by any kind of labor or recreation.

"8. As ardent spirits have invariably proved the bane of every community into which they have been introduced, we solemnly pledge ourselves that we will neither buy, nor sell, nor use this article, except for medical purposes, and we will use all lawful means to keep it utterly out of the settlement.

"9. As we must necessarily endure many of those trials and privations which are incident to a settlement in a new country, we agree that we will do all in our power to befriend each other; we will esteem it not only a duty, but a privilege to sympathize with each other under all our trials, to do good and lend, hoping for nothing again, and to assist each other on all necessary occasions.". . .

CODE OF LAWS FOR THE COLONY

"The following votes and resolutions have been passed at the regular meetings of the colony, and are binding upon its members:

"1. Voted, That a committee of two be appointed, whose duty it shall be to make inquiry concerning the character of individuals who may wish to unite with the colony, and no person shall be admitted without the consent of this committee.

"2. Voted, That three agents be appointed to go into the western country and select a suitable location for the use of the colony, and purchase the same.

"3. Voted, That we hereby authorize our agents to purchase for the use of the colony three miles square, or 5,760 acres, and as much more as they may have funds to purchase.

"4. Voted, That the land, when purchased, be laid out by the agents so as to conform as nearly as the location and other circumstances will permit to the schedule adopted by the colony.

"5. Voted, That no individual member of the colony shall be allowed to take more than one farm lot of 160 acres, and one village lot of ten acres, within the limits of the settlement.

"6. Voted, That the agents be authorized to take a duplicate or certificate of the purchased lands in the name of the committee for raising funds; and the said committee shall hold the said lands in their possession until the first Monday in October, 1836, at which time the land shall be distributed among the settlers, according to some plan on which they may then agree; the village lots, however, may be taken up by the settlers when they first arrive, each one taking his choice of the unoccupied lots.

"7. Voted, That each individual shall be obligated to settle the lot which he takes by the first of October, 1837, and in case of delinquency in this respect both the village and the farm lot may be sold to some other person, in which case the purchase money shall be refunded by the agents of the colony, with interest from the time it was paid.

"8. Voted, That each of the settlers, when he unites with the colony, shall advance $212.50, for which he shall be entitled to a farm lot of 160 acres and a village lot of ten acres, to be assigned to him according to the rules of the colony; and if any settler shall find himself unable to advance this sum, he may pay in $106.25, for which he shall be entitled to a farm lot of eighty acres and one-half of a village lot; and in case no money is paid before the departure of the agents, those who are delinquent shall give a note to the committee for raising funds, payable on the 25th day of June next, with interest for three months.

"9. Voted, That each settler, when he receives a deed of his village lot, shall give a note to the agents of the colony, payable in two years from the first of September, 1836, for the sum of twenty-five dollars, and this sum shall be appropriated towards defraying the expenses of building a meeting-house for the use of the colony.

"10. Voted, That an eighty-acre lot be reserved for a parsonage, out of the purchase, to be selected by the agents.

". . . finally adopted March 28, 1836, at Castleton, Vt."

* * *

The Mississippi Valley West had a strong attraction for many of the four million Europeans who migrated to the United States between 1815 and 1860. By 1860 more than half of the nation's foreign-born population were living west of the Alleghenies. The availability of cheap land on the fringe of settlement was the West's major appeal to these newcomers, an appeal which was made articulate by agents of transportation companies or of immigration offices of the Western states, who frequently button-holed the immigrant at the docks. For some foreign-born groups—especially the Germans —the still open lands of the West offered space where whole communities of their countrymen could enjoy the freedom as well as the economic opportunity of the New World; and still others were pulled west by the need for workers on railroads and canals. Germans were the most numerous of the West's foreign-born element. Cincinnati, Milwaukee, Chicago, and St.

Louis were centers of German migration; and on the perimeter
of settlement, from Texas through Missouri to Iowa and Wis-
consin, German communities flourished. As earlier, the British
Isles supplied a substantial number of settlers; and Scandina-
vians, though less numerous, put the stamp of their culture on
the upper Mississippi Valley, especially on Minnesota. Fred-
erick Law Olmsted, touring the ante-bellum South as a special
correspondent for the New York Times, *came upon a German*
community, in the vicinity of Neu-Braunfels, as he traveled
through south central Texas early in 1854. His observations,
as reported in his A Journey Through Texas, or a Saddle-Trip
on the Southwestern Frontier, *suggest the extent to which*
newcomers from Europe shaped the cultural patterns of the
developing West.

The first German settlers we saw, we knew at once. They
lived in little log cabins, and had inclosures of ten acres of
land about them. The cabins were very simple and cheap
habitations, but there were many little conveniences about
them, and a care to secure comfort in small ways evident, that
was very agreeable to notice. So, also, the greater variety of the
crops which had been grown upon their allotments, and the
more clean and complete tillage they had received contrasted
favorably with the patches of corn-stubble, overgrown with
crab-grass, which are usually the only gardens to be seen adjoining the cabins of the poor whites and slaves. . . .

We were entering the valley of the Guadalupe river, . . .
and had passed a small brown house with a turret and cross
upon it, which we learned was a Lutheran church, when we
were overtaken by a good-natured butcher, who lived in Neu-
Braunfels, whence he had ridden out early in the morning to
kill and dress the hogs of one of the large farmers. . . .

He had been in this country eight years. . . . The Germans, generally, were doing well, and were contented. They
had had a hard time at first, but they were all doing well now
—getting rich. He knew but one German who had bought a
slave; they did not think well of slavery; they thought it better
that all men should be free; besides, the negroes would not
work so well as the Germans. They were improving their condition very rapidly, especially within the last two years. . . .

There were Catholics and Protestants among them; as for himself, he was no friend to priests, whether Catholic or Protestant. He had had enough of them in Germany. They could not tell him anything new, and he never went to any church. . . .

We had still nearly a mile to ride before entering the town, and in this distance met eight or ten large wagons, each drawn by three or four pairs of mules or five or six yokes of oxen, each carrying under its neck a brass bell. They were all driven by Germans, somewhat uncouthly but warmly and neatly dressed; all smoking and all good-humored, giving us "good morning" as we met. Noticing the strength of the wagons, I observed that they were made by Germans, probably.

"Yes," said the butcher, "the Germans make better wagons than the Americans; the Americans buy a great many of them. *There are seven wagon-manufactories in Braunfels.*"

The main street of the town, which we soon entered upon, was very wide—three times as wide, in effect, as Broadway in New York. The houses, with which it was thickly lined on each side for a mile, were small, low cottages, of no pretensions to elegance, yet generally looking neat and comfortable. Many were furnished with verandahs and gardens, and the greater part were either stuccoed or painted. There were many workshops of mechanics and small stores, with signs oftener in English than in German; and bare-headed women, and men in caps and short jackets, with pendent pipes, were everywhere seen at work.

We had no acquaintance in the village, and no means of introduction, but, in hopes that we might better satisfy ourselves of the condition of the people, we agreed to stop at an inn and get dinner, instead of eating a cold snack in the saddle, without stopping at noon, as was our custom. "Here," said the butcher, "is my shop"—indicating a small house, at the door of which hung dressed meat and beef sausages—"and if you are going to stop, I will recommend you to my neighbor, there, Mr. Schmitz." It was a small cottage of a single story, having the roof extended so as to form a verandah, with a sign swinging before it, "Guadalupe Hotel, J. Schmitz."

I never in my life, except, perhaps, in awakening from a

dream, met with such a sudden and complete transfer of asso-
ciations. Instead of loose boarded or hewn log walls, with
crevices stuffed with rags or daubed with mortar, which we
have been accustomed to see during the last month, on staving
in a door, where we have found any to open; instead, even, of
four bare, cheerless sides of whitewashed plaster, which we
have found twice or thrice only in a more aristocratic American residence, we were—in short, we were in Germany.

There was nothing wanting; there was nothing too much,
for one of those delightful little inns which the pedestrian
who has tramped through the Rhine land will ever remember
gratefully. A long room, extending across the whole front of
the cottage, the walls pink, with stenciled panels, and scroll
ornaments in crimson, and with neatly-framed and glazed
pretty lithographic prints hanging on all sides; a long, thick,
dark oak table, with rounded ends, oak benches at its sides;
chiseled oak chairs; a sofa, covered with cheap pink calico,
with a small vine pattern; a stove in the corner; a little
mahogany cupboard in another corner, with pitcher and glasses
upon it; a smoky atmosphere; and finally, four thick-bearded
men, from whom the smoke proceeds, who all bow and say
"Good morning," as we lift our hats in the doorway.

The landlady enters; she does not readily understand us,
and one of the smokers rises immediately to assist us. Dinner
we shall have immediately, and she spreads the white cloth at
an end of the table, before she leaves the room, and in two
minutes' time, by which we have got off our coats and warmed
our hands at the stove, we are asked to sit down. An excellent
soup is set before us, and in succession there follow two
courses of meat, neither of them pork and neither of them
fried, two dishes of vegetables, salad, compote of peaches,
coffee with milk, wheat bread from the loaf, and beautiful
and sweet butter—not only such butter as I have never tasted
south of the Potomac before, but such as I have been told a
hundred times it was impossible to make in southern climate.
What is the secret? I suppose it is extreme cleanliness, beginning far back of where cleanliness usually begins at the South,
and careful and thorough *working*.

We then spent an hour in conversation with the gentlemen

who were in the room. They were all educated, cultivated, well-bred, respectful, kind, and affable men. All were natives of Germany, and had been living several years in Texas. Some of them were travelers, their homes being in other German settlements; some of them had resided long at Braunfels. . . .

In the afternoon [of the following day], we called upon the German Protestant clergyman, who received us kindly, and, though speaking little English, was very ready to give all the information he could about his people, and the Germans in Texas generally. We visited some of the workshops, and called on a merchant to ascertain the quality and amount of the cotton grown by the Germans in the neighborhood. . . .

As I was returning to the inn, about ten o'clock, I stopped for a few moments at the gate of one of the little cottages, to listen to some of the best singing I have heard for a long time, several parts being sustained by very sweet and well-trained voices. . . .

In the morning we found that our horses had been bedded, for the first time in Texas.

As we rode out of town, it was delightful to meet again troops of children, with satchels and knapsacks of books, and little kettles of dinner, all with ruddy, cheerful faces, the girls especially so, with their hair braided neatly, and without caps or bonnets, smiling and saluting us—"*guten morgen*"—as we met.

* * *

Texas, through which Frederick Law Olmsted traveled, had only recently become a part of the United States. As a result of its annexation in 1845 and the war with Mexico, which shortly followed, some 383,463 square miles (two-thirds of this in the State of Texas) were added to the American West. American pioneers had begun to settle in Texas in the 1820's, under an arrangement made by Spain, and later Mexico, with Moses and Stephen Austin and other colonizing agents known as empresarios. Pressure for independence among the American residents, after the early 1830's, led to the creation of the Republic of Texas in 1836. Mexican opposition to its annexation by the United States, as well as American concern for stability in the Southwest, created tensions that resulted in the

Mexican War (1846-1847). The correspondence of Moses Austin and his son Stephen, who carried out his father's plans, reveals the arrangements which facilitated the initial migration of Americans into Texas.

MOSES AUSTIN TO J.E.B. AUSTIN

St Louis Apr 8 1821

My Dear Son

. . . I much wish to see you return to this country before I leave it for the Spanish province of *Texas.* I have made a visit to St Antonio and obtained liberty to settle in that country—*as I am, ruined, in this,* I found nothing I could do would bring back my property again and to remain in a Country where I had enjoyed *welth* in a state of *poverty* I could Not submit to I therefore made an *exertion* and obtained what I asked for a right of settlement for myself and family the situation I have marked out is on the *Colorado* about 3 Days sale from New Orleans or rather from *the Belise* a *most* delightful situation. . . . I have asked for leave of settlement for 300 families and (200) Thousand Acres of Land to open a Port *Town* at the *mouth of the River* which has been granted me by the Governor of the Province of Texas and has gone on to the Vice King for his confirmation, I have been offered as many *Names* of respectable families as will make up the Number but untill I return I shall not admitt any as my wish is to have the lands survey'd before I introduce any families at all. I shall take with me about 30 young men to commence the settlement and return after your mother next year. . . .

Moses Austin

. . . .

STEPHEN F. AUSTIN TO MOSES AUSTIN

Nachitoches July 4 1821

. . . .

. . . The following is a rough Translation of the order from Arredondo to Martinez— . . .

"It is expedient to grant the permission which Moses Austin

solicited to establish himself with three hundred families in the Province of Texas, on the conditions specified in his memorial on this subject . . . provided that the following conditions be complied with—

1st All who emigrate under this permission must be *Catholics*, or agree to be so, before they remove—

2d They must take the oath of allegiance to be faithful to the King and Constitution etc

3 They must be *honest, industrious* farmers and mechanics —and the applicant M Austin, will be held responsible for their good conduct"

. . . .   S. F. Austin

. . . .

STEPHEN AUSTIN TO THE COLONISTS

Colarado River House of Mr Castlemans
August 6 1823.

Fellow Citizens,

I have once more the pleasure of addressing you a few lines from the Colorado— . . . The titles to your land is indisputable—the original grant for this settlement was made by the Spanish Government before the Revolution, it was then confirmed and the quantity of land designated by the decree of the Emperor Agustin Iturbide on the 18th of February last, and the whole was again approved and confirmed by the Sovereign Congress of the Mexican Nation on the 14 of April last after the fall of the Emperor. The titles . . . are then perfect and complete for ever, and each settler may sell his land the same as he could do in the United States.

. . . I wish the settlers to remember that the Roman Catholic is the religion of this nation, I have taken measures to have *Father Miness* [Maynes] formerly of Nachitoches, appointed our Curate, he is a good man and acquainted with the Americans—we must all be particular on this subject and respect the Catholic religion with all that attention due to its sacredness and to the laws of the land.

I have so far paid all the expenses attending this enterprise out of my own funds. . . . Those who have the means must pay me a little money on receipt of their titles; from those who have not money I will receive any kind of property that will not be a dead loss to me, such as horses, mules, cattle, hogs, peltry, Furs, bees wax, home made cloth, dressed deer skins, etc. Only a small part will be required in hand, for the balance I will wait one, two, and three years, according to the capacity of the person to pay— . . . The smallest quantity of land a family will receive is one thousand yards square which may be increased by me and the Commissioner without limit in proportion to the size of the family.

Young men must join and take land in the name of one. All thus united will be ranked as one family, they can then divide the land amongst themselves. . . . The settlers have now nothing to fear. . . . they must not be discouraged at any little depradations of Indians, they must remember that *American blood* flows in their veins, and that they must not dishonor that noble blood by yielding to trifling difficulties. . . .

Stephen F. Austin

*   *   *

The most dramatic episode in the movement for Texan independence was the heroic but futile defense of the Alamo, in which on March 6, 1836 a garrison of 187 men lost their lives, among them David Crockett and twelve volunteers who had followed him from Tennessee. "Remember the Alamo!" became the rallying cry of General Sam Houston and his men, when six weeks later they defeated Santa Anna in the Battle of San Jacinto to secure the independence of Texas. The author of what purport to be Crockett's "last words" is a matter of conjecture, but the account bears the gusty flavor of this rip-roaring, legend-making personality of the Mississippi Valley West.

I write this on the nineteenth of February, 1836, at San Antonio. We are all in high spirits, though we are rather short of provisions, for men who have appetites that could digest anything but oppression; but no matter, we have a prospect of soon getting our bellies full of fighting, and that is victuals and drink to a true patriot any day. . . .

February 22. The Mexicans, about sixteen hundred strong, with their President Santa Anna at their head, aided by Generals Almonte, Cos, Sesma, and Castrillon, are within two leagues of Bexar. . . .

February 23. Early this morning the enemy came in sight, marching in regular order, and displaying their strength to the greatest advantage, in order to strike us with terror. But that was no go; they'll find that they have to do with men who will never lay down their arms as long as they can stand on their legs. We held a short council of war, and, finding that we should be completely surrounded, and overwhelmed by numbers, if we remained in the town, we concluded to withdraw to the fortress of Alamo, and defend it to the last extremity. We accordingly filed off, in good order, having some days before placed all the surplus provisions, arms, and ammunition in the fortress. We have had a large national flag made; it is composed of thirteen stripes, red and white, alternately, on a blue ground with a large white star, of five points, in the center, and between the points the letters TEXAS. As soon as all our little band, about one hundred and fifty in number, had entered and secured the fortress in the best possible manner, we set about raising our flag on the battlements. . . .

February 24. Very early this morning the enemy commenced a new battery on the banks of the river, about three hundred and fifty yards from the fort, and by afternoon they amused themselves by firing at us from that quarter. . . .

March 3. We have given over all hopes of receiving assistance from Goliad or Refugio. Colonel Travis harangued the garrison, and concluded by exhorting them, in case the enemy should carry the fort, to fight to the last gasp, and render their victory even more serious to them than to us. This was followed by three cheers.

March 4. Shells have been falling into the fort like hail during the day, but without effect. About dusk, in the evening, we observed a man running toward the fort, pursued by about half a dozen of the Mexican cavalry. The bee-hunter immediately knew him to be the old pirate who had gone to Goliad, and, calling to the two hunters, he sallied out of the fort to the relief of the old man, who was hard pressed. I followed close after. Before we reached the spot the Mexicans were close on the heel of the old man, who stopped suddenly, turned short upon his pursuers, discharged his rifle, and one of the enemy fell from his horse. The chase was renewed, but finding that he would be overtaken and cut to pieces, he now turned again, and, to the amazement of the enemy, became the assailant in his turn. He clubbed his gun, and dashed among them like a wounded tiger, and they fled like sparrows. By this time we reached the spot, and, in the ardor of the moment, followed some distance before we saw that our retreat to the fort was cut off by another detachment of cavalry. Nothing was to be done but to fight our way through. We were all of the same mind. "Go ahead!" cried I, and they shouted, "Go ahead, Colonel!" We dashed among them, and a bloody conflict ensued. They were about twenty in number, and they stood their ground. After the fight had continued about five minutes, a detachment was seen issuing from the fort to our relief, and the Mexicans scampered off, leaving eight of their comrades dead upon the field. But we did not escape unscathed, for both the pirate and the bee-hunter were mortally wounded, and I received a saber cut across the forehead. The old man died, without speaking, as soon as we entered the fort. We bore my young friend to his bed, dressed his wounds, and I watched beside him. He lay, without complaint or manifesting pain, until about midnight, when he spoke, and I asked him if he wanted anything. "Nothing," he replied, but drew a sigh that seemed to rend his heart, as he added, "Poor Kate of Nacogdoches!" His eyes were filled with tears, as he continued: "Her words were prophetic, Colonel;" and then he sang in a low voice that resembled the sweet notes of his own devoted Kate,

> "But toom cam' the saddle, all bluidy to see,
> And hame cam' the steed, but hame never cam' he."

He spoke no more, and a few minutes after, died. Poor Kate, who will tell this to thee?

March 5.   Pop, pop, pop! Bom, bom, bom! throughout the day. No time for memorandums now. Go ahead! Liberty and independence forever!

[Here ends Colonel Crockett's manuscript.]

*   *   *

James K. Polk of Tennessee was elected President in 1844 on a platform which endorsed the "reannexation" of Texas. In his inaugural address he took pains to justify this step, with veiled allusions to the fact that Northerners objected to seeing the West contribute another slave state to the Union.

. . . Texas was once a part of our country—was unwisely ceded away to a foreign power—is now independent, and possesses an undoubted right to . . . merge her sovereignty as a separate and independent state in ours. . . . Foreign powers should . . . look on the annexation of Texas to the United States not as the conquest of a nation seeking to extend her dominions by arms and violence, but as the peaceful acquisition of a territory once her own, by adding another member to our confederation, with the consent of that member, thereby diminishing the chances of war and opening to them new and ever-increasing markets for their products.

To Texas the reunion is important, because the strong protecting arm of our Government would be extended over her, and the vast resources of her fertile soil and genial climate would be speedily developed, while the safety of New Orleans and of our whole southwestern frontier against hostile aggression . . . would be promoted by it. . . .

None can fail to see the danger to our safety and future peace if Texas remains an independent state or becomes an ally or dependency of some foreign nation more powerful than herself. . . . Whatever is good or evil in the local institutions of Texas will remain her own whether annexed to the United States or not. None of the present states will be responsible for them any more than they are for the local institutions of each other. They have confederated together for certain specified objects. Upon the same principle that they would refuse to form a perpetual union with Texas because of her local institutions our forefathers would have been prevented from forming our present Union.

*　　*　　*

The railroad contributed significantly to the "steam-engine" progress of the West in the forties and fifties. By the turn of the 1830's, railroads were being pushed westward from the Atlantic Coast; and by the early 1850's, eastern lines had

made connections with the Western waters at such points as
Buffalo, Dunkirk, Pittsburg, and Wheeling. In the West, the
first efforts at railroad building were interrupted by the Panic
of 1837, but construction was booming again by the late
1840's. During the 1850's, rails reached the Mississippi River
at several points, making possible through connections from
the East; and by 1856, the Illinois Central Railroad bisected
Illinois from Galena and Chicago southward to the junction
of the Ohio and the Mississippi. Relatively level terrain and
readily available timber facilitated railroad building in this
part of the West; but construction was often hindered by
problems of financing, political maneuvers attending the selec-
tion of routes, and a continuing scarcity of labor and of experienced construction and managerial personnel. This is
brought out in the letters of Charles Linsley, a twenty-one-
year-old Vermonter, who was engaged in 1852 to survey part
of the route of the Milwaukee and Mississippi, Wisconsin's
first railroad. His letters also illustrate the hazards and incon-
veniences of travel westward in the early 1850's.

Milwaukee, March 5th/52

My Dear Father:

. . . We left Cleveland on Monday last 1st March taking
the cars for Shelby, Ohio—a junction station on the Cleveland
& Cincinnati & Newark & Sandusky Roads—distance 67 miles.
The line is almost entirely straight & grades very light but
the track is rough & they were very slow. . . . We got
dinner at this place—waited about two hours & took cars for
Monroeville [Ohio] a small station on the Newark & Sandusky
Road distance about 35 miles I think. . . . We reached
Monroeville at 5:00. & left immediately for Toledo by stage
distance 62 miles. We found good coaches & smart horses
& by a little engineering six of us made out to get possession
of one coach. We went off smartly & soon struck a
McAdamized Road, went 12 miles & got supper. Started off
again about 9 o'clock for a nights seige. The night was stormy
& the prospect was that we should have a gloomy time as
sleeping was out of the question.—But you will see we made
out well. A gentleman who sat on the back seat lighted a
cigar with a wax taper & it burned for half a minute lighting
up the cabin & making it look cheerful indeed. Says I, "Wish

that could be kept up." "It can" says he, & immediately pulls
a sperm candle out of his carpet bag, which he proceeded to
light & we had made a strike surely. Now said I "if we had
some cards" & he pulls from the never failing carpet bag a
nice pack & we are fixed. Well we seated ourselves ("holding
candle" by turns) & first played Whist & then old sledge &c
&c till we got off the McAdamized Road which was only
about 10 miles from Toledo & the time was 4 o'clock Tuesday
morning. I need not say the night passed off very pleasantly
& we were not sleepy in the least. We reached Toledo at
6:00 & got breakfast. Left there at 10:00 (two hours bihind
time engine being broke) taking the Michigan Southern for
Chicago,   the first 30 miles was an old Road the oldest
in the state, which is leased by the M.S.R.R. [Michigan
Southern Railroad]. It is laid with a strap rail & in miserable
order which together with a fall of snow the night before
hindered us a good deal & we were four hours going the 30
miles. When we struck the Trail we went quite smart for
this country, & reached Laporte, Indiana, at 6:00 P.M.
where we took coaches for Michigan City 12 miles over a
plank road & reached there at 12.M.   after much trouble
we succeeded in getting a bed & a good sleep. Left there
next morning (Wednesday) by cars & reached Chicago at
11 o'clock. . . . We found that a boat had been out to
Milwaukee once but was then shut in by ice & there was no
way for us but to take stage. . . . We left there at 6 o'clock
Wednesday evening & rode all night & all day yesterday &
arrived here last night at 7 o'clock distance 90 miles fare
$5.00. It was a very hard ride as the Roads were rough & the
weather pretty cold . . . even at this season. We tipped over
once but came out safe—driver a little hurt—& we had reason
to be thankful that we were not all hurt as there were seven
of us inside a coach shut up tight & heavily loaded with
baggage but we went over a level spot & were going slow at
the time. The axeltree breaking close to the wheel was the
cause of the accident. . . .

Whitewater, Walworth County, Wis. March 10th/52
. . . Mr. Edgerton . . . told me to come on & take charge
of the locating party from this place [Whitewater] to Rock

River & gave me an introduction to Mr. Shields an assistant
on construction who is stopping at this place. . . . I . . .
made my appearance in the (apoligy for) Engineers Office
which was over a store. among the Paper Rags & crockery
leather flour &c a small low bench or table set near two small
windows constituted the Engineers corner. Not a chair in the
garret but seats provided on raisin boxes &c if they hadn't
been split into kindling wood. I found they never had a sheet
of profile paper since the Road was commenced but all
profiles were made by scale & dividers—I found Shields to be
a very clever fellow, a Scotchman who came to this country
at the time the road was commencing & has been on ever
since. . . . he is about 22 I should judge. he has charge of
a division from this place east. . . . There were only two
men engaged for axemen &c. Well I commenced, had a very
good transit & made some progress. . . . They pay here,
Rodman, axeman, & all $30.00 per month making no distinc-
tion which is a very poor plan. they employ Irish & Scotch
mostly & they are a lazy set to work. . . . much is lost by
improper management & by not having a proper head. Mr.
Edgerton appears to be a very fine man, of good education,
& a well read man but no experience in building Rail Roads.
came on as a land surveyor at first & knew nothing about the
true practical economy of Railroading. Conkey [who had the
contract to build the road] says that when he came on here
to lay track for them (that was done a year ago) he never saw
so green a set, not an engineer that ever saw any track laid
& all were in a fix & that is the way he came to get the job
so easily. he says he was but two hours concluding the
bargain. They never had an engineer on here that had ever
been on another railroad. It seems that the . . . former
Presdt was a scoundrel (to speak it plainly as it is said to me)
& sunk a good deal of money for the Company. He appointed
himself Chief Engineer & made a miserable location from
Milwaukee to Waukesha, very crooked & about four miles
out of the way. . . .

I find that the Co. is amazingly poor. None of the Engineers
that I have seen have been paid scarcely anything for a year
& they now owe them for a years work nearly. . . .

Chicago, Ill., Aug. 6, 1852

. . . It is absolutely impossible to get men here now on account of cholera, as there are none coming in at all. . . . try and forward some even if you have to make a trip to Boston for that purpose. I wrote some time since to M. L. Ray of Boston (an emigrant agent) to forward us 100 Munster men at once. We have heard nothing from him yet. I have been doing my best to get a gang in this city but have only succeeded in raising a half dozen. I fear I can raise no more at all. . . . tell them there is no cholera within 100 miles of our work.

*　　*　　*

The availability of railroads encouraged migration and speeded the development of the Western economy. Some of the companies actually became colonizing agencies, as is illustrated in the efforts of the Illinois Central to induce settlers to migrate to Illinois. This company was the beneficiary of a grant of two and a half million acres of government land to be located along the right of way of the road. To sell these lands, and thus finance construction, the company engaged in a far-flung advertising campaign, both in the United States and in Europe, extolling the advantages of farming in Illinois. As a result of its promotional activities, thousands of migrants were attracted to this part of the West. Typical of its advertisements is one referring to Illinois as "The Garden State of the West."

HOMES FOR THE INDUSTRIOUS IN THE GARDEN STATE OF THE WEST

The Illinois Central Railroad Co., have for sale 1,200,000 ACRES OF RICH FARMING LANDS, In Tracts of Forty Acres and upward on Long Credit and at Low Prices.

The attention of the enterprising and industrious portion of the community is directed to the following statements and liberal inducements offered them by the ILLINOIS CENTRAL RAILROAD COMPANY, which, as they will perceive, will enable them, by proper energy, perseverance and industry, to provide comfortable homes for themselves and families, with, comparatively speaking, very little capital.

LANDS OF ILLINOIS. No State in the Valley of the Mississippi offers so great an inducement to the settler as the State of Illinois. There is no portion of the world where all the conditions of climate and soil so admirably combine to produce those two great staples, CORN and WHEAT, as the Prairies of Illinois.

EASTERN AND SOUTHERN MARKETS. These lands are contiguous to a railroad 700 miles in length, which connects with other roads and navigable lakes and rivers, thus affording an unbroken communication with the Eastern and Southern markets.

RAILROAD SYSTEM OF ILLINOIS. Over $100,000,000 of private capital have been expended on the railroad system of Illinois. Inasmuch as part of the income from several of these works . . . go[es] to diminish the State expenses; the TAXES ARE LIGHT, and must consequently every day decrease. . . .

PRESENT POPULATION. The State is rapidly filling up with population; 868,025 persons having been added since 1850, making the present population 1,723,663, a ratio of 102 per cent. in ten years.

AGRICULTURAL PRODUCTS. The Agricultural Products of Illinois are greater than those of any other State. . . . The wheat crop of 1860 approaches 35,000,000 bushels, while the corn crop yields not less than 140,000,000 bushels.

FERTILITY OF THE SOIL. Nowhere can the industrious farmer secure such immediate results for his labor as upon these prairie soils, they being composed of a deep rich loam, the fertility of which is unsurpassed by any on the globe.

TO ACTUAL CULTIVATORS. *Since 1854 the Company have sold 1,300,000 acres. They sell only to actual cultivators, and every contract contains an agreement to cultivate. The road has been constructed through these lands at an expense of $30,000,000. In 1850 the population of forty-nine counties, through which it passes, was only 335,598 since which 479,293 have been added; making the whole population 814,891, a gain of 143 per cent. . . .*

PRICES AND TERMS OF PAYMENT. The prices of these lands vary from $6 to $25 per acre, according to location, quality, &c. First class farming lands sell for about $10 to $12 per acre; and the relative expense of subduing prairie land as compared with wood land is in the ratio of 1 to 10 in favor of the former. The terms of sale for the bulk of these lands will be

ONE YEAR'S INTEREST IN ADVANCE, at six per cent per annum, and six interest notes at six per cent., payable respectively in one, two, three, four, five and six years from date of sale; and four notes for principal, payable in four, five, six and seven years from date of sale; the contract stipulating that one-tenth of the tract purchased shall be fenced and cultivated, each and every year, for five years from date of sale, so that at the end of five years one-half shall be fenced and under cultivation.

TWENTY PER CENT. WILL BE DEDUCTED from the valuation for cash.

* * *

The flow of population westward by rail, lake, and canal threatened the primacy of the Western cities on the Ohio River route. In the 1840's and 1850's it was the urban communities of the Great Lakes whose rapid growth excited the popular imagination. And none of these, in this rising railroad age, was in a position to benefit more than Chicago. According to Hunt's Merchant's Magazine and Commercial Review, *for January, 1861, Chicago's spectacular growth was a result of the "immense concentration, not only of railroads at that point, but of the expenditure for railroad construction on a radius of 100 miles," all of which had "reflected upon Chicago as a focus." Chicago, like all Western cities, had grown "out of nothing in a short space of time," as one European visitor put it. It took shape in the mid-1830's on the site of Fort Dearborn, which was first occupied in 1803. By the mid-1850's, Chicago was reputed to be "the great feature of the new Western world." James Stirling, an Englishman who sojourned there in October, 1856, called it "a city, not in growth, but in revolution"; growth was "much too slow a word for the transformation of a hamlet of log-huts into a western New York, in the space of a few years." Its population —112,172 in 1860—had grown from a mere 4,470, twenty years earlier. Brooklyn's popular preacher, Henry Ward*

*Beecher, visited Chicago in October of 1855. He was enough
impressed with the expanding city to make it the subject of
one of the articles he wrote for the New York Ledger, in the
series, "Thoughts as they Occur, by one who keeps his Eyes
and Ears open."*

No man has seen the West who has not seen Chicago.
Nature has done little for its harbor, and government has
done less. The ground was not meant for a city. The place
has no adaptations for a fine city. It is low, flat, muddy, or
dusty. But such is the concentration of enormous business
here, that before many years all natural difficulties will have
been overcome. The grade will be raised artificially; the streets
paved; the sidewalks, now of wood, converted to stone; the
river tunnelled; the harbor cleaned out and enlarged, and the
whole river, in both its branches, be wharfed in and lined
with lumber-yards and warehouses. But as yet Chicago is
anything but a city of desirable aspect to the eye or the feet.
It would seem to be a merchant's *beau ideal* of paradise. It
fairly smokes and roars with business. There is no room for
the caravans of teams. The river is choked with craft, and
the harbor is filled with vessels. The streets are filled up with
boxes and bales, the stores are like hives in spring weather,
with swarms going in and out with incessant activity;—
buying and selling, buying and selling, buying and selling,—
that is Chicago. The merchant cannot get goods from the
East fast enough. His yesterday's arrivals are gone to-day, or
picked over and made thin. The warehouses cannot hold the
grain; the shipping cannot convey it away fast enough; and
demand, on every side, drives up the business-men with
incessant importunity. Huge hotels, that seem large enough
to accommodate an army, were running over; and having
occasion to stop a moment at the Briggs House, we found the
hall leading to the dining-room packed with scores of men,
though yet fifteen minutes to dinner, waiting for the opening
of the door. But it was the Agricultural Fair that had, without doubt, made such a terrific crush in town, during the
few days that we tarried there.

*　　*　　*

*Issues arising in the Middle West fired the tensions that
resulted in the Civil War. The most aggravating of these was
the question of slavery in the territories, for states in the making constituted a sphere of potential influence in which both
North and South hoped to gain the advantage. The issue came
to a head in the contest of the two contending sections to
dominate Kansas. In enacting the Kansas-Nebraska Bill, providing government for these two territories, Congress lifted
the prohibition on slavery that had been customary in the
upper part of the West and left the decision to "squatter
sovereignty"—the vote of the local residents. This precipitated
movements, generated in both the North and the South, to
supply Kansas with settlers who would espouse the point of
view of the respective section. Emigrant aid societies, originally organized by a Massachusetts abolitionist, Eli Thayer,
undertook to promote settlement by migrants hostile to
slavery. The South countered by encouraging the migration of
slaveholders into the area. Kansas "bled" during the conflict;
but the settlement of the West went on. Edward Everett
Hale, Unitarian minister and advocate of many causes, recalled
the activities of the Northern aid societies in his* Memories of
a Hundred Years.

When, . . . in the beginning of the year 1854, with a
sublime audacity, won by success, the Southern leaders determined to overthrow the Missouri Compromise, the opportunity for the direction of free emigration presented itself. . . .

The "Nebraska Bill". . . . violated the promises of the
Missouri Compromise by throwing open the territory west of
Arkansas and Missouri and Iowa to the institution of slavery.
The North was on fire at once at a violation so disgraceful
of a compact which had been loyally respected for thirty-four
years. And Eli Thayer, a school-master of Worcester, Massachusetts, called on the [Massachusetts] Legislature to organize
the Massachusetts Emigrant Aid Company. . . . It authorized a capital of five million dollars in establishing
settlements at the West. The charter . . . was signed by
Governor Washburn on the 26th day of April, 1854. This
was a month before the Nebraska Bill was signed by Franklin
Pierce, then President. On the 4th of May the petitioners

accepted the charter. Massachusetts picked up the gauntlet, it has been said, before it was thrown down.

In point of fact, the friends of the movement acted under a quiet, private organization through the whole of the year 1854, and a more valuable working charter was obtained for the New England Emigrant Aid Company in the next winter. . . . Before May, 1855, thirty thousand dollars were subscribed and spent. . . . The first company of emigrants went under the direction of its executive in August of 1854. Dr. Charles Robinson, who afterward became Governor of Kansas, was the leader.

When this New England Emigrant Aid Company was organized, the largest subscriber was John Carter Brown, a millionnaire merchant of Providence. He was chosen the first President of the new organization.

Mr. Eli Thayer was a near neighbor of mine in Worcester, and as soon as I knew of his prompt and wise movement I . . . told him I was ready to take hold anywhere. . . . There was enough for all of us to do. We called meetings in all available places, and went to speak or sent speakers wherever we were called for. Colonies formed themselves in all the larger towns of New England, and before the end of 1855 we had sent out four or five thousand settlers into Kansas. . . .

The books of the Emigrant Aid Companies show that the Central Company spent in the year 1854 $23,623.73. Before the spring of the next year the expenditure had been $96,956.01. In 1862 the company sold all its property in Kansas. It had then raised and expended $136,000. . . .

Local societies were formed in various sections—working in their own fashion. Mr. Thayer arranged for a meeting in the city of New York among other places. It was not large but it was enthusiastic. . . .

Most fortunately for the country the Southern oligarchy and their coadjutors in Missouri took the alarm more seriously than they needed to have done. Mr. Thayer had boldly named five million dollars as the capital for his new company. While we were doing our best to bring together the twenty thousand dollars which we spent in 1854, every paper in Missouri and farther South was announcing that we had five millions at our command. This announcement answered our purpose almost as well as if it had been true. And I think that no single cause stimulated the Western emigration into Kansas more than the announcement and belief that rich New England capitalists were investing five million dollars there.

The plan of Mr. Thayer was very simple. . . . We would announce at our office that, say, on the 3d of August we should send a company to Kansas. We corresponded with the railway companies to know which would give us the cheapest terms. We peddled through tickets to the people who came to us at the wholesale price. Then we appointed a competent person to take charge of the party. In this way men who went forward with the first parties could send their women or even their little children in subsequent parties, without coming back to take them over the route. . . .

We never gave a penny to a settler unless he was engaged to do work for us. And the people who said that we took out paupers did not know how many substantial men and women were eager to go into Kansas.

We offered a prize for the best marching song for emigrants. . . . Whittier wrote for us [another] capital marching song or "song of degrees":

> "We cross the prairie as of old
> Our fathers crossed the sea,
> To make the West, as they the East,
> The homestead of the free."

When one of these companies came to the new territory, our business with the individuals of whom it was composed was at an end. But, naturally, people who had started out together liked to keep together, and such people would take up their lands together. . . .

Wherever agents could, they established a steam engine for cutting lumber. In Lawrence we assisted Dr. George N. Brown, who established a printing-press at which the *Herald of Freedom* was printed. . . . I remember that the handbills which we circulated for calling meetings, at some of which I spoke, were headed "Sawmills and Liberty." The theory

which we were impressing was that towns were the bulwarks
of freedom; that if people would help the settlers by establishing their sawmills, they would form so many central
points where freedom would gather; and all this proved
precisely true. . . .

The first election in the Territory showed that armed men
from Missouri meant to take its organization into their
hands. The settlers had to arm themselves; and at their
request our officers made the purchase of Sharp's rifles, which
won a place in history. At one time Henry Ward Beecher
was nicknamed Sharp's Rifle Beecher, because he had contributed to the Rifle Fund.

*   *   *

*Similar societies, made up of pro-slavery elements, attempted
to hold the line for slavery in the new Territory; but it was
less easy to induce slaveholders to migrate than it was to per-
suade Northern farmers unencumbered with slaves. DeBow's
Review for May, 1856, printed an appeal from the Lafayette
Emigration Society of western Missouri urging the South as
a whole to face up to its obligation to "Settle the Territory
with emigrants from the south."*

KANSAS MATTERS—APPEAL TO THE SOUTH.

TO THE PEOPLE OF THE SOUTH: On the undersigned,
managers of the "Lafayette Emigration Society," has devolved
the important duty of calling the attention of the people
of the slaveholding States, to the absolute necessity of immediate action on their part, in relation to the settlement of
Kansas Territory. The crisis is at hand. Prompt and decisive
measures must be adopted, or farewell to southern rights and
independence.

The western counties of Missouri have, for the last two
years, been heavily taxed, both in money and time, in fighting the battles of the South. Lafayette county alone has
expended more than $100,000 in money, and as much, or
more, in time. Up to this time, the border counties of
Missouri have upheld and maintained the rights and interests
of the South in this struggle, unassisted, and unsuccessfully.

But the abolitionists, staking their all upon the Kansas issue, and hesitating at no means, fair or foul, are moving heaven and earth to render that beautiful Territory not only a "free State," so called, but a den of negro thieves and "higher law" incendiaries.

Missouri, we feel confident, has done her duty, and will still be found ready and willing to do all she can, fairly and honorably, for the maintainance of the integrity of the South. But the time has come when she can no longer stand up, single handed, the lone champion of the South, against the myrmidons of the entire North. It requires no great foresight to perceive that if the "higher law" men succeed in this crusade, it will be but the commencement of a war upon the institutions of the South, which will continue until slavery shall cease to exist in any of the States, or the Union is dissolved.

How, then, shall these impending evils be avoided? The answer is obvious. *Settle the Territory with emigrants from the south.* The population of the Territory at this time is about equal—as many pro-slavery settlers as abolitionists; but the fanatics have emissaries in all the free States—in almost every village—and by misrepresentation and falsehood are engaged in collecting money and enlisting men to tyranize over the south. Is it in the nature of southern men to submit without resistance, to look to the north for their laws and institutions? We do not believe it! If, then, the south is influenced by a spirit of self-respect and independence, *let societies be formed to assist emigrants.* Those who cannot emigrate can contribute money to assist those who can. We have such societies in Missouri, and we can induce more people to emigrate than we are able to support. If the whole south would adopt this system, we would succeed; Kansas would be a slave State, and the slavery agitation would cease. If we permit the north to make an abolition State of Kansas, the whole south must submit to be governed by the north. Will the south help us?

The great struggle will come off at the next election, in October, 1856, and unless the south can at that time maintain her ground, all will be lost. We repeat it, the crisis has arrived. The time has come for action—*bold, determined action;*

words will no longer do any good; we must have men in Kansas; and that too by tens of thousands. A few will not answer. If we should need ten thousand, and lack one of that number, all will count nothing. Let all then, who can come, do so at once. Those who cannot come, must give their money to help others to come. There are hundreds of thousands of broad acres of rich land, worth from $5 to $20 per acre, open to settlement and pre-emption, at $1.25 per acre. Let, then, the farmer come and bring his slaves with him. There are now one thousand slaves in Kansas, whose presence there strengthens our cause. Shall we allow these rich lands and this beautiful country to be overrun by our abolition enemies? We know of a surety that they have emissaries and spies in almost every town, village and city in the south, watching our movements, and tampering with our slaves. Let us, then, be vigilant and active in the cause; we must maintain our ground. The loss of Kansas to the south will be the death knell of our dear Union.

Missouri has done nobly, thus far, in overcoming the thousands who have been sent out by Abolition Aid Societies; we cannot hold out much longer unless the whole South will come to the rescue. We need men; we need money; send us both, and that quickly. Do not delay; come as individuals, come in companies, come by thousands.

Our hearts have been made glad by the late arrival of large companies from South Carolina and Alabama. They have responded promptly to our call for help. . . . We tell you now, and tell you frankly, that unless you come quickly, and come by thousands, we are gone. The elections once lost, we are lost forever. Then farewell to our southern cause, and farewell to our glorious Union.

PART VI

ACROSS THE WIDE MISSOURI

"Away, away, I'm bound away
Across the wide Missouri."

*While farmers and town-makers were filling in the Mississippi
Valley, migrating America was already moving onward toward
the Pacific. The forerunners in this advance were the explorers,
trappers, and merchandisers who made the initial contacts with
the region beyond the bend of the Missouri. The purchase of
Louisiana in 1803 added to the United States a vaguely defined domain of more than 840,000 square miles, stretching
from the Mississippi River to the Rockies; negotiations with
Britain secured the Oregon country in 1846; and the expansive Southwest was acquired in 1848 at the close of the
Mexican War and by the Gadsden Purchase of 1853. By 1860,
the census takers could find more than 600,000 Americans in
the Mountain and Pacific West. Thomas Jefferson's interest in
the trans-Mississippi country, even before the purchase of
Louisiana, led him to propose an expedition across the Continent, ostensibly for scientific purposes. Accordingly, Meri-
wether Lewis, Jefferson's private secretary, and William Clark,
younger brother of George Rogers Clark, embarked from St.
Louis, in the Spring of 1804, with a party which included
twenty-six soldiers, George Drouillard and Toussaint Charbonneau, interpreters, Charbonneau's squaw-wife, Sacajawea
(the Bird Woman), her infant son, and Clark's Negro servant.
After wintering in what is now central North Dakota, they set
out again in April, 1805, to explore the uncharted far Northwest. On August 12, they crossed the Continental Divide by
way of Lemhi Pass, and Lewis could exult in having reached
the "distant fountain of the . . . mighty Missouri" and
tasted the "cold Clear water" of the westward-flowing
Columbia.*

April 7th. 1805

. . . Our vessels consisted of six small canoes, and two
large perogues. This little fleet altho' not quite so rispectable
as those of Columbus or Capt. Cook, were still viewed by us

with as much pleasure as those deservedly famed adventurers ever beheld theirs; and I dare say with quite as much anxiety for their safety and preservation. we were now about to penetrate a country at least two thousand miles in width, on which the foot of civilized man had never trodden; the good or evil it had in store for us was for experiment yet to determine, and these little vessells contained every article by which we were to expect to subsist or defend ourselves. . . . enterta[in]ing as I do, the most confident hope of succeeding in a voyage which had formed a da[r]ling project of mine for the last ten years, I could but esteem this moment of my departure as among the most happy of my life. The party are in excellent health and sperits, zealously attached to the enterprise, and anxious to proceed; not a whisper of murmur or discontent to be heard among them, but all act in unison, and with the most perfect harmony. Capt. Clark myself the two Interpretters and the woman and child sleep in a tent of dressed skins. this tent is in the Indian stile, formed of a number of dressed Buffaloe skins sewed together with sinues. it is cut in such manner that when foalded double it forms the quarter of a circle, and is left open at one side here it may be attatched or loosened at pleasure by strings which are sewed to its sides for the purpose. . . .

August 8th 1805.
. . . the Indian woman recognized the point of a high plain to our right which she informed us was not very distant from the summer retreat of her nation on a river beyond the mountains which runs to the west [Lemhi Pass through the Bitterroot Mountains]. this hill she says her nation calls the beaver's head from a conceived re[se]mblance of it's figure to the head of that animal. she assures us that we shall either find her people on this river or on the river immediately west of it's source; which from it's present size cannot be distant. as it is now all important with us to meet with those people as soon as possible I determined to proceed tomorrow with a small party to the source of the principal stream of this river and pass the mountains to the Columbia; and down that river untill I found the Indians; in short it is my resolusion to find

them or some others, who have horses if it should cause me a trip of one month. for without horses we shall be obliged to leave a great part of our stores, of which, it appears to me that we have a stock already sufficiently small for the length of the voyage before us. . . .

August 11th 1805.

The track which we had pursued last evening soon disappeared. I therefore resolved to proceed to the narrow pass on the creek about 10 miles West in hopes that I should again find the Indian road at the place, accordingly I proceeded through the level plain directly to the pass. I now sent Drewyer [Drouillard] to keep near the creek to my right and Shields to my left, with orders to surch for the road which if they found they were to notify me by placing a hat in the muzzle of their gun. I kept McNeal with me; after having marched in this order for about five miles I discovered an Indian on horse back about two miles distant coming down the plain towards us. with my glass I discovered from his dress that he was of a different nation from any that we had yet seen, and was satisfyed of his being a Sosone [Shoshone]; his arms were a bow and quiver of arrows, and was mounted on an eligant horse without a saddle, and a small string which was attatched to the under jaw of the horse which answered as a bridle.

I was overjoyed at the sight of this stranger and had no doubt of obtaining a friendly introduction to his nation provided I could get near enough to him to convince him of our being whitemen. I therefore proceeded towards him at my usual pace. when I had arrived within about a mile he mad[e] a halt which I did also and unloosing my blanket from my pack, I mad[e] him the signal of friendship known to the Indians of the Rocky mountains and those of the Missouri, which is by holding the mantle or robe in your hands at two corners and then th[r]owing [it] up in the air higher than the head bringing it to the earth as if in the act of spreading it, thus repeating three times. this signal of the robe has arrisen from a custom among all those nations of spreading a robe or skin for ther gests to set on when they are visited. this signal had not the desired effect, he still kept his position and

seemed to view Drewyer an[d] Shields who were now coming
in sight on either hand with an air of suspicion, I wo[u]ld
willingly have made them halt but they were too far distant to
hear me and I feared to make any signal to them lest it should
increase the suspicion in the mind of the Indian of our having
some unfriendly design upon him. I therefore haistened to take
out of my sack some b[e]ads a looking glas and a few trinkets
which I had brought with me for this purpose and leaving my
gun and pouch with McNeal advanced unarmed towards him.
he remained in the same stedfast poisture untill I arrived in
about 200 paces of him when he turn[ed] his ho[r]se about
and began to move off slowly from me; I now called to him in
as loud a voice as I could command repeating the word
tab-ba-bone, which in their language signifyes *whiteman*.
but lo[o]king over his sholder he still kept his eye on Drewyer
and Sheilds who wer still advancing neither of them haveing
segacity enough to recollect the impropriety of advancing
when they saw me thus in parley with the Indian.

I now made a signal to these men to halt, Drewyer obeyed
but Shields who afterwards told me that he did not obse[r]ve
the signal still kept on the Indian halted again and turned
his ho[r]se about as if to wait for me, and I beleive he would
have remained untill I came up with him had it not been for
Shields who still pressed forward. whe[n] I arrived within
about 150 paces I again repeated the word tab-ba-bone and
held up the trinkits in my hands and striped up my shirt sleve
to give him an opportunity of seeing the colour of my skin
and advanced leasure[ly] towards him but he did not remain
untill I got nearer than about 100 paces when he suddonly
turned his ho[r]se about, gave him the whip leaped the creek
and disapeared in the willow brush in an instant and with him
vanished all my hopes of obtaining horses for the preasent. . . .

we now set out on the track of the horse hoping by that
means to be lead to an indian camp, the trail of inhabitants
of which should they abscond we should probably be enabled
to pursue to the body of the nation to which they would most
probably fly for safety. this rout led us across a large Island
framed by nearly an equal division of the creek in this bottom;
after passing to the open ground on the N. side of the creek

we observed that the track made out toward the high hills about 3 M. distant in that direction. I thought it probable that their camp might probably be among those hills & that they would reconnoiter us from the tops of them, and that if we advanced haistily towards them that they would become allarmed and probably run off; I therefore halted in an elivated situation near the creek had a fire kindled of willow brush cooked and took breakfast.   during this leasure I prepared a small assortment of trinkits consisting of some mockkerson awls a few strans of several kinds of b[e]ads some paint a looking glass &c which I attatched to the end of a pole and planted it near our fire in order that should the Indians return in surch of us the[y] might from this token discover that we were friendly and white persons. . . .

Monday August 12th 1805.

This morning I sent Drewyer out as soon as it was light, he followed the track of the horse we had pursued yesterday to the mountain wher it had ascended, and returned to me in about an hour and a half. I now determined to pursue the base of the mountains which form this cove to the S.W. in the expectation of finding some Indian road which lead over the Mountains, accordingly I sent Drewyer to my right and Shields to my left with orders to look out for a road or the fresh tracks of horses either of which we should first meet with I had determined to pursue.   at the distance of about 4 miles we passed 4 small rivulets near each other on which we saw som resent bowers or small conic lodges formed with willow brush.   near them the indians had geathered a number of roots from the manner in which they had toarn up the ground; but I could not discover the root which they seemed to be in surch of.

near this place we fell in with a large and plain Indian road which came into the cove from the N.E. and led along the foot of the mountains to the S.W. o[b]liquely approaching the main stream which we had left yesterday.   this road we now pursued to the S.W.   at 5 miles it passed a stout stream which is a principal fork of the ma[i]n stream and falls into it just above the narrow pass between the two clifts before men-

tioned and which we now saw below us. here we halted and
breakfasted on the last of our venison, having yet a small peice
of pork in reserve. after eating we continued our rout
through the low bottom of the main stream along the foot of
the mountains   on our right the valley for 5 Mls. further in a
S.W. direction was from 2 to 3 miles wide   the main stream
now after discarding two stream[s] on the left in this valley
turns abruptly to the West through a narrow bottom be-
twe[e]n the mountains. the road was still plain, I therefore
did not dispair of shortly finding a passage over the mountains
and of taisting the waters of the great Columbia this evening.
at the distance of 4 miles further the road took us to the
most distant fountain of the waters of the Mighty Missouri in
surch of which we have spent so many toilsome days and
wristless nights. thus far I had accomplished one of those
great objects on which my mind has been unalterably fixed
for many years,   judge then of the pleasure I felt in all[a]ying
my thirst with this pure and icecold water which issues from
the base of a low mountain or hill of a gentle ascent for ½ a
mile. the mountains are high on either hand leave this gap
at the head of this rivulet through which the road passes.
here I halted a few minutes and rested myself. two miles
below McNeal had exultingly stood with a foot on each side
of this little rivulet and thanked his god that he had lived to
bestride the mighty & heretofore deemed endless Missouri.
after refreshing ourselves we proceeded on to the top of the
dividing ridge from which I discovered immence ranges of
high mountains still to the West of us with their tops partially covered with snow. I now decended the mountain about
¾ of a mile which I found much steeper than on the opposite
side, to a handsome bold runing Creek of cold Clear water.
here I first tasted the water of the great Columbia river.
after a short halt of a few minutes we continued our march
along the Indian road which lead us over steep hills and deep
hollows to a spring on the side of a mountain where we found
a sufficient quantity of dry willow brush for fuel,   here we
encamped for the night.

*   *   *

Of all the individualists bred on the American frontier, the trappers—or "mountain men"—of the Far West were probably the most individual. In the vanguard of the westward advance, these sovereigns of the wilderness became almost a part of the primitive and often perilous environment in which they lived. Organized trapping parties began to ascend the Missouri as early as 1807, carrying goods to be exchanged for peltries. After 1825, an annual rendezvous, at centrally located points in the mountains, provided a place where Indians, individual traders, and fur company agents could meet to carry on the trade. Some of the mountain men, like Kit Carson, James Bridger, Thomas Fitzpatrick, and Jedediah Smith, played an important role in the exploration and conquest of the West. This pathfinding breed of Western men found a congenial chronicler in George Frederick Ruxton, an English traveler who spent the Winter and Spring of 1847 in the Colorado country, absorbing the flavor of the fur-trade frontier. His Life in the Far West, *which is fictionized history, ran serially in* Blackwood's Edinburgh Magazine *from June to November, 1848, was published as a book in 1849, and went through many editions.*

Independence [Missouri] may be termed the "prairie port" of the western country. . . . Here, . . . the Indian traders and the Rocky-Mountain trappers rendezvous, collecting in sufficient force to ensure their safe passage through the Indian country. At the seasons of departure and arrival of these bands, the little town presents a lively scene of bustle and confusion. The wild and dissipated mountaineers get rid of their last dollars in furious orgies, treating all comers to galore of drink, and pledging each other, in horns of potent whisky, to successful hunts and "heaps of beaver." When every cent has disappeared from their pouches, the free trapper often makes away with rifle, traps, and animals, to gratify his "dry" (for your mountaineer is never "thirsty"); and then, "hos and beaver" gone, is necessitated to hire himself to one of the leaders of big bands, and hypothecate his services for an equipment of traps and animals. . . .

The rendezvous, which was encamped on a little stream beyond the town [consisted of] upwards of forty huge waggons, of Conostoga and Pittsburg build, and covered with snow-white tilts, [which] were ranged in a semicircle, or rather a horse-shoe form, on the flat open prairie, their long "tongues" (poles) pointing outwards; with the necessary harness for four pairs of mules, or eight yoke of oxen, lying on the ground beside them, spread in ready order for "hitching up." Round the waggons groups of teamsters, tall stalwart young Missourians, were engaged in busy preparation for the start, greasing the wheels, fitting or repairing harness, smoothing ox-

bows, or overhauling their own moderate kits or "possibles." They were all dressed in the same fashion: a pair of "homespun" pantaloons, tucked into thick boots reaching nearly to the knee, and confined round the waist by a broad leathern belt, which supported a strong butcher-knife in a sheath. A coarse checked shirt was their only other covering, with a fur cap on the head.

Numerous camp-fires surrounded the waggons, and near them lounged wild-looking mountaineers, easily distinguished from the "greenhorn" teamsters by their dresses of buckskin, and their weather-beaten faces. . . .

In another part, the merchants of the caravan and the Indian traders superintended the lading of the waggons, or mule packs. They were dressed in civilised attire, and some were even bedizened in St Louis or Eastern City dandyism, to the infinite disgust of the mountain men, who look upon a bourge-way (bourgeois) with most undisguised contempt, despising the very simplest forms of civilisation. The picturesque appearance of the encampment was not a little heightened by the addition of several Indians from the neighbouring Shawnee settlement, who, mounted on their small active horses, on which they reclined, rather than sat, in negligent attitudes, quietly looked on at the novel scene, indifferent to the "chaff" in which the thoughtless teamsters indulged at their expense. Numbers of mules and horses were picketed at hand, whilst a large herd of noble oxen were being driven towards the camp—the wo-ha of the teamsters sounding far and near, as they collected the scattered beasts in order to yoke up. . . .

[*The favorite wintering-ground of Ruxton's trappers was at Brown's Hole, an enclosed valley, abounding in game, that extended from the northwest border of Colorado into Utah.*]

Singly, and in bands numbering from two to ten, the trappers dropped into the rendezvous; some with many pack-loads of beaver, others with greater or less quantity, and more than one on foot, having lost his animals and peltry by Indian thieving. Here were soon congregated many mountaineers, whose names are famous in the history of the Far West. Fitzpatrick and Hatcher, and old Bill Williams, well known leaders of trapping parties, soon arrived with their bands. Sublette came in with his men from Yellow Stone, and many of Wyeth's New Englanders were there. Chabonard with his halfbreeds, Wah-keitchas all, brought his peltries from the lower country; and half-a-dozen Shawanee and Delaware Indians, with a Mexican from Taos, one Marcelline, a fine strapping fellow, the best trapper and hunter in the mountains, and ever first in the fight. Here, too, arrived the "Bourgeois" traders of the "North West" * Company, with their superior equipments, ready to meet their trappers, and purchase the beaver at an equitable value; and soon the trade opened, and the encampment assumed a busy appearance.

A curious assemblage did the rendezvous present, and representatives of many a land met there. A son of *La belle France* here lit his pipe from one proffered by a native of New Mexico. An Englishman and a Sandwich Islander cut a quid from the same plug of tobacco. A Swede and an "old Virginian" puffed together. A Shawanee blew a peaceful cloud with a scion of the "Six Nations." One from the Land of Cakes—a canny chiel—sought to "get round" (in trade) a right "smart" Yankee, but couldn't "shine."

The beaver went briskly, six dollars being the price paid per lb. in goods—for money is seldom given in the mountain market, where "beaver" is cash, for which the articles supplied by the traders are bartered. In a very short time peltries of every description had changed hands, either by trade, or by gambling with cards and betting. . . .

[Having left the rendezvous, the hunters] came upon a party of French† trappers and hunters, who were encamped [on Horse Creek] with their lodges and Indian squaws, and formed quite a village. Several old companions were amongst them; and, to celebrate the arrival of a "camarade," a splendid dog-feast was prepared in honour of the event. To effect this, the squaws sallied out of their lodges to seize upon sundry of the younger and plumper of the pack, to fill the kettles for the approaching feast. With a presentiment of the fate in store for them, the curs slunk away with tails between their legs, and declined the pressing invitations of the anxious squaws. These shouldered their tomahawks and gave chase; but the cunning pups outstripped them, and would have fairly beaten the kettles, if some of the mountaineers had not stepped out with their rifles and quickly laid half-a-dozen ready to the knife. A cayeute, attracted by the scent of blood, drew near, unwitting of the canine feast in progress, and was likewise

* The Hudson's Bay Company is so called by the American trappers.
† Creoles of St. Louis, and French Canadians.

soon made *dog* of, and thrust into the boiling kettle with the rest.

The feast that night was long protracted; and so savoury was the stew, and so agreeable to the palates of the hungry hunters, that at the moment the last morsel was drawn from the pot, when all were regretting that a few more dogs had not been slaughtered, a wolfish-looking cur, who incautiously poked his long nose and head under the lodge skin, was pounced upon by the nearest hunter, who in a moment drew his knife across the animal's throat, and threw it to a squaw to skin and prepare for the pot. The wolf had long since been vigorously discussed, and voted by all hands to be "good as dog."

"Meat's meat," is a common saying in the mountains, and from the buffalo down to the rattlesnake, including every quadruped that runs, every fowl that flies, and every reptile that creeps, nothing comes amiss to the mountaineer. Throwing aside all the qualms and conscientious scruples of a fastidious stomach, it must be confessed that *dog-meat* takes a high rank in the wonderful variety of cuisine afforded to the gourmand and the gourmet by the prolific "mountains." Now, when the bill of fare offers such tempting viands as buffalo beef, venison, mountain mutton, turkey, grouse, wildfowl, hares, rabbits, beaver and their tails, &c. &c., the station assigned to "dog" as No. 2 in the list can be well appreciated— No. 1, in delicacy of flavour, richness of meat, and other good qualities, being the flesh of *panthers*, which surpasses every other, and all put together.

* * *

Independence, Missouri, outfitting post for the trappers, was also the point of departure for Santa Fe, another magnet of trade which drew Americans into the trans-Missouri West. The trade flourished from 1821 to 1843, when it was interrupted for a time by decree of the Mexican Government. As repeated use gave form to the Santa Fe trail, it ran for some 780 miles, from Independence, in Missouri, southwestward to the Arkansas River, along the north bank of the Arkansas to Bent's Fort, and thence through Raton Pass to Santa Fe. In

*time, many caravans took a cut-off by way of the Cimarron
Valley. A classic description of the trade was written by Josiah
Gregg, a Tennesseean who settled in Independence in the later
1820's. For reasons of health he joined the Spring caravan in
1831 and for the next eight years participated regularly in the
trade. His* Commerce of the Prairies, *published in 1844, pro-
vides a precise account of the preparations for the trip, the
organization of the caravan at Council Grove, incidents of life
en route, and the excitement and hub-bub attending the
arrival at the long anticipated destination.*

The new town of INDEPENDENCE, but twelve miles
from the Indian border and two or three south of the Missouri
river, being the most eligible point, soon began to take the
lead as a place of debarkation, outfit and departure. . . . It
is to this beautiful spot, already grown up to be a thriving
town, that the prairie adventurer, whether in search of
wealth, health or amusement, is latterly in the habit of repairing, about the first of May, as the caravans usually set out
some time during that month. Here they purchase their provisions for the road, and many of their mules, oxen, and
even some of their wagons—in short, load all their vehicles,
and make their final preparations for a long journey across the
prairie wilderness.

As Independence is a point of convenient access (the Missouri river being navigable at all times from March till November), it has become the general 'port of embarkation' for
every part of the great western and northern 'prairie ocean.'
Besides the Santa Fé caravans, most of the Rocky Mountain
traders and trappers, as well as emigrants to Oregon, take this
town in their route. During the season of departure, therefore, it is a place of much bustle and active business. . . .

The ordinary supplies for each man's consumption during
the journey, are about fifty pounds of flour, as many more of
bacon, ten of coffee and twenty of sugar, and a little salt.
Beans, crackers, and trifles of that description, are comfortable
appendages, but being looked upon as *dispensable* luxuries, are
seldom to be found in any of the stores on the road. The
buffalo is chiefly depended upon for fresh meat, and great is

the joy of the traveller when that noble animal first appears in sight.

The wagons now most in use upon the Prairies are manufactured in Pittsburg; and are usually drawn by eight mules or the same number of oxen. Of late years, however, I have seen much larger vehicles employed, with ten or twelve mules harnessed to each, and a cargo of goods of about five thousand pounds in weight. At an early period the horse was more frequently in use, as mules were not found in great abundance; but as soon as the means for procuring these animals increased, the horse was gradually and finally discarded, except occasionally for riding and the chase.

Oxen having been employed by Major Riley for the baggage wagons of the escort which was furnished the caravan of 1829, they were found, to the surprise of the traders, to perform almost equal to mules. Since that time, upon an average about half of the wagons in these expeditions have been drawn by oxen. They possess many advantages, such as pulling heavier loads than the same number of mules, particularly through muddy or sandy places; but they generally fall off in strength as the prairie grass becomes drier and shorter, and often arrive at their destination in a most shocking plight. In this condition I have seen them sacrificed at Santa Fé for ten dollars the pair; though in more favorable seasons, they sometimes remain strong enough to be driven back to the United States the same fall. Therefore, although the original cost of a team of mules is much greater, the loss ultimately sustained by them is usually less,—to say nothing of the comfort of being able to travel faster and more at ease. The inferiority of oxen as regards endurance is partially owing to the tenderness of their feet; for there are very few among the thousands who have travelled on the Prairies that ever knew how to shoe them properly. Many have resorted to the curious expedient of shoeing their animals with 'moccasins' made of raw buffalo-skin, which does remarkably well as long as the weather remains dry; but when wet, they are soon worn through. Even mules, for the most part, perform the entire trip without being shod at all; though the hoofs often become very smooth, which frequently renders all their movements on the dry grassy surface nearly as laborious as if they were treading on ice.

The supplies being at length procured, and all necessary preliminaries systematically gone through, the trader begins the difficult task of loading his wagons. Those who understand their business, take every precaution so to stow away their packages that no jolting on the road can afterwards disturb the order in which they had been disposed. The ingenuity displayed on these occasions has frequently been such, that after a tedious journey of eight hundred miles, the goods have been found to have sustained much less injury, than they would have experienced on a turnpike-road, or from the ordinary handling of property upon our western steamboats. . . .

It was on the 15th of May, 1831, . . . that our little party set out from Independence. The general rendezvous at Council Grove was our immediate destination. It is usual for the traders to travel thus far in detached parties, and to assemble there for the purpose of entering into some kind of organization, for mutual security and defence during the remainder of the journey. . . .

Early on the 26th of May we reached the long looked-for rendezvous of Council Grove, where we joined the main body of the caravan. . . .

The designation of 'Council Grove,' after all, is perhaps the most appropriate that could be given to this place; for *we* there held a 'grand council,' at which the respective claims of the different 'aspirants to office' were considered, leaders selected, and a system of government agreed upon,—as is the standing custom of these promiscuous caravans. One would have supposed that electioneering and 'party spirit' would hardly have penetrated so far into the wilderness: but so it was. Even in our little community we had our 'office-seekers' and their 'political adherents,' as earnest and as devoted as any of the modern school of politicians in the midst of civilization. After a great deal of bickering and wordy warfare, however, all the 'candidates' found it expedient to decline, and a gentleman by the name of Stanley, without seeking, or even desiring the 'office,' was unanimously proclaimed 'Captain of the Cara-

van.' The powers of this officer were undefined by any 'constitutional provision,' and consequently vague and uncertain:
orders being only viewed as mere requests, they are often
obeyed or neglected at the caprice of the subordinates. It is
necessary to observe, however, that the captain is expected to
direct the order of travel during the day, and to designate the
camping-ground at night; with many other functions of a general character, in the exercise of which the company find it
convenient to acquiesce. . . .

But after this comes the principal task of organizing. The
proprietors are first notified by 'proclamation' to furnish a list
of their men and wagons. The latter are generally apportioned
into four 'divisions,' particularly when the company is large—
and ours consisted of nearly a hundred wagons, besides a
dozen of dearborns and other small vehicles, and two small
cannons (a four and six pounder), each mounted upon a carriage. To each of these divisions, a 'lieutenant' was appointed,
whose duty it was to inspect every ravine and creek on the
route, select the best crossings, and superintend what is called
in prairie parlance, the 'forming' of each encampment.

Upon the calling of the roll, we were found to muster an
efficient force of nearly two hundred men without counting
invalids or other disabled bodies, who, as a matter of course,
are exempt from duty. There is nothing so much dreaded by
inexperienced travellers as the ordeal of guard duty. . . .

The usual number of watches is eight, each standing a
fourth of every alternate night. When the party is small the
number is generally reduced; while in the case of very small
bands, they are sometimes compelled for safety's sake to keep
one watch on duty half the night. With large caravans the
captain usually appoints eight 'sergeants of the guard,' each
of whom takes an equal portion of men under his command. . . .

The arrival [in Santa Fe] produced a great deal of bustle
and excitement among the natives. "*Los Americanos!*"—"*Los
carros!*"—"*La entrada de la caravana!*" were to be heard in
every direction; and crowds of women and boys flocked around
to see the new-comers; while crowds of *léperos* hung about as
usual to see what they could pilfer. The wagoners were by no

means free from excitement on this occasion. Informed of the 'ordeal' they had to pass, they had spent the previous morning in 'rubbing up;' and now they were prepared, with clean faces, sleek combed hair, and their choicest Sunday suit, to meet the 'fair eyes' of glistening black that were sure to stare at them as they passed. There was yet another preparation to be made in order to 'show off' to advantage. Each wagoner must tie a bran new 'cracker' to the lash of his whip; for, on driving through the streets and the *plaza pública*, every one strives to outvie his comrades in the dexterity with which he flourishes this favorite badge of his authority.

Our wagons were soon discharged in the warerooms of the Custom-house; and a few days' leisure being now at our disposal, we had time to take that recreation which a fatiguing journey of ten weeks had rendered so necessary. The wagoners, and many of the traders, particularly the novices, flocked to the numerous fandangoes, which are regularly kept up after the arrival of a caravan. But the merchants generally were anxiously and actively engaged in their affairs—striving who should first get his goods out of the custom-house, and obtain a chance at the 'hard chink' of the numerous country dealers, who annually resort to the capital on these occasions.

*   *   *

Bent's Fort, landmark on the Santa Fe trail, figured in the fur trade as well as in the "commerce of the prairies." Founded by William Bent and partners in about 1832, it became the outstanding trading post in the Southwest. Ruxton's description of it, included in his Life in the Far West, *was based on observations during his visit there in the Spring of 1847.*

Bent's Fort is situated on the left or northern bank of the river Arkansa[s], about one hundred miles from the foot of the Rocky Mountains—on a low and level bluff of the prairie which here slopes gradually to the water's edge. The walls are built entirely of adobes—or sun-burned bricks—in the form of a hollow square, at two corners of which are circular flanking towers of the same material. The entrance is by a large gateway into the square, round which are the rooms occupied by the traders and employés of the host. These are small in size, with walls coloured by a white-wash made of clay found in the prairie. Their flat roofs are defended along the exterior by parapets of adobe, to serve as a cover to marksmen firing from the top; and along the coping grow plants of cactus of all the varieties common in the plains. In the centre of the square is the press for packing the furs; and there are three large rooms, one used as a store and magazine, another as a council-room, where the Indians assemble for their "talks," whilst the third is the common dining-hall, where the traders, trappers, and hunters, and all employés, feast upon the best provender the game-covered country affords. Over the culinary department presided of late years a fair lady of colour, Charlotte by name, who was, as she loved to say, "de onlee lady in de dam Injun country," and who moreover was celebrated from Long's Peak to the Cumbres Espanolás for slapjacks and pumpkin pies.

Here congregate at certain seasons the merchants of the plains and mountains, with their stocks of peltry. Chiefs of the Shian, the Kioway, and Arapahó, sit in solemn conclave with the head traders, and smoke the "calumet" over their real and imaginary grievances. Now O-cun-no-whurst, the Yellow Wolf, grand chief of the Shian, complains of certain grave offences against the dignity of his nation! A trader from the "big lodge" (the fort) has been in his village, and before the trade was opened, in laying the customary chief's gift "on the prairie" * has not "opened his hand," but "squeezed out his present between his fingers," grudgingly, and with too sparing measure. This was hard to bear, but the Yellow Wolf would say no more!

Tah-kai-buhl, or, "he who jumps," is deputed from the Kioway to warn the white traders not to proceed to the Canadian to trade with the Comanche. That nation is mad—a "heap mad" with the whites, and has "dug up the hatchet" to "rub out" all who enter its country. The Kioway loves the paleface, and gives him warning (and "he who jumps" looks as if he deserves something "on the prairie" for his information).

* Indian expression for a free gift.

Shawh-noh-qua-mish, "the peeled lodge-pole," is there to excuse his Arapahó braves, who lately made free with a band of horses belonging to the fort. He promises the like shall never happen again, and he, Shawh-noh-qua-mish, speaks with a "single tongue." Over clouds of tobacco and kinnik-kinnik, these grave affairs are settled and terms arranged.

In the corral, groups of leather-clad mountaineers, with "decks" of "euker" and "seven up" gamble away their hard-earned peltries. The employés—mostly St. Louis Frenchmen and Canadian voyageurs—are pressing packs of buffalo skins, beating robes, or engaged in other duties of a trading fort. Indian squaws, the wives of mountaineers, strut about in all the pride of beads and fofarrow, jingling with bells and bugles, and happy as paint can make them. Hunters drop in with animals packed with deer or buffalo meat to supply the fort; Indian dogs look anxiously in at the gateway, fearing to enter and encounter their natural enemies, the whites: and outside the fort, at any hour of the day or night, one may safely wager to see a dozen cayeutes or prairie wolves loping round, or seated on their haunches, and looking gravely on, waiting patiently for some chance offal to be cast outside. Against the walls, groups of Indians, too proud to enter without an invitation, lean, wrapped in their buffalo robes, sulky and evidently ill at ease to be so near the whites without a chance of fingering their scalp-locks; their white lodges shining in the sun, at a little distance from the river-banks; their horses feeding in the plain beyond.

The appearance of the fort is very striking, standing as it does hundreds of miles from any settlement, on the vast and lifeless prairie, surrounded by hordes of hostile Indians, and far out of reach of intercourse with civilised man; its mud-built walls inclosing a little garrison of a dozen hardy men, sufficient to hold in check the numerous tribes of savages ever thirsting for their blood. Yet the solitary stranger passing this lone fort, feels proudly secure when he comes within sight of the "stars and stripes" which float above the walls.

*   *   *

As the trade with Santa Fe was reaching its peak, American pioneers were beginning to travel another highway into the

"Far West," this one to Oregon. Fertile soil, rather than trade, was the primary attraction that drew men and their families in this direction; but Protestant missionaries played an important role in advertising the region and guiding migrants to it. A Methodist mission was established on the Willamette River in 1834; and two years later Dr. Marcus Whitman set up another on the Walla Walla. In heading for Oregon, pioneers followed a route which had been used by fur-trading outfits for many years. It ran for some 2,000 miles from Independence, Missouri, to the Columbia River, by way of the valleys of the Blue, Platte, Sweetwater, Bear, and Snake. By the mid-1840's, the Oregon "fever" was running so high that societies were formed to undertake organized expeditions; and smaller groups often were within sight of other parties on the way. The throng that converged on Independence, Missouri, in 1843, was so numerous that, once on the trail, the travelers were divided into two units, one for those encumbered with cattle and the other for those who were not. The details of travel with the more slowly moving "Cow Column" were later recorded by its commander, Jesse Applegate.

The migrating body numbered over one thousand souls, with about one hundred and twenty wagons, drawn by six-ox teams, averaging about six yokes to the team, and several thousand loose horses and cattle.

The emigrants first organized and attempted to travel in one body, but it was soon found that no progress could be made with a body so cumbrous and as yet so averse to all discipline. And at the crossing of the "Big Blue," it divided into two columns, which traveled in supporting distance of each other as far as Independence Rock, on the Sweet Water.

From this point, all danger from Indians being over, the emigrants separated into small parties better suited to the narrow mountain paths and small pastures on their front. . . . Some of the emigrants had only their teams, while others had large herds in addition which must share the pastures and be guarded and driven by the whole body. . . . Those not encumbered with or having but few loose cattle attached themselves to the light column; those having more than four or five cows had of necessity to join the heavy or cow column. Hence the cow column, being much larger than the other and encumbered with its large herds, had to use greater exertion and observe a more rigid discipline to keep pace with its more agile consort.

It is with the cow or more clumsy column that I propose to journey with the reader for a single day.

It is four o'clock; the sentinels on duty have discharged their rifles—the signal that the hours of sleep are over; and every wagon and tent is pouring forth its night tenants, and slow-kindling smokes begin largely to rise and float away on the morning air. Sixty men start from the corral, spreading as they make through the vast herd of cattle and horses that form a semicircle around the encampment, the most distant perhaps two miles away.

The herders pass to the extreme verge and carefully examine for trails beyond, to see that none of the animals have strayed or been stolen during the night. This morning no trails lead beyond the outside animals in sight, and by five o'clock the herders begin to contract the great moving circle, and the well-trained animals move slowly towards camp. . . . In about an hour, five thousand animals are close up to the encampment, and the teamsters are busy selecting their teams and driving them inside the "corral" to be yoked. The corral is a circle one hundred yards deep, formed with wagons connected strongly with each other; the wagon in the rear being connected with the wagon in front by its tongue and oxchains. It is a strong barrier that the most vicious ox cannot break, and in case of an attack of the Sioux would be no contemptible entrenchment.

From six to seven o'clock is a busy time; breakfast is to be eaten, the tents struck, the wagons loaded, and the teams yoked and brought up in readiness to be attached to their respective wagons. All know when, at seven o'clock, the signal to march sounds, that those not ready to take their proper places in the line of march must fall into the dusty rear for the day.

There are sixty wagons. They have been divided into fifteen divisions or platoons of four wagons each, and each platoon is entitled to lead in its turn. The leading platoon of today will be the rear one of tomorrow, and will bring up

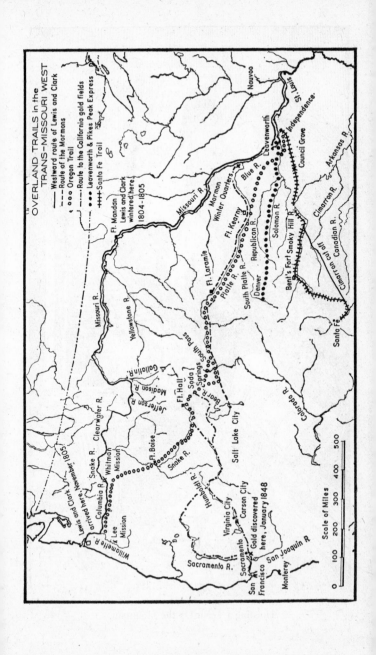

Hoisting a Team Up the Mountain.

the rear unless some teamster, through indolence or negligence, has lost his place in the line, and is condemned to that uncomfortable post. It is within ten minutes of seven; the corral but now a strong barricade is everywhere broken, the teams being attached to the wagons. The women and children have taken their places in them. The pilot (a borderer who has passed his life on the verge of civilization, and has been chosen to the post of leader from his knowledge of the savage and his experience in travel through roadless wastes) stands ready in the midst of his pioneers and aids to mount and lead the way. Ten or fifteen young men, not today on duty, form another cluster. They are ready to start on a buffalo hunt, are well mounted and well armed, as they need be, for the unfriendly Sioux have driven the buffalo out of the Platte, and the hunters must ride fifteen or twenty miles to reach them. The cow-drivers are hastening, as they get ready, to the rear of their charges, to collect and prepare them for the day's march.

It is on the stroke of seven; the rushing to and fro, the cracking of the whips, the loud command to oxen, and what seemed to be the inextricable confusion of the last ten minutes has ceased. Fortunately every one has been found and every teamster is at his post. The clear notes of a trumpet sound in the front; the pilot and his guards mount their horses; the leading division of wagons move out of the encampment and take up the line of march, the rest fall into their places with the precision of clockwork, until the spot so lately full of life sinks back into that solitude that seems to reign over the broad plain and rushing river as the caravan draws its lazy length toward the distant El Dorado. . . .

The caravan has been about two hours in motion and is now extended as widely as a prudent regard for safety will permit. First, near the bank of the shining river, is a company of horsemen; they seem to have found an obstruction, for the main body has halted while three or four ride rapidly along the bank of a creek or slough. They are hunting a favorable crossing for the wagons; while we look they have succeeded; it has apparently required no work to make it passable, for all but one of the party have passed on, and he has raised a flag, no doubt a signal to the wagons to steer their course to where he stands. The leading teamster sees him, though he is yet two miles off, and steers his course directly towards him, all the wagons following in his track. They (the wagons) form a line three-quarters of a mile in length; some of the teamsters ride upon the front of their wagons, some march beside their teams; scattered along the line companies of women and children are taking exercise on foot. . . . Next comes a band of horses; two or three men or boys follow them, the docile and sagacious animals scarce needing this attention, for they have learned to follow in the rear of the wagons. . . . Not so with the large herd of horned beasts that bring up the rear; lazy, selfish and unsocial, it has been a task to get them in motion, the strong always ready to domineer over the weak, halt in the front and forbid the weaker to pass them. . . . Nothing of the moving panorama, smooth and orderly as it appears, has more attractions for the eye than that vast square column in which all colors are mingled, moving here slowly and there briskly, as impelled by horsemen riding furiously in front and rear.

But the picture, in its grandeur, its wonderful mingling of colors and distinctness of detail, is forgotten in contemplation of the singular people who give it life and animation. No other race of men with the means at their command would undertake so great a journey; none save these could successfully perform it, with no previous preparation, relying only on the fertility of their invention to devise the means to overcome each danger and difficulty as it arose. They have undertaken to perform, with slow-moving oxen, a journey of two thousand miles. The way lies over trackless wastes, wide and deep rivers, rugged and lofty mountains, and is beset with hostile savages. Yet, whether it were a deep river with no tree upon its banks, a rugged defile where even a loose horse could not pass, a hill too steep for him to climb, or a threatened attack of an enemy, they are always found ready and equal to the occasion, and always conquerors. May we not call them men of destiny? They are people changed in no essential particulars from their ancestors, who have followed closely on the footsteps of the receding savage, from the Atlantic seaboard to the great valley of the Mississippi. . . .

The pilot, by measuring the ground and timing the speed of the wagons and the walk of his horses, has determined the rate of each, so as to enable him to select the nooning place as near as the requisite grass and water can be had at the end of five hours' travel of the wagons. Today, the ground being favorable, little time has been lost in preparing the road, so that he and his pioneers are at the nooning place an hour in advance of the wagons, which time is spent in preparing convenient watering places for the animals, and digging little wells near the bank of the Platte. As the teams are not unyoked, but simply turned loose from the wagons, a corral is not formed at noon, but the wagons are drawn up in columns, four abreast, the leading wagon of each platoon on the left—the platoon being formed with that in view. This brings friends together at noon as well as at night.

Today, an extra session of the Council is being held, to settle a dispute that does not admit of delay, between a proprietor and a young man who has undertaken to do a man's service on the journey for bed and board. Many such engagements exist, and much interest is taken in the manner this high court, from which there is no appeal, will define the right of each party in such engagements. The Council was a high court in the most exalted sense. It was a Senate, composed of the ablest and most respected fathers of the emigration. It exercised both legislative and judicial powers, and its laws and decisions proved it equal and worthy of the high trust reposed in it. Its sessions were usually held on days when the caravan was not moving. It first took the state of the little commonwealth into consideration; revised or repealed rules defective or obsolete, and exacted such others as exigencies seemed to require. The common weal being cared for, it next resolved itself into a court to hear and settle private disputes and grievances. The offender and the aggrieved appeared before it; witnesses were examined, and the parties were heard by themselves and sometimes by council. The judges, thus being made fully acquainted with the case, and being in no way influenced or cramped by technicalities, decided all cases according to their merits. There was but little use for lawyers before this court, for no plea was entertained which was calculated to hinder or defeat the ends of justice. . . .

It is now one o'clock; the bugle has sounded, and the caravan has resumed its westward journey. It is in the same order, but the evening is far less animated than the morning march; a drowsiness has fallen apparently on man and beast; teamsters drop asleep on their perches and even walking by their teams, and the words of command are now addressed to the slowly creeping oxen in the softened tenor of women or the piping treble of children, while the snores of the teamsters make a droning accompaniment.

But a little incident breaks the monotony of the march. An emigrant's wife whose state of health has caused Doctor Whitman to travel near the wagon for the day, is now taken with violent illness. The Doctor has had the wagon driven out of the line, a tent pitched and a fire kindled. Many conjectures are hazarded in regard to this mysterious proceeding and as to why this last wagon is to be left behind.

And we must leave it, hasten to the front, and note the proceedings, for the sun is now getting low in the west and at length the painstaking pilot is standing ready to conduct the train in the circle which he has previously measured and marked out, which is to form the invariable fortification for the night. The leading wagons follow him so nearly round the circle, that but a wagon length separates them. Each wagon follows in its track, the rear closing on the front, until its tongue and ox-chains will perfectly reach from one to the other, and so accurate the measurement and perfect the practice, that the hindmost wagon of the train always precisely closes the gateway as each wagon is brought into position. It is dropped from its team, (the teams being inside into position) the team unyoked, and the yokes and chains are used to connect the wagon strongly with that in its front. Within ten minutes from the time the leading wagon halted, the barricade is formed, the teams unyoked and driven out to pasture. Everyone is busy preparing fires of buffalo chips to cook the evening meal, pitching tents and otherwise preparing for the night. There are anxious watchers for the absent wagon, for there are many matrons who may be afflicted like its inmate before the journey is over; and they fear the strange and startling practice of this Oregon doctor will be dangerous. But as the sun goes down, the absent wagon rolls into camp, the bright, speaking face and cheery look of the doctor, who rides in advance, declare without words that all is well and both mother and child are comfortable. . . .

All able to bear arms in the party have been formed into three companies, and each of these into four watches; every third night it is the duty of one of these companies to keep watch and ward over the camp, and it is so arranged that each watch takes its turn of guard duty through the different watches of the night. Those forming the first watch tonight will be second not on duty, then third and fourth, which brings them through all the watches of the night. They begin at 8 o'clock, P.M., and end at 4 o'clock, A.M.

It is not yet eight o'clock when the first watch is to be set; the evening meal is just over, and the corral now free from the intrusion of cattle or horses, groups of children are scattered over it. The larger are taking a game of romps; "the wee toddling things" are being taught that great achievement that distinguishes man from the lower animals. Before a tent near the river a violin makes lively music, and some youths and maidens have improvised a dance upon the green; in another quarter a flute gives its mellow and melancholy notes to the still night air, which as they float away over the quiet river, seem a lament for the past rather than a hope for the future. It has been a prosperous day; more than twenty miles have been accomplished of the great journey. . . .

But time passes; the watch is set for the night, the council of old men has broken up, and each has returned to his own quarter. The flute has whispered its last lament to the deepening night. The violin is silent, and the dancers have dispersed. Enamored youth have whispered a tender "good night" in the ear of blushing maidens, or stolen a kiss from the lips of some future bride—for Cupid here as elsewhere has been busy bringing together congenial hearts, and among those simple people he alone is consulted in forming the marriage tie. . . . All is hushed and repose from the fatigues of the day, save the vigilant guard, and the wakeful leader, who still has cares upon his mind that forbid sleep.

* * *

The traffic on the Trail, in the Spring of 1846, obviously annoyed Francis Parkman, author of the most famous account of of the Oregon migration. Late in April of that year, Parkman set out from St. Louis for the Rockies, on a tour of curiosity and amusement. Disdaining the many emigrant parties then embarking on the "Road to Oregon," he and his French-Canadian companion, Henry Chatillon, teamed up with three Englishmen engaged in a hunting expedition. Parkman was keenly interested in the Indians (especially the Dakotas), whom they met from time to time. He seems to have had more respect for some of them than for his Oregon-bound countrymen, despite the hardships of travel he saw them enduring along the way. His The Oregon Trail: Sketches of Prairie and Rocky-Mountain Life *first appeared in 1847.*

About dark a sallow-faced fellow descended the hill on horseback, and splashing through the pool, rode up to the tents. He was enveloped in a huge cloak, and his broad felt hat was weeping about his ears with the drizzling moisture of the evening. Another followed, a stout, square-built, intelligent-looking man, who announced himself as leader of an emigrant party, encamped a mile in advance of us. About twenty wagons, he said, were with him; the rest of his party were on the other side of the Big Blue, waiting for a woman who was in the pains of childbirth, and quarrelling meanwhile among themselves.

These were the first emigrants that we had overtaken, although we had found abundant and melancholy traces of their progress throughout the course of the journey. Sometimes we passed the grave of one who had sickened and died on the way. The earth was usually torn up, and covered thickly with wolf-tracks. Some had escaped this violation. One morning, a piece of plank, standing upright on the summit of a grassy hill, attracted our notice, and riding up to it, we found the following words very roughly traced upon it, apparently with a red-hot piece of iron:—

MARY ELLIS.
Died May 7th, 1845.
aged two months.

Such tokens were of common occurrence.

We were late in breaking up our camp on the following morning, and scarcely had we ridden a mile when we saw, far in advance of us, drawn against the horizon, a line of objects stretching at regular intervals along the level edge of the prairie. An intervening swell soon hid them from sight, until, ascending it a quarter of an hour after, we saw close before us the emigrant caravan, with its heavy white wagons creeping on in slow procession, and a large drove of cattle following behind. Half a dozen yellow-visaged Missourians, mounted on horseback, were cursing and shouting among them, their lank angular proportions enveloped in brown homespun, evidently cut and adjusted by the hands of a domestic female tailor. As we approached, they called to us: "How are ye, boys? Are ye for Oregon or California?"

As we pushed rapidly by the wagons, children's faces were thrust out from the white coverings to look at us; while the care-worn, thin-featured matron, or the buxom girl, seated in front, suspended the knitting on which most of them were engaged to stare at us with wondering curiosity. By the side of each wagon stalked the proprietor, urging on his patient oxen, who shouldered heavily along, inch by inch, on their interminable journey. It was easy to see that fear and dissension prevailed among them; some of the men—but these, with one exception, were bachelors—looked wistfully upon us as we rode lightly and swiftly by, and then impatiently at their own lumbering wagons and heavy-gaited oxen. Others were unwilling to advance at all, until the party they had left behind should have rejoined them. Many were murmuring against the leader they had chosen, and wished to depose him; and this discontent was fomented by some ambitious spirits, who had hopes of succeeding in his place. The women

were divided between regrets for the homes they had left and
fear of the deserts and savages before them. . . .

Some days elapsed, and brought us near the Platte. . . .
late [one] afternoon, in the midst of a gloomy and barren
prairie, we came suddenly upon the great trail of the Pawnees,
leading from their villages on the Platte to their war and
hunting grounds to the southward. Here every summer passes
the motley concourse: thousands of savages, men, women,
and children, horses and mules, laden with their weapons
and implements, and an innumerable multitude of unruly
wolfish dogs, who have not acquired the civilized accomplishment of barking, but howl like their wild cousins of the
prairie.

The permanent winter villages of the Pawnees stand on the
lower Platte, but throughout the summer the greater part of
the inhabitants are wandering over the plains,—a treacherous,
cowardly banditti, who, by a thousand acts of pillage and
murder, have deserved chastisement at the hands of government. . . .

On the eighth of June, at eleven o'clock, we reached the
South Fork of the Platte, at the usual fording-place. For
league upon league the desert uniformity of the prospect was
almost unbroken; the hills were dotted with little tufts of
shrivelled grass, but betwixt these the white sand was glaring
in the sun; and the channel of the river, almost on a level
with the plain, was but one great sand-bed, about half a mile
wide. It was covered with water, but so scantily that the
bottom was scarcely hidden; for, wide as it is, the average
depth of the Platte does not at this point exceed a foot and
a half. Stopping near its bank, we gathered *bois de vache*,
and made a meal of buffalo-meat. Far off, on the other side,
was a green meadow, where we could see the white tents and
wagons of an emigrant camp; and just opposite to us we
could discern a group of men and animals at the water's
edge. Four or five horsemen soon entered the river, and in ten
minutes had waded across and clambered up the loose sand-
bank. They were ill-looking fellows, thin and swarthy, with
care-worn anxious faces, and lips rigidly compressed. They

had good cause for anxiety; it was three days since they first encamped here, and on the night of their arrival they had lost a hundred and twenty-three of their best cattle, driven off by the wolves, through the neglect of the man on guard. This discouraging and alarming calamity was not the first that had overtaken them. Since leaving the settlements they had met with nothing but misfortune. Some of their party had died; one man had been killed by the Pawnees; and about a week before they had been plundered by the Dahcotahs of all their best horses, the wretched animals on which our visitors were mounted being the only ones that were left. They had encamped, they told us, near sunset, by the side of the Platte, and their oxen were scattered over the meadow, while the horses were feeding a little farther off. Suddenly the ridges of the hills were alive with a swarm of mounted Indians, at least six hundred in number, who came pouring with a yell down towards the camp, rushing up within a few rods, to the great terror of the emigrants; when, suddenly wheeling, they swept around the band of horses, and in five minutes disappeared with their prey through the openings of the hills. . . .

The emigrants recrossed the river, and we prepared to follow. First the heavy ox-wagons plunged down the bank, and dragged slowly over the sand-beds; sometimes the hoofs of the oxen were scarcely wet by the thin sheet of water; and the next moment the river would be boiling against their sides, and eddying around the wheels. Inch by inch they receded from the shore, dwindling every moment, until at length they seemed to be floating far out in the middle of the river. A more critical experiment awaited us; for our little mule-cart was ill-fitted for the passage of so swift a stream. We watched it with anxiety, till it seemed a motionless white speck in the midst of the waters; and it was motionless, for it had stuck fast in a quicksand. The mules were losing their footing, the wheels were sinking deeper and deeper, and the water began to rise through the bottom and drench the goods within. All of us who had remained on the hither bank galloped to the rescue; the men jumped into the water, adding their strength to that of the mules, until by much effort the cart was extricated, and conveyed in safety across. . . .

At last we gained the Platte. Following it for about five miles, we saw, just as the sun was sinking, a great meadow, dotted with hundreds of cattle, and beyond them an encampment of emigrants. A party of them came out to meet us, looking upon us at first with cold and suspicious faces. Seeing four men, different in appearance and equipment from themselves, emerging from the hills, they had taken us for the van of the much-dreaded Mormons, whom they were very apprehensive of encountering. We made known our true character, and then they greeted us cordially. They expressed much surprise that so small a party should venture to traverse that region, though in fact such attempts are often made by trappers and Indian traders. We rode with them to their camp. The wagons, some fifty in number, with here and there a tent intervening, were arranged as usual in a circle; the best horses were picketed in the area within, and the whole circumference was glowing with the dusky light of fires, displaying the forms of the women and children who were crowded around them. . . .

For three days we travelled without interruption, and on the evening of the third encamped by the well-known spring on Scott's Bluff.

Henry Chatillon and I rode out in the morning, and, descending the western side of the Bluff, were crossing the plain beyond. Something that seemed to me a file of buffalo came into view, descending the hills several miles before us. But Henry reined in his horse, and, peering across the prairie with a better and more practised eye, soon discovered its real nature. "Indians!" he said. "Old Smoke's lodges, I b'lieve. Come; let us go! Wah! get up, now, 'Five Hundred Dollar.'" And laying on the lash with good will, he galloped forward, and I rode by his side. Not long after, a black speck became visible on the prairie, full two miles off. It grew larger and larger; it assumed the form of a man and horse; and soon we could discern a naked Indian, careering at full gallop towards us. When within a furlong he wheeled his horse in a wide circle, and made him describe various mystic figures upon the prairie; Henry immediately compelled "Five Hundred Dollar" to execute similar evolutions. "It *is* Old Smoke's village," said he, interpreting these signals; "didn't I say so?" . . .

[Our visitor] was a young fellow, of no note in his nation; yet in his person and equipments he was a good specimen of a Dahcotah warrior in his ordinary travelling dress. Like most of his people, he was nearly six feet high; lithely and gracefully, yet strongly proportioned; and with a skin singularly clear and delicate. He wore no paint; his head was bare; and his long hair was gathered in a clump behind, to the top of which was attached transversely, both by way of ornament and of talisman, the mystic whistle, made of the wing-bone of the war-eagle, and endowed with various magic virtues. From the back of his head descended a line of glittering brass plates, tapering from the size of a doubloon to that of a half-dime, a cumbrous ornament, in high vogue among the Dahcotahs, and for which they pay the traders a most extravagant price; his chest and arms were naked, the buffalo robe, worn over them when at rest, had fallen about his waist, and was confined there by a belt. This, with the gay moccasins on his feet, completed his attire. For arms he carried a quiver of dog-skin at his back, and a rude but powerful bow in his hand. His horse had no bridle; a cord of hair, lashed around his jaw, served in place of one. The saddle was made of wood covered with raw hide, and both pommel and cantle rose perpendicularly full eighteen inches, so that the warrior was wedged firmly in his seat, whence nothing could dislodge him but the bursting of the girths.

Advancing with our new companion, we found more of his people, seated in a circle on the top of a hill; while a rude procession came straggling down the neighboring hollow, men, women, and children, with horses dragging the lodge-poles behind them. All that morning, as we moved forward, tall savages were stalking silently about us. At noon we reached Horse Creek. The main body of the Indians had arrived before us. On the farther bank stood a large and strong man, nearly naked, holding a white horse by a long cord, and eying us as we approached. This was the chief, whom Henry called "Old Smoke." Just behind him, his youngest and favorite squaw sat astride a fine mule, covered with caparisons of whitened skins, garnished with blue and white beads, and fringed with little ornaments of metal that tinkled with every movement of the animal. The girl had a light clear complexion, enlivened by a spot of vermilion on each cheek; she smiled, not to say grinned, upon us, showing two gleaming rows of white teeth. In her hand she carried the tall lance of her unchivalrous lord, fluttering with feathers; his round white shield hung at the side of her mule; and his pipe was slung at her back. Her dress was a tunic of deer-skin, made beautifully white by means of a species of clay found on the prairie, ornamented with beads, arranged in figures more gay than tasteful, and with long fringes at all the seams. Not far from the chief stood a group of stately figures, their white buffalo-robes thrown over their shoulders, gazing coldly upon us; and in the rear, for several acres, the ground was covered with a temporary encampment. Warriors, women, and children swarmed like bees; hundreds of dogs, of all sizes and colors, ran restlessly about; and, close at hand, the wide shallow stream was alive with boys, girls, and young squaws, splashing, screaming, and laughing in the water. At the same time a long train of emigrants with their heavy wagons was crossing the creek, and dragging on in slow procession by the encampment of the people whom they and their descendants, in the space of a century, are to sweep from the face of the earth.

The encampment itself was merely a temporary one during the heat of the day. None of the lodges were pitched; but their heavy leather coverings, and the long poles used to support them, were scattered everywhere, among weapons, domestic utensils, and the rude harness of mules and horses. The squaws of each lazy warrior had made him a shelter from the sun, by stretching a few buffalo-robes, or the corner of a lodge-covering, upon poles; and here he sat in the shade, with a favorite young squaw, perhaps, at his side, glittering with all imaginable trinkets. Before him stood the insignia of his rank as a warrior, his white shield of bull-hide, his medicine-bag, his bow and quiver, his lance and his pipe, raised aloft on a tripod of poles. Except the dogs, the most active and noisy tenants of the camp were the old women, ugly as Macbeth's witches, with hair streaming loose in the wind, and nothing but the tattered fragment of an old buffalo-robe to hide their shrivelled limbs. The day of their favoritism passed two generations ago; now the heaviest labors of the camp devolved upon them; they must harness the horses, pitch the lodges, dress the buffalo-robes, and bring in meat for the hunters. With the cracked voices of these hags, the clamor of dogs, the shouting and laughing of children and girls, and the listless tranquillity of the warriors, the whole scene had an effect too lively and picturesque to be forgotten.

* * *

The remoteness of the Far West in the 1840's gave it appeal for the Mormons, long suffering adherents of the Church of Jesus Christ of the Latter Day Saints. Almost from the moment their Church was organized, in 1830, the Mormons were beset by local resistance. During the 1830's they moved successively from New York to Ohio, to Missouri, and back to Nauvoo, Illinois. There, by the mid-1840's, the opposition of the "Gentiles" was so violent as to prompt them to consider transporting their Kingdom of Zion to the Far West, possibly in an area under Mexican control. Early in 1846, thousands of loyal Mormons left Nauvoo and established temporary settlements on the Missouri River, in the vicinity of what are now Omaha and Council Bluffs. In the Spring of 1847, Brigham Young led an exploratory party westward to the Great Salt Lake Basin, which they chose as the site for their wilderness Zion. Within a decade, some 22,000 Saints were residing in the vicinity of the Great Salt Lake or in towns along the "Mormon Corridor," a result of the largest organized migration in the history of the American West. Their unusual religious practices, the development of Salt Lake City, and their planned economy—something of a novelty on the traditionally individualistic frontier—prompted description of the Mormon settlements by many visitors, among them Benjamin G. Ferris, who resided there during the Winter of 1852-1853, as secretary of Utah Territory, and Jules Remy and Julius Brenchley, French travelers who visited Salt Lake City in 1855.

If the design of the Mormon rulers in selecting the Great
Basin as the seat of their power was to isolate their people
from the rest of the world, they certainly made a happy
choice. The Mormon capital is unapproachable from any
civilized point except by a tedious journey of from eight
hundred to one thousand miles. In a severe winter it is
entirely inaccessible. . . .

Great Salt Lake City presents a very singular appearance to
the eye of a stranger. It is built of adobe or sun-dried bricks,
and is of a uniform lead color, with the single exception of
the house of Brigham Young, the prophet and seer, which is
white, and standing on the most prominent point in the city,
may be seen at a great distance. The streets are eight rods
wide, and cross each other at right angles. . . . A mountain
stream called "City Creek," originally ran through the centre
of the town, but by numerous ditches its water is distributed
through almost every street, according to the inclination of
the land. The buildings are very ordinary in their style of
construction, generally of one story, and are, many of them,
mere huts. It is not uncommon to see a long, low building,
with from two to half a dozen entrances, which is a sure
indication that the owner is the husband of sundry wives,
after the fashion of the prophet Joseph. There are a few
dwellings of a larger class and fair appearance, among which
are those of Brigham Young, . . . Heber C. Kimball, Parley
P. Platt [Pratt], Ezra T. Benson, and other dignitaries of the
Mormon hierarchy.

The public buildings are few—the Council House, where
the Legislative Assembly and the courts are held; the Tithing-
office, where tithes are received, in a room of which is the
Post-office; the Social Hall, where theatrical performances
are had, in which the Saints are accommodated with conveniences for dances and social parties; and the Tabernacle,
a long, low building on Temple Block, the Mormon place of
worship, . . . capable of seating an audience of three thousand.

Temple Block . . . has a range of workshops belonging to
the Church [the Public Works], in which various mechanical
employments are carried on. . . . The poor emigrating Saint

is, through the "Perpetual Emigrating Fund Company," furnished with the means of performing the great journey, but, when he gets to Zion, he is without food, raiment, or shelter. A house is speedily built for him, and he is placed in the "Public Works" to work out the debt, during which process he is furnished with the necessaries of life from the Tithing-office. . . .

The whole of this small nation occupy themselves as usefully as the working bees of a hive, perfectly justifying the emblem erected by the President of the Church on the summit of his mansion. . . . The idle or unemployed are not to be met with here. Every one, from the lowest of the faithful up to the bishop and even the apostle, is occupied in manual labour. . . . Each works for himself or his family, under the triple incentive of necessity, of his own and the public welfare.

Although there are neither grog shops nor dealers in any kind of drinks to be met with, it does not follow that the Saints refrain from the moderate use of spirituous or fermented liquors. . . . Many of them take beer, to make which they cultivate hops in their valleys; others drink wine when they can get it, and some even indulge in whisky, which they distil from the potato. In the evening their families generally pass their time together, conversing, singing, preaching, reading the Bible and sacred works, as well as the periodicals published by their leaders. . . .

There are in Great Salt Lake City—and we enumerate them according to the numerical importance of the contingent furnished by each nation,—English, Scotch, Canadians, Americans . . . . Danes, Swedes, Norwegians, Germans, Swiss, Poles, Russians, Italians, French, Negroes, Hindoos, and Australians; we even saw a Chinese there. All these people, bred in different and often adverse faiths, . . . flock together every day, to live more than brothers in perfect harmony, in the centre of the American continent, where they form a new nation, independent, compact, and, in fact, as little under the control of the government of the United States which takes them under its protection, as of the firmans of the Grand Turk. . . .

Brigham Young is the supreme President of the Church of Latter-Day Saints throughout the world. He is the Mormon pope; he is at the same time, by election of the people, a prophet, "revelator," and seer; and still more, he was, at the time of our journey, Governor of the territory of Utah, and recognized in that capacity by the President of the United States. He is . . . fair, of moderate height, stout almost to obesity. . . . His general appearance is that of an honest farmer, and nothing in his manners indicates a man of the higher classes. Of superior intellect, though uneducated, Brigham has given proofs of remarkable talent and profound ability, in combining the heterogeneous elements of which his people are made up. Joseph Smith, the founder of the Church, said of Brigham Young that *"he could eat more eggs, and beget more children, than any man in the State of Illinois. . . ."* Brother Brigham—he is thus styled among the Saints—has a seraglio of seventeen women of various ages. . . . The number of his children is unknown. In the preceding spring he had nine born to him in one week. Everyone extols the solicitude of this model of patriarchs for his numerous progeny. . . .

We were made much of everywhere; we were called Brother Brenchley, Brother Remy. This tickled us so mightily that we thought it good fun not to undeceive them. . . . Once the Church musicians came and gave us a serenade; a Sicilian, named Ballo, conducted the orchestra. They played *La Marseillaise*, God save the Queen, Yankee Doodle, Hail Columbia, sacred pieces from Mehul and Mozart, and bits from the operas of Meyerbeer and Rossini. The music, we should observe to the credit of the Mormons, was very good, and better than what one meets with in most provincial towns in Europe. A ball, too, was given us, at which every gentleman danced with two ladies at once, an ingenious innovation, and not the only one with which Mormonism aspires to endow society, with a view to its reformation. . . .

Nothing in their organization or in their customs approaches [communism] . . . , which the Mormons have been accused of practising. . . . If there is seen in their remote establishments a sort of transient association, it is due to the necessity which is imposed on them by the Indians, of living under the shelter of the same walls, under pain of being easily surprised and plundered. But property always remains rigidly personal, and every one receives the fruit of his labour.

* * *

Gold was the magnet that turned the tide of migration toward California; but for a few Americans the pull of this part of the Far West antedated the eventful discovery of 1848. Yankee merchants were trading there as early as the late eighteenth century, when it was under Spanish rule; and they continued to do so after Mexico assumed control. A number of them settled permanently in the Pacific province, espoused the Catholic faith, Hispanicized their names, and took California wives. In time their letters praising the California climate attracted pioneers from the Missouri frontier. On the eve of the Mexican War, when steps were taken to acquire the area for the United States, Americans in California's mixed population numbered close to 700. Young Richard Henry Dana, taking time out from Harvard to ship as a common sailor on a hide and tallow trader, visited Mexican California in 1835 and 1836. He described the society there in his Two Years Before the Mast.

I certainly never saw so much silver at one time in my life, as during the week that we were at Monterey. The truth is, they have no credit system, no banks, and no way of investing money but in cattle. They have no circulating medium but silver and hides—which the sailors call "California bank notes." Everything that they buy they must pay for in one or the other of these things. The hides they bring down dried and doubled, in clumsy ox-carts or upon mules' backs, and the money they carry tied up in a handkerchief;—fifty, eighty, or an hundred dollars and half dollars. . . .

Monterey, as far as my observation goes, is decidedly the pleasantest and most civilized-looking place in California. In the centre of it is an open square, surrounded by four lines of one-story plastered buildings, with half a dozen cannon in the centre; some mounted, and others not. This is the "Presidio," or fort. Every town has a presidio in its centre; or rather, every presidio has a town built around it; for the forts were first built by the Mexican government, and then the people built near them for protection. The presidio here was entirely open and unfortified. There were several officers with long titles, and about eighty soldiers, but they were poorly paid, fed, clothed, and disciplined. The governor-general, or, as he is commonly called, the "general," lives here; which makes it the seat of government. He is appointed by the central government at Mexico, and is the chief civil and military officer. In addition to him, each town has a commandant, who is the chief military officer, and has charge of the fort, and of all transactions with foreigners and foreign vessels; and two or three alcaldis and corregidores, elected by the inhabitants, who are the civil officers. Courts and jurisprudence they have no knowledge of. Small municipal matters are regulated by the alcaldis and corregidores, and everything relating to the general government, to the military, and to foreigners, by the commandants, acting under the governor-general. Capital cases are decided by him, upon personal inspection, if he is near; or upon minutes sent by the proper officers, if the offender is at a distant place. No Protestant has any civil rights, nor can he hold any property, or, indeed remain more than a few weeks on shore, unless he belong to some vessel. Consequently, the Americans and English who intend to reside here become Catholics, to a man; the current phrase among them being,—"A man must leave his conscience at Cape Horn."

But to return to Monterey. The houses here, as everywhere else in California, are of one story, built of clay made into large bricks, about a foot and a half square and three or four inches thick, and hardened in the sun. These are cemented together by mortar of the same material, and the whole are of a common dirt-color. The floors are generally of earth, the windows grated and without glass; and the doors, which are seldom shut, open directly into the common room; there being no entries. Some of the more wealthy inhabitants have glass to their windows and board floors; and in Monterey nearly all the houses are plastered on the outside. The better houses, too, have red tiles upon the roofs.

The common ones have two or three rooms which open into each other, and are furnished with a bed or two, a few chairs and tables, a looking-glass, a crucifix of some material or other, and small daubs of paintings enclosed in glass and representing some miracle or martyrdom. They have no chimneys or fire-places in the houses, the climate being such as to make a fire unnecessary; and all their cooking is done in a small cook-house, separated from the house. The Indians . . . do all the hard work, two or three being attached to each house; and the poorest persons are able to keep one, at least, for they have only to feed them and give them a small piece of coarse cloth and a belt, for the males; and a coarse gown, without shoes or stockings, for the females.

In Monterey there are a number of English and Americans (English or "Ingles" all are called who speak the English language) who have married Californians, become united to the Catholic Church, and acquired considerable property. Having more industry, frugality, and enterprise than the natives, they soon get nearly all the trade into their hands. They usually keep shops, in which they retail the goods purchased in larger quantities from our vessels, and also send a good deal into the interior, taking hides in pay, which they again barter with our vessels. In every town on the coast there are foreigners engaged in this kind of trade, while I recollect but two shops kept by natives. The people are naturally suspicious of foreigners, and they would not be allowed to remain, were it not that they became good Catholics, and by marrying natives, and bringing up their children as Catholics and Spaniards, and not teaching them the English language, they quiet suspicion, and even became popular and leading men. The chief alcaldis in Monterey and Santa Barbara were both Yankees by birth.

The men in Monterey appeared to me to be always on horseback. Horses are as abundant here as dogs and chickens were in Juan Fernandez. There are no stables to keep them in, but they are allowed to run wild and graze wherever they please, being branded, and having long leather ropes, called "lassos," attached to their necks and dragging along behind them, by which they can be easily taken. The men usually catch one in the morning, throw a saddle and bridle upon him, and use him for the day, and let him go at night, catching another the next day. When they go on long journeys, they ride one horse down, and catch another, throw the saddle and bridle upon him, and after riding him down, take a third, and so on to the end of the journey. There are probably no better riders in the world. They get upon a horse when only four or five years old, their little legs not long enough to come halfway over his sides; and may almost be said to keep on him until they have grown to him. The stirrups are covered or boxed up in front, to prevent their catching when riding through the woods; and the saddles are large and heavy, strapped very tight upon the horse, and have large pommels, or loggerheads, in front, round which the "lasso" is coiled when not in use. They can hardly go from one house to another without getting on a horse, there being generally several standing tied to the door-posts of the little cottages. When they wish to show their activity, they make no use of their stirrups in mounting, but striking the horse, spring into the saddle as he starts, and sticking their long spurs into him, go off on the full run. Their spurs are cruel things, having four or five rowels, each an inch in length, dull and rusty. The flanks of the horses are often sore from them, and I have seen men come in from chasing bullock with their horses' hind legs and quarters covered with blood. They frequently give exhibitions of their horsemanship, in races, bullbaitings, &c.; but as we were not ashore during any holyday, we saw nothing of it. Monterey is also a great place for cock-fighting, gambling of all sorts, fandangos, and every kind of amusement and knavery. Trappers and hunters, who occasionally arrive here from over the Rocky Mountains, with their valuable skins and furs, are often entertained with every sort of amusement and dissipation, until they have wasted their time and their money, and go back, stripped of everything.

*   *   *

The discovery of gold in California greatly speeded the settlement of the Pacific Coast West. The momentous find, on

January 24, 1848, was not announced in the New York papers until August; and it was the following January before ships from the Atlantic Coast were carrying gold-seekers to the new El Dorado. But by 1849, prospectors were descending upon California from every quarter of the globe. Before the beginning of Winter, close to 30,000 had taken the overland route across the plains; in Mexico, the whole state of Sonora was said to be on the move; and hundreds of Oregon pioneers abandoned newly found farms in the quest for gold. Probably more than 80,000 people came to California in 1848 and 1849; between 1846 and 1852 its population increased from 10,000 to 250,000, centered mainly in San Francisco and the gold fields. Drowsy California felt the impact of gold months before the arrival of the "Forty-niners." The social revolution caused when news of the discovery reached Monterey in May of 1848 was described by the Reverend Walter Colton, editor, teacher, clergyman—and alcalde of the California capital—in his Three Years in California, *written in 1850.*

Monday, May 29 [1848]. Our town [Monterey] was startled out of its quiet dreams today by the announcement that gold had been discovered on the American Fork. The men wondered and talked, and the women too; but neither believed. . . .

Monday, June 5. Another report reached us this morning from the American Fork. The rumor ran, that several workmen, while excavating for a millrace, had thrown up little shining scales of a yellow ore that proved to be gold; that an old Sonoranian, who had spent his life in gold mines, pronounced it the genuine thing. Still the public incredulity remained, save here and there a glimmer of faith, like the flash of a firefly at night. . . .

Tuesday, June 6. . . . I determined to put an end to the suspense and dispatched a messenger this morning to the American Fork. He will have to ride, going and returning, some four hundred miles, but his report will be reliable. We shall then know whether this gold is a fact or fiction—a tangible reality on the earth or a fanciful treasure at the base of some rainbow, retreating over hill and waterfall, to lure pursuit and disappoint hope. . . .

Monday, June 12. A straggler came in to-day from the

American Fork, bringing a piece of yellow ore weighing an ounce. The young dashed the dirt from their eyes, and the old from their spectacles. One brought a spyglass, another an iron ladle; some wanted to melt it, others to hammer it, and a few were satisfied with smelling it. All were full of tests; and many, who could not be gratified in making their experiments, declared it a humbug. One lady sent me a huge gold ring, in the hope of reaching the truth by comparison, while a gentleman placed the specimen on the top of his gold-headed cane and held it up, challenging the sharpest eyes to detect a difference. But doubts still hovered on the minds of the great mass. They could not conceive that such a treasure could have lain there so long undiscovered. The idea seemed to convict them of stupidity. . . .

Tuesday, June 20.—My messenger sent to the mines, has returned with specimens of the gold; he dismounted in a sea of upturned faces. As he drew forth the yellow lumps from his pockets and passed them around among the eager crowd, the doubts, which had lingered till now, fled. All admitted they were gold, except one old man, who still persisted they were some Yankee invention, got up to reconcile the people to the change of flag. The excitement produced was intense; and many were soon busy in their hasty preparations for a departure to the mines. The family who had kept house for me caught the moving infection. Husband and wife were both packing up; the blacksmith dropped his hammer, the carpenter his plane, the mason his trowel, the farmer his sickle, the baker his loaf, and the tapster his bottle. All were off for the mines, some on horses, some on carts, and some on crutches, and one went in a litter. An American woman, who had recently established a boarding-house here, pulled up stakes, and was off before her lodgers had even time to pay their bills. Debtors ran, of course. I have only a community of women left, and a gang of prisoners, with here and there a soldier, who will give his captain the slip at the first chance. I don't blame the fellow a whit; seven dollars a month, while others are making two or three hundred a day! that is too much for human nature to stand.

Saturday, July 15. The gold fever has reached every servant

in Monterey; none are to be trusted in their engagement beyond a week, and as for compulsion, it is like attempting to drive fish into a net with the ocean before them. Gen. Mason, Lieut. Lanman, and myself, form a mess; we have a house and all the table furniture and culinary apparatus requisite, but our servants have run, one after another, till we are almost in despair: even Sambo, who we thought would stick by from laziness, if no other cause, ran last night; and this morning, for the fortieth time, we had to take to the kitchen, and cook our own breakfast. A general of the United States Army, the commander of a man-of-war, and the Alcalde of Monterey, in a smoking kitchen, grinding coffee, toasting a herring, and peeling onions! These gold mines are going to upset all the domestic arrangements of society, turning the head to the tail, and the tail to the head. Well, it is an ill wind that blows nobody any good; the nabobs have had their time, and now comes that of the "niggers." We shall all live just as long, and be quite as fit to die.

Tuesday, July 18. Another bag of gold from the mines and another spasm in the community. It was brought down by a sailor from Yuba river, and contains a hundred and thirty-six ounces. It is the most beautiful gold that has appeared in the market; it looks like the yellow scales of the dolphin, passing through his rainbow hues at death. My carpenters, at work on the school-house, on seeing it, threw down their saws and planes, shouldered their picks, and are off for the Yuba. Three seamen ran from the Warren, forfeiting their four years' pay; and a whole platoon of soldiers from the fort left only their colors behind. One old woman declared she would never again break an egg or kill a chicken without examining yolk and gizzard.

Saturday, Aug. 12. My man Bob, who is of Irish extraction, and who had been in the mines about two months, returned to Monterey four weeks since, bringing with him over two thousand dollars, as the proceeds of his labor. Bob, while in my employ, required me to pay him every Saturday night, in gold, which he put into a little leather bag and sewed into the lining of his coat, after taking out just twelve and a half cents, his weekly allowance for tobacco. But now he took rooms and began to branch out; he had the best horses, the richest viands, and the choicest wines in the place. He never drank himself, but it filled him with delight to brim the sparkling goblet for others. I met Bob to-day, and asked him how he got on. "Oh, very well," he replied, "but I am off again for the mines." "How is that, Bob? You brought down with you over two thousand dollars; I hope you have not spent all that: you used to be very saving; twelve and a half cents a week for tobacco, and the rest you sewed into the lining of your coat." "Oh, yes," replied Bob, "and I have got *that* money yet; I worked hard for it; and the diel can't get it away; but the two thousand dollars came asily by good luck, and has gone as asily as it came." Now Bob's story is only one of a thousand like it in California, and has a deeper philosophy in it than meets the eye. Multitudes here are none the richer for the mines. He who can shake chestnuts from an exhaustless tree, won't stickle about the quantity he roasts.

Thursday, Aug. 16. Four citizens of Monterey are just in from the gold mines on Feather River, where they worked in company with three others. They employed about thirty wild Indians who are attached to the rancho owned by one of the party. They worked precisely seven weeks and three days, and have divided seventy-six thousand eight hundred and forty-four dollars,—nearly eleven thousand dollars to each. Make a dot there, and let me introduce a man, well known to me, who has worked on the Yuba River sixty-four days, and brought back, as the result of his individual labor, five thousand three hundred and fifty-six dollars. Make a dot there, and let me introduce another townsman, who has worked on the North Fork fifty-seven days, and brought back four thousand five hundred and thirty-four dollars. Make a dot there, and let me introduce a boy, fourteen years of age, who has worked on the Mokelumne fifty-four days, and brought back three thousand four hundred and sixty-seven dollars. Make another dot there, and let me introduce a woman, of Sonoranian birth, who has worked in the dry diggins forty-six days, and brought back two thousand one hundred and twenty-five dollars. Is not this enough to make a man throw down his le[d]ger and shoulder a pick? But the deposits which yielded these harvests were now opened for the first time; they were the accumulations of ages; only the foot-prints of the elk and wild savage had passed over them. Their slumber was broken for the first time by the sturdy arms of the American emigrant.

Tuesday, Aug. 28. The gold mines have upset all social and domestic arrangements in Monterey; the master has become his own servant, and the servant his own lord.

* * *

Inflation set the tone of San Francisco as "Forty-niners" swarmed into the once placid Pacific trading post. Traveling with the gold-seeking throng was the American poet, novelist, and travel writer, Bayard Taylor, on commission from Horace Greeley to report the gold rush in letters to the New York Tribune. Reaching San Francisco in July, 1849, Taylor was struck with the jerry-built appearance of the mushrooming community, with its turbulent, cosmopolitan society, and with the high cost of living which easy gold had imposed upon it. His visit to the once rich Mokelumne Diggings impressed him with the hard labor necessary to wrest pay dirt from worked over mines. He reserved many of his reactions to California for his book, El Dorado, *which was published by G. P. Putnam of New York in 1850.*

The Ohio's boat put us ashore at the northern point of the anchorage, at the foot of a steep bank, from which a high pier had been built into the bay. A large vessel lay at the end, discharging her cargo. We scrambled up through piles of luggage, and among the crowd collected to witness our arrival, picked out two Mexicans to carry our trunks to a hotel. The barren side of the hill before us was covered with tents and canvas houses, and nearly in front a large two-story building displayed the sign: "Fremont Family Hotel."

As yet, we were only in the suburbs of the town. Crossing the shoulder of the hill, the view extended around the curve of the bay, and hundreds of tents and houses appeared, scattered all over the heights, and along the shore for more than a mile. A furious wind was blowing down through a gap in the hills, filling the streets with clouds of dust. On every side stood buildings of all kinds, begun or half-finished, and the greater part of them mere canvas sheds, open in front, and covered with all kinds of signs, in all languages. Great quantities of goods were piled up in the open air, for want of a place to store them. The streets were full of people, hurrying to and fro, and of as diverse and bizarre a character as the houses: Yankees of every possible variety, native Californians in *sarapes* and sombreros, Chilians, Sonorians, Kanakas from Hawaii, Chinese with long tails, Malays armed with their everlasting creeses, and others in whose embrowned and bearded visages it was impossible to recognize any especial nationality. We came at last into the plaza, now dignified by the name of Portsmouth Square. It lies on the slant side of the hill, and from a high pole in front of a long one-story adobe building used as the Custom House, the American flag was flying. On the lower side stood the Parker House—an ordinary frame house of about sixty feet front—and towards its entrance we directed our course.

Our luggage was deposited on one of the rear porticos, and we discharged the porters, after paying them two dollars each —a sum so immense in comparison to the service rendered that there was no longer any doubt of our having actually landed in California. There were no lodgings to be had at the Parker House—not even a place to unroll our blankets; but one of the proprietors accompanied us across the plaza to the City Hotel, where we obtained a room with two beds at $25 per week, meals being in addition $20 per week. I asked the landlord whether he could send a porter for our trunks. "There is none belonging to the house," said he; "every man is his own porter here." I returned to the Parker House, shouldered a heavy trunk, took a valise in my hand and carried them to my quarters, in the teeth of the wind. Our room was in a sort of garret over the only story of the hotel; two cots, evidently of California manufacture, and covered only with a pair of blankets, two chairs, a rough table and a small looking-glass, constituted the furniture. There was not space enough between the bed and the bare rafters overhead, to sit upright, and I

gave myself a severe blow in rising the next morning without
the proper heed. . . .

Many of the passengers began speculation at the moment of
landing. The most ingenious and successful operation was
made by a gentleman of New York, who took out fifteen hundred copies of The Tribune and other papers, which he disposed of in two hours, at one dollar a-piece! Hearing of this I
bethought me of about a dozen papers which I had used to
fill up crevices in packing my valise. There was a newspaper
merchant at the corner of the City Hotel, and to him I proposed the sale of them, asking him to name a price. "I shall
want to make a good profit on the retail price," said he, "and
can't give more than ten dollars for the lot." I was satisfied
with the wholesale price, which was a gain of just four thousand per cent! . . .

. . . It may be interesting to give here a few instances of
the enormous and unnatural value put upon property at the
time of my arrival. The Parker House rented for $110,000
yearly, at least $60,000 of which was paid by gamblers, who
held nearly all the second story. Adjoining it on the right was
a canvas-tent fifteen by twenty-five feet, called "Eldorado,"
and occupied likewise by gamblers, which brought $40,000.
On the opposite corner of the plaza, a building called the
"Miner's Bank," used by Wright & Co., brokers, about half the
size of a fire-engine house in New York, was held at a rent of
$75,000. A mercantile house paid $40,000 rent for a one-
story building of twenty feet front; the United States Hotel,
$36,000; the Post-Office, $7,000, and so on to the end of the
chapter. A friend of mine, who wished to find a place for a
law-office, was shown a cellar in the earth, about twelve feet
square and six deep, which he could have at $250 a month.
One of the common soldiers at the battle of San Pasquale was
reputed to be among the millionaires of the place, with an
income of $50,000 *monthly*. A citizen of San Francisco died
insolvent to the amount of $41,000 the previous Autumn. His
administrators were delayed in settling his affairs, and his real
estate advanced so rapidly in value meantime, that after his
debts were paid his heirs had a yearly income of $40,000.

These facts were indubitably attested; every one believed them, yet hearing them talked of daily, as matters of course, one at first could not help feeling as if he had been eating of "the insane root."

The prices paid for labor were in proportion to everything else. The carman of Mellus, Howard & Co. had a salary of $6,000 a year, and many others made from $15 to $20 daily. Servants were paid from $100 to $200 a month, but the wages of the rougher kinds of labor had fallen to about $8. Yet, notwithstanding the number of gold-seekers who were returning enfeebled and disheartened from the mines it was difficult to obtain as many workmen as the forced growth of the city demanded. A gentleman who arrived in April told me he then found but thirty or forty houses; the population was then so scant that not more than twenty-five persons would be seen in the streets at any one time. Now, there were probably five hundred houses, tents and sheds, with a population, fixed and floating, of six thousand. People who had been absent six weeks came back and could scarcely recognize the place. Streets were regularly laid out, and already there were three piers, at which small vessels could discharge. It was calculated that the town increased daily by from fifteen to thirty houses; its skirts were rapidly approaching the summits of the three hills on which it is located. . . .

Business was over about the usual hour, and then the harvest-time of the gamblers commenced. Every "hell" in the place and I did not pretend to number them, was crowded, and immense sums were staked at the monte and faro tables. A boy of fifteen, in one place, won about $500, which he coolly pocketed and carried off. One of the gang we brought in the Panama won $1,500 in the course of the evening, and another lost $2,400. A fortunate miner made himself conspicuous by betting large piles of ounces on a single throw. His last stake of 100 oz. was lost, and I saw him the following morning dashing through the streets, trying to break his own neck or that of the magnificent *garañon* he bestrode. . . .

Dr. Gillette . . . related to me the manner of his finding the rich gulch which attracted so many to the Mokelumne Diggings. . . . About two months previous to our arrival, Dr.

Gillette came down from the Upper Bar with a companion, to "prospect" for gold among the ravines in the neighborhood. There were no persons there at the time, except some Indians. . . . One day at noon, while resting in the shade of a tree, Dr. G. took a pick and began carelessly turning up the ground. Almost on the surface, he struck and threw out a lump of gold of about two pounds' weight. Inspired by this unexpected result, they both went to work, laboring all that day and the next, and even using part of the night to quarry out the heavy pieces of rock. At the end of the second day they went to the village on the Upper Bar and weighed their profits, which amounted to fourteen pounds! They started again the third morning under pretense of hunting, but were suspected and followed by the other diggers, who came upon them just as they commenced work. The news rapidly spread, and there was soon a large number of men on the spot, some of whom obtained several pounds per day, at the start. The gulch had been well dug up for the large lumps, but there was still great wealth in the earth and sand, and several operators only waited for the wet season to work it in a systematic manner. . . .

We found many persons at work in the higher part of the gulch, searching for veins and pockets of gold, in the holes which had already produced their first harvest. Some of these gleaners, following the lodes abandoned by others as exhausted, into the sides of the mountain, were well repaid for their perseverance. Others, again, had been working for days without finding anything. Those who understood the business obtained from one to four ounces daily. Their only tools were the crowbar, pick, and knife, and many of them, following the veins under strata of rock which lay deep below the surface, were obliged to work while lying flat on their backs, in cramped and narrow holes, sometimes kept moist by springs. They were shielded, however, from the burning heats, and preserved their health better than those who worked on the bars of the river. . . .

From all I saw and heard, while at the Mokelumne Diggings, I judged there was as much order and security as could be attained without a civil organization. The inhabitants had elected one of their own number Alcalde, before whom all culprits were tried by a jury selected for the purpose. Several thefts had occurred, and the offending parties been severely punished after a fair trial. Some had been whipped and cropped, or maimed in some other way, and one or two of them hung. Two or three who had stolen largely had been shot down by the injured party, the general feeling among the miners justifying such a course when no other seemed available. We met near Livermore's Ranche, on the way to Stockton, a man whose head had been shaved and his ears cut off, after receiving one hundred lashes, for stealing ninety-eight pounds of gold. It may conflict with popular ideas of morality, but nevertheless, this extreme course appeared to have produced good results. In fact, in a country without not only bolts and bars, but any effective system of law and government, this Spartan severity of discipline seemed the only security against the most frightful disorder. The result was that, except some petty acts of larceny, thefts were rare. Horses and mules were sometimes taken, but the risk was so great that such plunder could not be carried on to any extent. The camp or tent was held inviolate, and like the patriarchal times of old, its cover protected all it enclosed. Among all well-disposed persons there was a tacit disposition to make the canvas or pavilion of rough oak boughs as sacred as once were the portals of a church.

*   *   *

Operations at the mines—from staking the claim to working the lode—were reported with a woman's eye for detail in the letters of Mrs. Louise A. Clappe, whose physician husband opened an office at Rich Bar in the Feather River Canyon on the northern fringe of the gold region, in 1851. Although this somewhat straitlaced New England housewife professed to be baffled by such terms as "Long Toms," "riddles," "tailings," and "riffle boxes," for the layman her account of mining methods would be hard to improve upon. Her letters, signed "Dame Shirley," were published serially in The Pioneer *Magazine of San Francisco in 1854 and 1855. Bret Harte used them in writing several of his best stories on the Gold Rush.*

. . . first, let me explain to you the "claiming" system. As there are no State laws upon the subject, each mining community is permitted to make its own. Here, they have decided that no man may "claim" an area of more than forty feet square. This he "stakes off" and puts a notice upon it, to the effect that he "holds" it for mining purposes. If he does not choose to "work it" immediately, he is obliged to renew the notice every ten days; for without this precaution, any other person has a right to "jump it," that is, to take it from him. There are many ways of evading the above law. For instance, an individual can "hold" as many "claims" as he pleases, if he keeps a man at work in each, for this workman represents the original owner. I am told, however, that the laborer, himself, can "jump" the "claim" of the very man who employs him, if he pleases so to do. This is seldom, if ever, done; the person who is willing to be hired, generally prefers to receive the six dollars *per diem*, of which he is *sure* in any case, to running the risk of a "claim" not proving valuable. After all, the "holding of claims" by proxy is considered rather as a carrying out of the spirit of the law, than as an evasion of it. But there are many ways of *really* outwitting this rule, though I cannot stop now to relate them, which give rise to innumerable arbitrations, and nearly every Sunday, there is a "miners' meeting" connected with this subject.

Having got our gold mines discovered and "claimed," I will try to give you a faint idea of how they "work" them. Here, in the mountains, the labor of excavation is extremely difficult, on account of the immense rocks which form a large portion of the soil. Of course, no man can "work out" a "claim" alone. For that reason, and also for the same that makes partnerships desirable, they congregate in companies of four or six, generally designating themselves by the name of the place from whence the majority of the members have emigrated; as for example, the "Illinois," "Bunker Hill," "Bay State," etc., companies. In many places the surface-soil, or in mining phrase, the "top dirt," "pays" when worked in a "Long Tom." This machine, (I have never been able to discover the derivation of its name,) is a trough, generally about twenty feet in length, and eight inches in depth, formed of wood, with the exception of six feet at one end, called the "riddle," (query, why riddle?) which is made of sheet-iron, perforated with holes about the size of a large marble. Underneath this cullender-like portion of the "long-tom," is placed another trough, about ten feet long, the sides six inches perhaps in height, which divided through the middle by a slender slat, is called the "riffle-box." It takes several persons to manage, properly, a "long-tom." Three or four men station themselves with spades, at the head of the machine, while at the foot of it, stands an individual armed "wid de shovel and de hoe." The spadesmen throw in large quantities of the precious dirt, which is washed down to the "riddle" by a stream of water leading into the "long-tom" through wooden gutters or "sluices." When the soil reaches the "riddle," it is kept constantly in motion by the man with the hoe. Of course, by this means, all the dirt and gold escapes through the perforations into the "riffle-box" below, one compartment of which is placed just beyond the "riddle." Most of the dirt washes over the sides of the "riffle-box," but the gold being so astonishingly heavy remains safely at the bottom of it. When the machine gets too full of stones to be worked easily, the man whose business it is to attend to them throws them out with his shovel, looking carefully among them as he does so for any pieces of gold, which may have been too large to pass through the holes of the "riddle." I am sorry to say that he generally loses his labor. At night they "pan out" the gold, which has been collected in the "riffle-box" during the day. Many of the miners decline washing the "top dirt" at all, but try to reach as quickly as possible the "bed-rock," where are found the richest deposits of gold. The river is supposed to have formerly flowed over this "bed-rock," in the "crevices" of which, it left, as it passed away, the largest portions of the so eagerly sought for ore. . . .

When a company wish to reach the bed rock as quickly as possible, they "sink a shaft," (which is nothing more nor less than digging a well,) until they "strike" it. They then commence "drifting coyote holes" (as they call them) in search of "crevices," which, as I told you before, often pay immensely. These "coyote holes" sometimes extend hundreds of feet into the side of the hill. Of course they are obliged to use lights in working them. They generally proceed, until the air is so impure as to extinguish the lights, when they return to the entrance of the excavation, and commence another, perhaps close to it. When they think that a "coyote hole" has been faithfully "worked," they "clean it up," which is done by scraping the surface of the "bed rock" with a knife,—lest by chance they have overlooked a "crevice,"—and they are often richly rewarded for this precaution.

Now I must tell you how those having "claims" on the hills procure the water for washing them. The expense of raising it in any way from the river, is too enormous to be thought of for a moment. In most cases it is brought from ravines in the mountains. A company, to which a friend of ours belongs, has dug a ditch about a foot in width and depth, and more than three miles in length, which is fed in this way. . . . When it reaches the top of the hill, [it] is divided into five or six branches, each one of which supplies one, two, or three "long-toms." There is an extra one, called the "waste-ditch," leading to the river, into which the water is shut off at night and on Sundays. This "race" (another and peculiar name for it) has already cost the company more than five thousand dollars. They sell the water to others at the following rates: Those that have the first use of it pay ten per cent. upon all the gold that they take out. As the water runs off from their machine, (it now goes by the elegant name of "tailings,") it is taken by a company lower down; and as it is not worth so much as when it was clear, the latter pay but seven per cent. If any others wish the "tailings," now still less valuable than at first, they pay four per cent. on all the gold which they take out, be it much or little. The water companies are constantly in trouble, and the arbitrations on that subject are very frequent. . . .

Gold mining is Nature's great lottery scheme. A man may work in a claim for many months, and be poorer at the end of the time than when he commenced; or he may "take out" thousands in a few hours. It is a mere matter of chance. A friend of ours, a young Spanish surgeon from Guatemala, a person of intelligence and education, told us that, after "working a claim" for six months, he had taken out but six ounces.

It must be acknowledged, however, that if a person "work

his claim" himself, is economical and industrious, keeps his health, and is satisfied with small gains, he is "bound" to make money. And yet, I cannot help remarking, that almost all with whom we are acquainted seem to have *lost*. Some have had their "claims" jumped; many holes which had been excavated, and prepared for working at a great expense, caved in during the heavy rains of the fall and winter. Often after a company has spent an immense deal of time and money in "sinking a shaft," the water from the springs, (the greatest obstacle which the miner has to contend with in this vicinity) rushes in so fast, that it is impossible to work in them, or to contrive any machinery to keep it out, and for that reason only, men have been compelled to abandon places where they were at the very time "taking out" hundreds of dollars a day. If a fortunate or an unfortunate (which shall I call him?) *does* happen to make a "big strike," he is almost sure to fall into the hands of the professed gamblers, who soon relieve him of all care of it. They have not troubled the Bar much during the winter, but as the spring opens, they flock in like ominous birds of prey. Last week one left here, after a stay of four days, with over a thousand dollars of the hard-earned gold of the miners. But enough of these best-beloved of Beelzebub, so infinitely worse than the robber or murderer;—for surely it would be kinder to take a man's life, than to poison him with the fatal passion of gambling.

Perhaps you would like to know what class of men is more numerous in the mines. As well as I can judge, there are upon this river as many foreigners as Americans. The former, with a few exceptions, are extremely ignorant and degraded; though we have the pleasure of being acquainted with three or four Spaniards of the highest education and accomplishments. Of the Americans, the majority are of the better class of mechanics. Next to these, in number, are the sailors and the farmers. There are a few merchants and steamboat-clerks, three or four physicians, and one lawyer. We have no ministers, though fourteen miles from here there is a "Rancho," kept by a man of distinguished appearance, an accomplished monte-dealer and horse-jockey, who is *said* to have been—in the States—a preacher of the Gospel. I know not if this be true; but at any rate, such things are not uncommon in California.

* * *

The movement of population into the Far West in the 1840's lent support to the view—long held in some quarters—that it was the nation's "manifest destiny" to occupy the Continent from coast to coast. In 1845, the editor of the Democratic Review *spoke of "our manifest destiny to overspread the Continent allotted by Providence for the free development of our yearly multiplying millions." This argument sustained the agitation to acquire Texas and Oregon and the nation's participation in the Mexican War. It found extreme expression in the writing of the Missourian, William Gilpin, who envisioned the advance of the American pioneer as not only fulfilling the nation's "manifest destiny" but assuring the United States a commanding position among the nations of the globe. Gilpin took part in the convention for establishing a government for Oregon, became an adviser to such expansionist statesmen as Benton and Polk, and served as a major in the Mexican War. He was appointed by Lincoln as the first governor of Colorado Territory. From the mid-1840's to 1860, as author and orator, he developed the theme that American soldiers and farmer-pioneers were the standard bearers in the movement across the Continent by which the United States was to fulfill its historical destiny. Portions of Gilpin's speeches and writings constitute a classic statement of the expansionist point of view.*

Everybody is acquainted with the history of the American people. . . . Restricted heretofore in its development, to so much of our continent as belongs to the Atlantic, a point of progress is reached, whence our energies, overflowing toward the west, expand to embrace the regions of the Pacific Ocean and establish direct and familiar relations with Asia. . . .

Up to . . . 1840, the progress whereby twenty-six States and four Territories had been established . . . had amounted to a solid strip of twenty-five miles in depth, added annually, along the western face of the Union from Canada to the Gulf. This occupation of wild territory, accumulating outward like the annual rings of our forest trees, proceeds with all the solemnity of a Providential ordinance. It is at this moment sweeping onward to the Pacific with accelerated activity and force, like a deluge of men, rising unabatedly, and daily pushed onward by the hand of God. . . . Fronting the Union on every side is a vast *army* of pioneers. This vast body, numbering 500,000 at least, has the movements and obeys the discipline of a perfectly organized military force. It is momentarily recruited by single individuals, families, and in some instances, communities, from every village, county, city, and State in the Union, and by emigrants from other nations. Each man in this moving throng is in force a platoon. He makes a farm upon the outer edge of the settlements which he occupies for a year, and then sells to the leading files of the mass pressing up to him from behind. He again advances twenty-five miles, renews his farm, is again overtaken, and again sells. As individuals fall out from the front rank, or fix themselves permanently, others rush from behind, pass to the front, and assail the wilderness in their turn.

Previous to the late war with Mexico, this busy throng was engaged at one point in occupying the peninsula of Florida and lands vacated by emigrant Indian tribes—at another in reaching the copper region of Lake Superior—in absorbing Iowa and Wisconsin. From this very spot had gone forth a forlorn hope to occupy Oregon and California; Texas was thus annexed, the Indian country pressed upon its flanks, and spy companies reconnoitering New and Old Mexico. Even then, obeying that mysterious and uncontrollable impulse which drives our nation to its goal, a body of the hardiest race that ever faced varied and unnumbered privations and dangers, embarked upon the trail to the Pacific coast, forced their way to the end, encountering and defying dangers and difficulties unparalleled, with a courage and success the like to which the world has not heretofore seen. Thus, then, *overland* sweeps this tide-wave of population, absorbing in its thundering march the glebe, the savages, and the wild beasts of the wilderness, scaling the mountains and debouching down upon the seaboard. Upon the high Atlantic sea-coast, the pioneer force has thrown itself into ships, and found in the ocean-fisheries food for its creative genius. The whaling fleet is the *marine* force of the pioneer army. These two forces, by land and sea, have both worked steadily onward to the North Pacific. They now reunite in the harbors of Oregon and California, about to bring into existence upon the Pacific a commercial grandeur identical with that which has followed them upon the Atlantic.

National wars stimulate progress, for they are the consequences of indiscreet opposition and jealousy of its march. . . . Then it is that the young pioneers, entering the armies of the frontier, rush out and reconnoitre the unpruned wilderness. During the Revolution, little armies, issuing down the Alleghanies, passed over Kentucky, Tennessee, and the Northwest Territory. These new countries were reconnoitred and admired. With hardy frames, confirmed health, and recruited by a year or two of peace, these soldiers returned to occupy the choice spots which had been their bivouac and camping-grounds. From the campaigns of war grew the settlements of peace, and populous States displaced the wilderness. Another war came with another generation. Armies penetrated into Michigan, Upper Illinois, and through Mississippi. The great Mississippi river, crossed at many points, ceased to be a barrier, and the steamboat appeared plowing its yellow flood. Five great States, five Territories, and three millions of people now emblazon its western side!

And now again has come another generation and another war. Your armies have scaled the icy barriers of the "Mother Mountain" and the Andes. Hid for a time in the mazes of their manifold peaks and ridges, they have issued out at many points upon the beach of the blue Pacific. Passing round by the great oceans, a military marine simultaneously strikes the shore, and lends them aid. Thus is the wilderness reconnoitred in war, its geography illustrated, and its conquerors disciplined. Your young soldiers, resting for a moment at home, resuming the civic wreath and weapons of husbandry, have sallied forth again to give to you great roads for commerce and a sisterhood of maritime States on the new-found ocean. Only four years ago, the nation, misled by prejudices artfully instilled into the general mind, regarded the great western wilds uninhabitable, and the new ocean out of reach. War [with Mexico] came—100,000 soldiers, and as many citizens, went forth, penetrated everywhere, and returned to relate in every open ear the won-

derful excellence of the climates and countries they had seen.
Hence have come already these new States, this other seaboard, and the renewed vivacity of progress with which the
general heart now palpitates. Will this cease or slacken? Has
the pouring forth of the stream from Europe ever ceased since
the day of Columbus? Has the grass obliterated the trails
down the Alleghanies or across the Mississippi? Rather let
him who doubts seat himself upon the bank of our magnificent
river and await the running dry of its yellow waters—for
sooner shall he see this, than a cessation in the crowd now
flowing loose to the western seaboard! Gold is dug; lumber is
manufactured; pastoral and arable agriculture grow apace; a
marine flashes into existence; commerce resounds; the fisheries are prosecuted; vessels are built; steam pants through all
the waters. Each interest, stimulating all the rest, and per-
petually creating novelties, a career is commenced to which,
as it glances across the Pacific, the human eye assigns no
term. . . .

The most remarkable feature of America is the Basin of the
Mississippi. . . . The population is at present [1858] twelve
millions. The capacity for population is indefinite. . . .
When, therefore, this interval of North America shall be filled
up, the affiliation of mankind will be accomplished, proximity
recognized, the distraction of intervening oceans and equa-
torial heats cease, the remotest nations be grouped together
and fused into one universal and convenient system of immediate relationship. . . .

In contrast [to the continents of Europe and Asia] the interior of North America presents towards heaven an expanded bowl, to receive and fuse into harmony whatsoever
enters within its rim. So each of the other continents, present-
ing a bowl reversed, scatter everything from a central apex into
radiant distraction. Political societies and empires have in all
ages conformed themselves to these emphatic geographical
facts. The democratic republican empire of North America is
then predestined to expand and fit itself to the continent; to
control the oceans on either hand, and eventually the continents beyond them. Much is uncertain, yet through all the
vicissitudes of the future this much of eternal truth is dis-

cernible. In geography, the antithesis of the old world; in society, we are and will be the reverse. Our North America will rapidly accumulate a population equalling that of the rest of the world combined: A people one and indivisible, identical in manners, language, customs, and impulse; preserving the same civilization, the same religion; imbued with the same opinions; and having the same political liberties. . . .

Behold, then, rising now, as in the future, the empire which industry and self-government create. The growth of half a century, hewed out of the wilderness—its weapons, the axe and plough; the tactics, labor and energy; its soldiers, free and equal citizens. Behold the oracular goal to which our eagles march, and whither the phalanx of our States and people moves harmoniously on to plant a hundred States and consummate their civic greatness.

Sod House, Custer County, Nebraska (1889)

Part VII

FILLING IN THE LAST WEST

> "Up to and including 1880 the country had a frontier of settlement, but at present the settled area has been so broken into by isolated bodies of settlement, that there can hardly be said to be a frontier line." (*Census of 1890*)

The rush to California and the settlement of the Far West bolstered the demand for improved communication across the Continent. As a result, by 1870 the western segment of a transcontinental railroad spanned the open spaces from the bend of the Missouri to California; and its haunting whistle as it crossed the Plains signalled the impending occupation of America's last West. By the mid-1880's additional lines laced the once unsettled country, encroaching upon the last retreat of its Indian occupants and encouraging the agricultural development of an area formerly shunned by farmers as an arid, grassy waste. By 1890 the settlement of the West had become so general that the census takers, for the first time in the nation's history, were unable to identify a traditional "frontier." Before the day of the railroad, facilities for relatively fast communication with the Far West were limited to the stage coach and the pony express. By 1859, some six stage lines carried mail and passengers westward, by routes that could be traveled to California in about twenty-five days. The pony express, which operated during 1860 and 1861, when it was superseded by the telegraph, accomplished the distance in eight to ten days. Mark Twain rode the overland stage and glimpsed the pony express as he traveled westward in 1861, to become a reporter on the Virginia City (Nevada) Territorial Enterprise. He described this experience in Roughing It.

The first thing we did on that glad evening that landed us at St. Joseph was to hunt up the stage-office, and pay a hundred and fifty dollars apiece for tickets per overland coach to Carson City, Nevada.

The next morning, bright and early, we took a hasty breakfast, and hurried to the starting-place. . . .

Our coach was a great swinging and swaying stage, of the most sumptuous description—an imposing cradle on wheels. It was drawn by six handsome horses, and by the side of the driver sat the "conductor," the legitimate captain of the craft; for it was his business to take charge and care of the mails, baggage, express matter, and passengers. We three were the only passengers, this trip. We sat on the back seat, inside. About all the rest of the coach was full of mail bags—for we had three days' delayed mails with us. Almost touching our knees, a perpendicular wall of mail matter rose up to the roof. There was a great pile of it strapped on top of the stage, and both the fore and hind boots were full. We had twenty-seven hundred pounds of it aboard, the driver said—"a little for Brigham, and Carson, and 'Frisco, but the heft of it for the Injuns, which is powerful troublesome 'thout they get plenty of truck to read." . . .

We changed horses every ten miles, all day long, and fairly flew over the hard, level road. We jumped out and stretched our legs every time the coach stopped, and so the night found us still vivacious and unfatigued. . . .

As the sun went down and the evening chill came on, we made preparation for bed. We stirred up the hard leather letter-sacks, and the knotty canvas bags of printed matter. . . . in such a way as to make our bed as level as possible. . . .

Whenever the stage stopped to change horses, we would wake up, and try to recollect where we were—and succeed—and in a minute or two the stage would be off again, and we likewise. . . .

The station buildings were long, low huts, made of sun-dried, mud-colored bricks, laid up without mortar (*adobes*, the Spaniards call these bricks, and Americans shorten it to '*dobies*). The roofs, which had no slant to them worth speaking of, were thatched and then sodded or covered with a thick layer of earth, and from this sprung a pretty rank growth of weeds and grass. It was the first time we had ever seen a man's front yard on top of his house. The buildings consisted of barns, stable-room for twelve or fifteen horses, and a hut for an eating-room for passengers. This latter had bunks in it for the station-keeper and a hostler or two. You could rest your elbow on its eaves, and you had to bend in order to get in at the door. . . .

Right here we suffered the first diminution of our princely state. We left our six fine horses and took six mules in their place. But they were wild Mexican fellows, and a man had to stand at the head of each of them and hold him fast while the driver gloved and got himself ready. And when at last he grasped the reins and gave the word, the men sprung suddenly away from the mules' heads and the coach shot from the station as if it had issued from a cannon. How the frantic animals did scamper! It was a fierce and furious gallop—and the gait never altered for a moment till we reeled off ten or twelve miles and swept up to the next collection of little station-huts and stables.

So we flew along all day. At 2 P.M. the belt of timber that fringes the North Platte and marks its windings through the vast level floor of the Plains came in sight. At 4 P.M. we crossed a branch of the river, and at 5 P.M. we crossed the Platte itself, and landed at Fort Kearney, *fifty-six hours out from St. Joe*—THREE HUNDRED MILES! . . .

In a little while all interest was taken up in stretching our necks and watching for the "pony-rider"—the fleet messenger who sped across the continent from St. Joe to Sacramento, carrying letters nineteen hundred miles in eight days! . . .

We had had a consuming desire, from the beginning, to see a pony-rider, but somehow or other all that passed us and all that met us managed to streak by in the night, and so we heard only a whiz and a hail, and the swift phantom of the desert was gone before we could get our heads out of the windows. But now we were expecting one along every moment, and would see him in broad daylight. Presently the driver exclaims:

"HERE HE COMES!"

Every neck is stretched further, and every eye strained wider. Away across the endless dead level of the prairie a black speck appears against the sky, and it is plain that it moves. Well, I should think so! In a second or two it becomes a horse and rider, rising and falling, rising and falling—sweeping toward us nearer and nearer—growing more and more distinct, more and more sharply defined—nearer and still nearer, and the flutter of the hoofs comes faintly to the ear—another instant a whoop and a hurrah from our upper deck, a wave of the rider's hand, but no reply, and man and horse burst past our excited faces, and go winging away like a belated fragment of a storm!

So sudden is it all, and so like a flash of unreal fancy, that but for the flake of white foam left quivering and perishing on a mail-sack after the vision had flashed by and disappeared, we might have doubted whether we had seen any actual horse and man at all, maybe. . . .

Toward dawn we got under way again, and presently, as we sat with raised curtains enjoying our early-morning smoke and contemplating the first splendor of the rising sun as it swept down the long array of mountain peaks, . . . we hove in sight of South Pass City. The hotel-keeper, the postmaster, the blacksmith, the mayor, the constable, the city marshal, and the principal citizen and property-holder, all came out and greeted us cheerily, and we gave him good day. He gave us a little Indian news, and a little Rocky Mountain news, and we gave him some Plains information in return. He then retired to his lonely grandeur and we climbed on up among the bristling peaks and the ragged clouds. South Pass City consisted of four log cabins, one of which was unfinished, and the gentleman with all those offices and titles was the chiefest of the ten citizens of the place. Think of hotel-keeper, postmaster, blacksmith, mayor, constable, city marshal and principal citizen all condensed into one person and crammed into one skin.

*   *   *

In less than a year after the termination of the pony express, Congress authorized the construction of a railroad to the Pacific. Its completion, in 1869, was probably the most monumental accomplishment in the history of the West. The road was to follow the Platte Valley route marked out by the overland migration to Utah and California. Two corporations, subsidized by gifts of land from the public domain and by loans from the Federal Government, were authorized to construct the road. One, the Union Pacific, built westward from the

vicinity of Omaha. The other, the Central Pacific, built east-
ward from Sacramento. In the Spring of 1869 the construction
crews came in sight of one another; and on May 10, at
Promontory Point, in Utah, the spikes were driven that con-
nected the continent-spanning rails. The magnitude as well as
the drama of this great achievement is revealed in the memoir
of Grenville M. Dodge, who became chief engineer of the line
in 1866.

The organization for work on the plains away from civilization was as follows: Each of our surveying parties consisted
of a chief, who was an experienced engineer, two assistants,
also civil engineers, rodmen, flagmen and chainmen, generally graduated civil engineers, but without personal experience in the field, besides axe men, teamsters and herders.
When the party was expected to live upon the game of the
country a hunter was added. Each party would thus consist of
from eighteen to twenty-two men, all armed. When operating
in a hostile Indian country they were regularly drilled, though
after the Civil War this was unnecessary, as most of them had
been in the army. Each party entering a country occupied by
hostile Indians was generally furnished with a military escort
of from ten men to a company under a competent officer. The
duty of this escort was to protect the party when in camp.
In the field the escort usually occupied prominent hills commanding the territory in which the work was to be done, so as
to head off sudden attacks by the Indians. Notwithstanding
this protection, the parties were often attacked, their chief, or
some of their men killed or wounded, and their stock run off.

In preliminary surveys in the open country a party would
run from eight to twelve miles of line in a day. On location in
an open country three or four miles would be covered, but in
a mountainous country generally not to exceed a mile. All
hands worked from daylight to dark, the country being recon-
noitered ahead of them by the chief, who indicated the
streams to follow, and the controlling points in summits and
river crossings. The party of location that followed the preliminary surveys, had the maps and profiles of the line
selected for location and devoted its energies to obtaining a

line of the lowest grades and the least curvature that the country would admit.

The location party in our work on the Union Pacific was followed by the construction corps, grading generally 100 miles at a time. That distance was graded in about thirty days on the plains, as a rule, but in the mountains we sometimes had to open our grading several hundred miles ahead of our track in order to complete the grading by the time the track should reach it. All the supplies for this work had to be hauled from the end of the track, and the wagon transportation was enormous. At one time we were using at least 10,000 animals, and most of the time from 8,000 to 10,000 laborers. The bridge gangs always worked from five to twenty miles ahead of the track, and it was seldom that the track waited for a bridge. To supply one mile of track with material and supplies required about forty cars, as on the plains everything—rails, ties, bridging, fastenings, all railway supplies, fuel for locomotives and trains, and supplies for men and animals on the entire work, had to be transported from the Missouri River. Therefore, as we moved westward, every hundred miles added vastly to our transportation. Yet the work was so systematically planned and executed that I do not remember an instance in all the construction of the line of the work being delayed a single week for want of material. . . .

Our Indian troubles commenced in 1864 and lasted until the track joined at Promontory. We lost most of our men and stock while building from Fort Kearney to Bitter Creek. At that time every mile of road had to be surveyed, graded, tied, and bridged under military protection. The order to every surveying corps, grading, bridging and tie outfit was never to run when attacked. All were required to be armed, and I do not know that the order was disobeyed in a single instance, nor did I ever hear that the Indians had driven a party permanently from its work. I remember one occasion when they swooped down on a grading outfit in sight of the temporary fort of the military some five miles away, and right in sight of the end of the track. The Government Commission to examine that section of the completed road had just arrived, and the Commissioners witnessed the fight. The graders had their arms stacked on the cut. The Indians leaped from the ravines, and, springing upon the workmen before they could reach their arms, cut loose the stock and caused a panic. General Frank P. Blair, General Simpson and Dr. White were the Commissioners, and they showed their grit by running to my car for arms to aid in the fight. We did not fail to benefit from this experience, for, on returning to the East the Commission dwelt earnestly on the necessity of our being protected. . . .

We made our plans to build to Salt Lake, 480 miles, in 1868, and to endeavor to meet the Central Pacific at Humboldt Wells, 219 miles west of Ogden, in the spring of 1869. I had extended our surveys during the years 1867 and 1868 to the California State line, and laid my plans before the company, and the necessary preparations were made to commence work as soon as frost was out of the ground, say about April 1st. Material had been collected in sufficient quantities at the end of the track to prevent any delay. During the winter ties and bridge timber had been cut and prepared in the mountains to bring to the line at convenient points, and the engineering forces were started to their positions before cold weather was over that they might be ready to begin their work as soon as the temperature would permit. I remember that the parties going to Salt Lake crossed the Wasatch Mountains on sledges, and that the snow covered the tops of the telegraph poles. We all knew and appreciated that the task we had laid out would require the greatest energy on the part of all hands. About April 1st, therefore, I went onto the plains myself and started our construction forces, remaining the whole summer between Laramie and the Humboldt Mountains. I was surprised at the rapidity with which the work was carried forward. Winter caught us in the Wasatch Mountains, but we kept on grading our road and laying our track in the snow and ice at a tremendous cost. I estimated for the company that the extra cost of thus forcing the work during that summer and winter was over $10,000,000, but the instructions I received were to go on, no matter what the cost. Spring found us with the track at Ogden, and by May 1st we had reached Promontory, 534 miles west of our starting point twelve months before. Work on our line was opened to Humboldt Wells, making in the year a grading of 754 miles of line.

The Central Pacific had made wonderful progress coming east, and we abandoned the work from Promontory to Humboldt Wells, bending all our efforts to meet them at Promontory. Between Ogden and Promontory each company graded a line, running side by side, and in some places one line was right above the other. The laborers upon the Central Pacific were Chinamen, while ours were Irishmen, and there was much ill-feeling between them. Our Irishmen were in the habit of firing their blasts in the cuts without giving warning to the Chinamen on the Central Pacific working right above them. From this cause several Chinamen were severely hurt. Complaint was made to me by the Central Pacific people, and I endeavored to have the contractors bring all hostilities to a close, but, for some reason or other, they failed to do so. One day the Chinamen, appreciating the situation, put in what is called a "grave" on their work, and when the Irishmen right under them were all at work let go their blast and buried several of our men. This brought about a truce at once. From that time the Irish laborers showed due respect for the Chinamen, and there was no further trouble.

When the two roads approached in May, 1869, we agreed to connect at the summit of Promontory Point, and the day was fixed so that trains could reach us from New York and California. We laid the rails to the junction point a day or two before the final closing. Coming from the East, representing the Union Pacific, were Thomas C. Durant, Vice President, Sidney Dillon, who had taken a prominent part in the construction of the road from the beginning, and John R. Duff, directors, together with the consulting engineer and a carload of friends. From the West the representatives of the Central Pacific were its President, Leland Stanford, Mr. Collis P. Huntington, Mr. Crocker, Mr. Hopkins, Mr. Colton, and other members of that company, and Mr. Montague, chief engineer, and a detachment of troops from Camp Douglass, Salt Lake City. The two trains pulled up facing each other, each crowded with workmen who sought advantageous positions to witness the ceremonies, and literally covered the cars.

The officers and invited guests formed on each side of the track leaving it open to the south. The telegraph lines had been brought to that point, so that in the final spiking as each blow was struck the telegraph recorded it at each connected office from the Atlantic to the Pacific. Prayer was offered, a number of spikes were driven in the two adjoining rails, each one of the prominent persons present taking a hand, but very few hitting the spikes, to the great amusement of the crowd. When the last spike was placed, light taps were given upon it by several officials, and it was finally driven home by the chief engineer of the Union Pacific railway. The engineers ran up their locomotives until they touched, the engineer upon each engine breaking a bottle of champagne upon the other one, and thus the two roads were wedded into one great trunk line from the Atlantic to the Pacific. Spikes of silver and gold were brought specially for the occasion, and later were manufactured into miniature spikes as mementoes of the occasion. It was a bright but cold day. After a few speeches we all took refuge in the Central Pacific cars, where wine flowed freely, and many speeches were made. . . .

Of late years there has been a great deal of criticism and comparison of the building of the Union Pacific and Central Pacific Railroads, favoring the latter. The theory is that because the Central Pacific had the Sierra Nevada Range to tackle at first, it was a more difficult problem, financially and physically, to handle than the Union Pacific end, but this is a very great mistake. The Union Pacific had to bring all of its material, ties, bridging, etc., from tide-water by rail or by river. They had to build the first 630 miles without any material on its line to aid them except the earth, and for this they only received $16,000 per mile in Government bonds. There was no settlement on the line to create any traffic or earnings along the whole distance, which was very difficult in appealing to the people to buy the bonds and furnish money for the company. In comparison to this, the Central Pacific started at Sacramento with a tide-water base coming right up to it, so that all the material that had to come from foreign or domestic ports had the cheapest rates by sea. Then from Sacramento they had built over the mountains to Virginia

City to the great Bonanza mines at Virginia City, which gave them a large traffic at high rates, and gave them very large earnings. Then again, only a few miles east of Sacramento, the east base of the Sierra Nevada Range commences, and they received immediately $48,000 in Government bonds per mile for the 150 miles, and $32,000 in Government bonds from there on to Salt Lake, a distance of barely 200 miles, more than the 630 miles that the Union Pacific had to build on $16,000 per mile. This favorable condition for the Central Pacific was such that the representatives of that road had very little difficulty in raising all the money they needed and having for nearly one-half of their road a fine traffic to help pay the interest on their bonds.

*   *   *

The Union Pacific spawned an unseemly brood of transient construction towns as it built westward across the Plains. A few became permanent centers of trade and commerce, but most of them declined and disappeared, or were literally picked up and carried forward, when construction crews moved on to complete the next leg of the road. While they flourished, they could hold their own with the mining towns and the cow towns as examples of the transient and uninhibited urbanism that frequently took shape in the rapidly changing Plains and Mountain West. In the Summer of 1868, J. H. Beadle, Western correspondent of the Cincinnati Commercial, *visited Benton, the temporary terminus of the Union Pacific, which was then nearly 700 miles west of Omaha. He later described the violence of Benton's short-lived, pre-fabricated existence in his book,* The Undeveloped West.

Here had sprung up in two weeks, as if by the touch of Aladdin's Lamp, a city of three thousand people; there were regular squares arranged into five wards, a city government of mayor and aldermen, a daily paper, and a volume of ordinances for the public health. It was the end of the freight and passenger, and beginning of the construction, division; twice every day immense trains arrived and departed, and stages left for Utah, Montana, and Idaho; all the goods formerly hauled across the plains came here by rail and were reshipped, and for ten hours daily the streets were thronged with motley crowds of railroad men, Mexicans and Indians, gamblers, "cappers," and saloon-keepers, merchants, miners, and mule-whackers. The streets were eight inches deep in white dust as I entered the city of canvas tents and pole-houses; the suburbs appeared as banks of dirty white lime, and a new arrival with black clothes looked like nothing so much as a cockroach struggling through a flour barrel.

It was sundown, and the lively notes of the violin and guitar were calling the citizens to evening diversions. Twenty-three saloons paid license to the evanescent corporation, and five dance-houses amused our elegant leisure. . . .

The regular routine of business, dances, drunks and fist-fights met with a sudden interruption on the 8th of August. Sitting in a tent door that day I noticed an altercation across the street, and saw a man draw a pistol and fire, and another stagger and catch hold of a post for support. The first was about to shoot again when he was struck from behind and the pistol wrenched from his hand. The wounded man was taken into a *cyprian's* tent near by and treated with the greatest kindness by the women, but died the next day. It was universally admitted that there had been no provocation for the shooting, and the general voice was, "Hang him!"

Next day I observed a great rush and cry in the street, and looking out, saw them dragging the murderer along towards the tent where the dead man lay. The entire population were out at once, plainsmen, miners and women mingled in a wild throng, all insisting on immediate hanging. Pale as a sheet and hardly able to stand, the murderer, in the grasp of two stalwart Vigilantes, was dragged through the excited crowd, and into the tent where the dead man lay, and forced to witness the laying out and depositing in the coffin. . . .

The great institution of Benton was the "Big Tent," sometimes, with equal truth but less politeness, called the "Gamblers' Tent." This structure was a nice frame, a hundred feet long and forty feet wide, covered with canvass and conveniently floored for dancing, to which and gambling it was entirely devoted. It was moved successively to all the mushroom terminus "cities," and during my stay was the great public resort of Benton. A description of one of these towns is a description of all; so let us spend one evening in the "Big Tent," and see how men amuse their leisure where home life and society are lacking.

As we enter, we note that the right side is lined with a splendid bar, supplied with every variety of liquors and cigars, with cut glass goblets, ice-pitchers, splendid mirrors, and pictures rivalling those of our Eastern cities. At the back end a space large enough for one cotillon is left open for dancing; on a raised platform, a full band is in attendance day and night, while all the rest of the room is filled with tables devoted to monte, faro, rondo coolo, fortune-wheels, and every other species of gambling known. . . .

During the day the "Big Tent" is rather quiet, but at night, after a few inspiring tunes at the door by the band, the long hall is soon crowded with a motley throng of three or four hundred miners, ranchmen, clerks, "bullwhackers," gamblers and "cappers." The brass instruments are laid aside, the string-music begins, the cotillons succeed each other rapidly, each ending with a drink, while those not so employed crowd around the tables and enjoy each his favorite game. To-night is one of unusual interest, and the tent is full, while from every table is heard the musical rattle of the dice, the hum of the wheel, or the eloquent voice of the dealer. . . .

To look on Benton, a motley collection of log and canvass tents, one would have sworn there was no trade; but in those canvass tents, immense sums changed hands. E. Block & Co., Wholesale Dealers in Liquors and Tobacco, with whom I lodged in Benton, in a frame and canvass tent, twenty by forty feet in extent, did a business of $30,000 a month. Others did far better. Ten months afterwards, I revisited the site. There was not a house or tent to be seen; a few rock piles and half destroyed chimneys barely sufficed to mark the ruins; the white dust had covered everything else, and desolation reigned supreme.

Transactions in real estate in all these towns were, of course, most uncertain; and everything that looked solid was a sham. Red brick fronts, brown stone fronts, and stuccoed walls, were found to have been made to order in Chicago and shipped in (pine) sections. Ready made houses were finally sent out in lots, boxed, marked, and numbered; half a dozen men could erect a block in a day, and two boys with screw-drivers put up a "habitable dwelling" in three hours. A very good graystone stucco front, with plain sides, twenty by forty tent, could be had for $300; and if your business happened to desert you, or the town moved on, you only had to take your store to pieces, ship it on a platform car to the next city, and set up again. There was a pleasing versatility of talent in the population of such towns.

An army officer told me that he went up the Platte Valley late in 1866 and observed a piece of rising ground near the junction of the two streams, where for miles not a live shrub or blade of grass was to be seen. Six months after he returned and the "Great and Growing City of the Platte" covered the site; three thousand people made the desert hum with business and pleasure; there were fine hotels, elegant restaurants, and billiard halls and saloons, while a hundred merchants jostled each other through banks and insurance offices. All the machinery of society was in easy operation; there were two daily papers, a Mayor and Common Council, an aristocracy and a common people, with old settlers, new comers, and first families. Six months after he returned and hunted for the site. A few piles of straw and brick, with debris of oyster cans nearly covered by the shifting sands, alone enabled him to find it. The "city" had got up and emigrated to the next terminus. . . .

Of all [the cities] which sprang up on the road, only two or three survive in anything like their first greatness. A speculative and uncertain character attached to all of them; lots in the "wickedest city," Julesburg, which once sold readily for a thousand dollars, are now the habitations of the owls and prairie dogs.

*   *   *

Procuring food for railroad construction gangs was one of the pursuits that made up the lively career of William F. Cody, the one, indeed, that allegedly earned him the title of "Buffalo Bill." Cody's early life epitomized the pre-farmer history of the Plains, as his "Wild West" shows, in later years, helped to imbed this history in the American tradition. At the

age of eleven, he was employed as a "cavvy boy" for the over-
land freighting firm of Russell, Majors, and Waddell; the gold
fever took him to Denver in 1859; by 1860 he was riding the
pony express; and in the ensuing decade he served as guide and
scout in the Army's efforts to control the Plains Indians. In
his buffalo hunting activities Cody used to advantage his faith-
ful horse, Brigham, and a breech-loading 50-caliber Spring-
field, which he called "Lucretia Borgia." He was reputed for
the skill, daring, and courage with which he rode alongside the
animal and shot downward to the heart. In his Autobiography,
which appeared in 1879, few of these qualities of his person-
ality are left to the reader's imagination.

It was about this time [1867] that the end of the Kansas
Pacific track was in the heart of the buffalo country, and the
company was employing about twelve hundred men in the
construction of the road. As the Indians were very troublesome, it was difficult to obtain fresh meat for the workmen,
and the company therefore concluded to engage the services
of hunters to kill buffaloes.

Having heard of my experience and success as a buffalo
hunter, Messrs. Goddard Brothers, who had the contract for
boarding the employees of the road, . . . made me a good
offer to become their hunter. . . . They said they would require about twelve buffaloes a day; that would be twenty-four
hams, as we took only the hind-quarters and hump of each
buffalo. The work was dangerous. . . . Indians . . . were
riding all over that section of the country, and as I would be
obliged to go from five to ten miles from the road each day
to hunt the buffaloes, accompanied by only one man with a
light wagon for the transportation of the meat, I . . . demanded a large salary. They could afford to remunerate me
well, because the meat would not cost them anything. They
agreed to give me five hundred dollars per month. . . .

I immediately began my career as a buffalo hunter for the
Kansas Pacific Railroad, and it was not long before I acquired a considerable notoriety. It was at this time that the
very appropriate name of "Buffalo Bill," was conferred upon
me by the road-hands. It has stuck to me ever since, and I
have never been ashamed of it.

During my engagement as hunter for the company—a period of less than eighteen months—I killed 4,280 buffaloes; and I had many exciting adventures with the Indians, as well as hair-breadth escapes, some of which are well worth relating.

One day, in the spring of 1868, I mounted Brigham and started for Smoky Hill River. After galloping about twenty miles I reached the top of a small hill overlooking the valley of that beautiful stream.

As I was gazing on the landscape, I suddenly saw a band of about thirty Indians nearly half a mile distant; I knew by the way they jumped on their horses that they had seen me as soon as I came into sight.

The only chance I had for my life was to make a run for it, and I immediately wheeled and started back towards the railroad. Brigham . . . struck out as if he comprehended that it was to be a run for life. . . . On reaching a ridge beyond, I looked back and saw the Indians coming for me full speed. . . . Brigham . . . did some of the prettiest running I ever saw. But the Indians were about as well mounted as I was, and one of their horses in particular—a spotted animal—was gaining on me all the time.

The Indian who was riding the spotted horse was armed with a rifle, and would occasionally send a bullet whistling along, sometimes striking the ground ahead of me. I saw that this fellow must be checked, or a stray bullet . . . might hit me or my horse; so suddenly stopping Brigham, . . . I raised old "Lucretia" to my shoulder, took deliberate aim at the Indian and his horse, hoping to hit one or the other, and fired. He was not over eighty yards from me at this time, and at the crack of my rifle down went his horse. Not waiting to see if he recovered, . . . we were again fairly flying towards our destination. We had urgent business just then and were in a hurry to attend to it.

The other Indians had gained on us while I was engaged in shooting at their leader. . . . To return their compliment I occasionally wheeled myself in the saddle and fired back at them, and one of my shots broke the leg of one of their horses. . . .

Only seven or eight Indians now remained in dangerous

proximity to me, and as their horses were beginning to lag somewhat, I checked my faithful old steed a little to allow him an opportunity to draw an extra breath or two. I had determined, if it should come to the worst, to drop into a buffalo wallow, where I could stand the Indians off for a while; but I was not compelled to do this, as Brigham carried me through most nobly.

The chase was kept up until we came within three miles of the end of the railroad track, where two companies of soldiers were stationed for the purpose of protecting the workmen from the Indians. One of the outposts saw the Indians chasing me across the prairie, and gave the alarm. In a few minutes I saw . . . men coming on foot, and cavalrymen, too, came galloping to our rescue. . . . The Indians turned and ran in the direction from which they had come. . . .

Captain Nolan, of the Tenth Cavalry, now came up with forty of his men, and upon learning what had happened he determined to pursue the Indians. He kindly offered me one of the cavalry horses, and . . . we started out after the flying Indians. . . . Before they had gone five miles we overtook and killed eight of their number. The others succeeded in making their escape. On coming to the place where I had killed the first horse—the spotted one— . . . I found that my bullet had struck him in the forehead and killed him instantly. He was a noble animal, and ought to have been engaged in better business.

On our return we found old Brigham grazing quietly and contentedly on the grass. He looked up at me as if to ask if we had got away with any of those fellows who had chased us. I believe he read the answer in my eyes.

*   *   *

The advent of the railroad on the Plains brought about the extinction of the buffalo, as it curtailed the freedom of movement of the Indians who had been guaranteed this part of the Continent as their permanent possession. Millions of buffalo roamed the Plains when the first pioneers moved toward the Far West, constituting a physical hazard as well as a source of food for travelers and migrants. The availability of railroads facilitated the sport of buffalo hunting as well as the shipment

*of hides once they were in demand as a source of commercial
leather. As a result of their exploitation for both sport and
profit the herds were virtually exterminated between 1867 and
1883. The buffalo, as yet relatively unmolested, were a novelty
to Horace Greeley as he journeyed toward San Francisco, via
the Pike's Peak Express, in 1859. For three days, late in May,
the stage threaded its way through great herds of these heavy,
stubborn beasts. Greeley described this experience in letters to
the* New York Tribune, *later published as* An Overland
Journey from New York to San Francisco in 1859.

On rising our first ridge this morning [May 29], a herd
of buffalo was seen grazing on the prairie some three miles
toward the Solomon [a branch of the Kansas River]; soon,
more were visible; then others. At length a herd of perhaps
a hundred appeared on the north. . . .

Thence, nearly all day, the buffalo in greater or less
numbers were visible among the bottoms of the Solomon on
our right—usually two to three miles distant. At length, about
5 P.M., we reached the crest of a "divide," . . . and saw
the whole region from half a mile to three miles south of our
road, and for an extent of at least four miles east and west,
fairly alive with buffalo. There certainly were not less than
ten thousand of them; I believe there were many more. Some
were feeding, others lying down, others pawing up the earth,
rolling on it, etc. . . .

We are near the heart of the buffalo region. The stages
from the west that met us here this evening report the sight
of millions within the last two days. Their trails chequer the
prairie in every direction. . . . All day yesterday [May 30],
they darkened the earth around us, often seeming to be
drawn up like an army in battle array. . . . Whenever
alarmed, they set off on their awkward but effective canter
to the greater herds still south. . . . This necessarily sends
those north of us across our roads often but a few rods in
front of us. . . . Of course, they sometimes stop and tack,
or, seeing us, sheer off and cross further ahead, or split into
two lines; but the general impulse, when alarmed, is to follow
blindly and at full speed, seeming not to inquire or consider
from what quarter danger is to be apprehended.

What strikes the stranger with most amazement is their immense numbers. I know a million is a great many, but I am confident we saw that number yesterday. Certainly, all we saw could not have stood on ten square miles of ground. Often, the country for miles on either hand seemed quite black with them. . . . Consider that we have traversed more than one hundred miles in width since we first struck them, and that for most of this distance the buffalo have been constantly in sight, and that they continue for some twenty-five miles further on—this being the breadth of their present range, which has a length of perhaps a thousand miles—and you have some approach to an idea of their countless myriads. . . .

The superintendent of this division . . . had a narrow escape day before yesterday. He was riding his mule along our road, utterly unconscious of danger, when a herd of buffalo . . . were stampeded by an emigrant train, and set off full gallop. . . . A slight ridge hid them from Mr. F.'s sight till their leader came full tilt against his mule, knocking him down, and going over him at full speed. Mr. F. of course fell with the dying mule, and I presume lay very snug by his side while the buffaloes made a clear sweep over the concern—he firing his revolver rapidly, and thus inducing many of the herd to shear off on one side or the other. . . .

Two nights ago, an immense herd came down upon a party of Pike's Peakers camped just across the creek from this station, and, (it being dark) were with difficulty prevented from trampling down tents, cattle, and people. Some fifty shots were fired into them before they could be turned.

*   *   *

The construction of the transcontinentals helped to precipitate the last test of strength between the white and the Indian civilizations; and the fate of many of the original occupants of the West was as drastic as that of the buffalo. By the 1850's the United States Government had abandoned its policy of guaranteeing the entire Plains country to the Indians and had begun to treat with the tribes to limit them to specific locations. Many, refusing to give up their nomadic freedom,

*showed their objections by raiding mining camps and mail
coaches, massacring settlers, and waging open warfare against
Federal troops in the West. They made one major final stand
in the Sioux War of 1875-1876. In this instance, their resistance was aggravated by the corruption of agents of the
Interior Department in handling Indian affairs, the menacing
advance of the Northern Pacific Railroad, and the encroachment of miners on Sioux lands following gold discoveries in
the Black Hills. It was in this conflict that Colonel George A.
Custer and his detachment were trapped and exterminated in
the Battle of the Little Big Horn (1876). In time, however,
the Sioux uprising met the same unhappy fate as that of
earlier Indian resistance movements. Custer was on the Plains
as early as 1867, when he was attached to a quasi-punitive
expedition, under the command of Major General Winfield S.
Hancock, designed to impress the Indians of western Kansas
with American strength. His account of this operation in his
book,* My Life on the Plains, *reveals the basic conflict of
attitudes which complicated relations between whites and
Indians in the trans-Missouri West.*

It may be asked, What had the Indians done to make this
incursion necessary? They had been guilty of numerous thefts
and murders during the preceding summer and fall, for none
of which had they been called to account. They had attacked
the stations of the overland mail route, killed the employees,
burned the station, and captured the stock. Citizens had been
murdered in their homes on the frontier of Kansas; murders
had been committed on the Arkansas route. The principal
perpetrators of these acts were the Cheyennes and Sioux. . . .
It was not to punish for these sins of the past that the expedition was set on foot, but rather by its imposing appearance and its early presence in the Indian country to check
or intimidate the Indians from a repetition of their late
conduct. This was deemed particularly necessary from the
fact that the various tribes from which we had greatest
cause to anticipate trouble had during the winter, through
their leading chiefs and warriors, threatened that as soon as
the grass was up in spring a combined outbreak would take
place along our entire frontier, and especially against the
main routes of travel. [A council was thought to be called for,

and] word was sent early in March to the agents of those tribes whom it was desirable to meet. The agents sent runners to the villages inviting them to meet us at some point near the Arkansas river. . . .

[As we approached the Indian encampment, on Pawnee Fork, above Fort Larned] we witnessed one of the . . . most imposing military displays, prepared according to the Indian art of war, which it has ever been my lot to behold. It was nothing more nor less than an Indian line of battle drawn directly across our line of march; as if to say, Thus far and no further. Most of the Indians were mounted; all were bedecked in their brightest colors, their heads crowned with the brilliant war-bonnet, their lances bearing the crimson pennant, bows strung, and quivers full of barbed arrows. In addition to these weapons, which with the hunting-knife and tomahawk are considered as forming the armament of the warrior, each one was supplied with either a breech-loading rifle or revolver, sometimes with both—the latter obtained through the wise foresight and strong love of fair play which prevails in the Indian Department, which, seeing that its wards are determined to fight, is equally determined that there shall be no advantage taken, but that the two sides shall be armed alike; proving, too, in this manner the wonderful liberality of our Government, which not only is able to furnish its soldiers with the latest improved style of breech-loaders to defend it and themselves, but is equally able and willing to give the same pattern of arms to their common foe. . . . In the line of battle before us there were several hundred Indians, while further to the rear and at different distances were other organized bodies acting apparently as reserves. . . . As far as the eye could reach small groups or individuals could be seen in the direction of the village; these were evidently parties of observation, whose sole object was to learn the result of our meeting with the main body and hasten with the news to the village.

For a few moments appearances seemed to foreshadow anything but a peaceful issue. The infantry was in the advance, followed closely by the artillery, while my command, the cavalry, was marching on the flank. General Hancock, who was riding with his staff at the head of the column, coming suddenly in view of the wild fantastic battle array, . . . hastily sent orders to the infantry, artillery, and cavalry to form line of battle, evidently determined that if war was intended we should be prepared. The cavalry, being the last to form on the right, came into line on a gallop, and, without waiting to align the ranks carefully, the command was given to "draw sabre." . . . Here in battle array, facing each other, were the representatives of civilized and barbarous warfare. The one, with but few modifications, stood clothed in the same rude style of dress, bearing the same patterned shield and weapon that his ancestors had borne centuries before; the other confronted him in the dress and supplied with the implements of war which the most advanced stage of civilization had pronounced the most perfect. . . .

After a few moments of painful suspense, General Hancock, accompanied by General A. J. Smith and other officers, rode forward, and through an interpreter invited the chiefs to meet us midway, for the purpose of an interview. In response to this invitation Roman Nose, bearing a white flag, accompanied by Bull Bear, White Horse, Gray Beard, and Medicine Wolf on the part of the Cheyennes, and Pawnee Killer, Bad Wound, Tall Bear that Walks under the Ground, Left Hand, Little Bear, and Little Bull on the part of the Sioux, rode forward to the middle of the open space between the two lines. Here we shook hands with all of the chiefs, most of them exhibiting unmistakable signs of gratification at this apparently peaceful termination of our rencounter. General Hancock very naturally inquired the object of the hostile attitude displayed before us, saying to the chiefs that if war was their object we were ready then and there to participate. Their immediate answer was that they did not desire war, but were peacefully disposed. They were then told that we would continue our march toward the village, and encamp near it, but would establish such regulations that none of the soldiers would be permitted to approach or disturb them.

* * *

*Despite Hancock's assurances, the Indians departed before the
council could be held. Custer, with eight troops of cavalry, was
sent in pursuit. He learned that the Indians, after abandoning
their village, had attacked and burned a mail station, killed
and disembowelled the white men they found there, fired into
another station, and tried to gain admittance to a third. On
receiving Custer's report, General Hancock punished the
Indians by destroying their village. Meanwhile Custer had
word of an Indian attack upon a wagon train and its military
escort of forty-eight men returning from Fort Wallace to
Hancock's camp with supplies. Accompanying the wagon train
was William Comstock, whom Custer described as "the favorite and best known scout on the central plains." Custer's account of this incident is second-hand, but it depicts in a
graphic way the nature of Indian warfare on the Plains.*

Comstock and the officers . . . were astonished to perceive that between six and seven hundred warriors were bearing down upon them, and in a few minutes would undoubtedly commence the attack. Against such odds, and upon
ground so favorable for the Indian mode of warfare, it seemed
unreasonable to hope for a favorable result. Yet the entire
escort, officers and men, entered upon their defence with
the determination to sell their lives as dearly as possible. . . .

Lieutenant Robbins at once set about preparing to receive
his unwelcome visitors. Colonel Cook formed the train in
two parallel columns, leaving ample space between for the
horses of the cavalry. Lieutenant Robbins then dismounted
his men and prepared to fight on foot. The led horses, under
charge of the fourth trooper, were placed between the two
columns of wagons, and were thus in a measure protected
from the assaults which the officers had every reason to
believe would be made for their capture. The dismounted
cavalrymen were thus formed in a regular circle enclosing the
train and horses. . . .

. . . Suddenly, with a wild ringing war-whoop, the entire
band of warriors bore down upon the train and its little
party of defenders.

On came the savages, filling the air with their terrible yells.
Their first object, evidently, was to stampede the horses and
draught animals of the train; then, in the excitement and

consternation which would follow, to massacre the escort and drivers. The wagonmaster in immediate charge of the train had been ordered to keep his two columns of wagons constantly moving forward and well closed up. This last injunction was hardly necessary, as the frightened teamsters, glancing at the approaching warriors and hearing their savage shouts, were sufficiently anxious to keep well closed upon their leaders.

The first onslaught of the Indians was made on the flank which was superintended by Colonel Cook. They rode boldly forward as if to dash over the mere handful of cavalrymen, who stood in skirmishing order in a circle about the train. Not a soldier faltered as the enemy came thundering upon them, but waiting until the Indians were within short rifle range of the train, the cavalrymen dropped upon their knees, and taking deliberate aim poured a volley from their Spencer carbines into the ranks of the savages, which seemed to put a sudden check upon the ardor of their movements and forced them to wheel off to the right. Several of the warriors were seen to reel in their saddles, while the ponies of others were brought down or wounded by the effectual fire of the cavalrymen.

Those of the savages who were shot from their saddles were scarcely permitted to fall to the ground before a score or more of their comrades dashed to their rescue and bore their bodies beyond the possible reach of our men. This is in accordance with the Indian custom in battle. They will risk the lives of a dozen of their best warriors to prevent the body of any one of their number from falling into the white man's possession. The reason for this is the belief, which generally prevails among all the tribes, that if a warrior loses his scalp he forfeits his hope of ever reaching the happy hunting-ground.

As the Indians were being driven back by the well-directed volley of the cavalrymen, the latter, overjoyed at their first success, became reassured, and sent up a cheer of exultation, while Comstock, who had not been idle in the fight, called out to the retreating Indians in their native tongue, taunting them with their unsuccessful assault.

The Attack Upon the Train.

Cattle Drive, Dodge City (1878).

The Indians withdrew to a point beyond the range of our carbines, and there seemed to engage in a parley. Comstock, who had closely watched every movement, remarked that "There's no sich good luck for us as to think them Injuns mean to give it up so. Six hundred red devils ain't agoin' to let fifty men stop them from gettin' at the coffee and sugar that is in these wagons. And they ain't agoin' to be satisfied until they get some of our scalps to pay for the bucks we popped out of their saddles a bit ago.". . .

But little time was spent at the parley. Again the entire band of warriors, except those already disabled, prepared to renew the attack, and advanced as before—this time, however, with greater caution, evidently desiring to avoid a reception similar to the first. When sufficiently near to the troops the Indians developed their new plan of attack. It was not to advance *en masse*, as before, but fight as individuals, each warrior selecting his own time and method of attack. This is the habitual manner of fighting among all Indians of the Plains, and is termed "circling." First the chiefs led off, followed at regular intervals by the warriors, until the entire six or seven hundred were to be seen riding in single file as rapidly as their fleet-footed ponies could carry them. Preserving this order, and keeping up their savage chorus of yells, war-whoops, and taunting epithets, this long line of mounted barbarians was guided in such manner as to envelop the train and escort, and make the latter appear like a small circle within a larger one.

The Indians gradually contracted their circle, although maintaining the full speed of their ponies, until sufficiently close to open fire upon the soldiers. At first the shots were scattering and wide of their mark; but, emboldened by the silence of their few but determined opponents, they rode nearer and fought with greater impetuosity. Forced now to defend themselves to the uttermost, the cavalrymen opened fire from their carbines, with most gratifying results. The Indians, however, moving at such a rapid gait and in single file, presented a most uncertain target. To add to this uncertainty, the savages availed themselves of their superior— almost marvellous—powers of horsemanship. Throwing them-

selves upon the sides of their well-trained ponies, they left no
part of their persons exposed to the aim of the troopers except the head and one foot, and in this posture they were
able to aim the weapons either over or under the necks of
their ponies, thus using the bodies of the latter as an effective shield against the bullets of their adversaries.

At no time were the Indians able to force the train and its
escort to come to a halt. The march was continued at an uninterrupted gait. This successful defence against the Indians
was in a great measure due to the presence of the wagons,
which, arranged in the order described, formed a complete
barrier to the charges and assaults of the savages; and, as a
last resort, the wagons could have been halted and used as
a breastwork, behind which the cavalry, dismounted, would
have been almost invincible against their more numerous
enemies. There is nothing an Indian dislikes more in warfare
than to attack a foe, however weak, behind breastworks of
any kind. Any contrivance which is an obstacle to his pony
is a most serious obstacle to the warrior.

The attack of the Indians, aggravated by their losses in
warriors and ponies, as many of the latter had been shot
down, was continued without cessation for three hours. The
supply of ammunition of the cavalry was running low. The
"fourth troopers," who had remained in charge of the led
horses between the two columns of wagons, were now replaced from the skirmishers, and the former were added to
the list of active combatants. If the Indians should maintain
the fight much longer, there was serious ground for apprehension regarding the limited supply of ammunition.

If only night or reinforcements would come! was the
prayerful hope of those who contended so gallantly against
such heavy odds. . . . The Indians, although apparently
turning all their attention to the little band inside, had
omitted no precaution to guard against interference from
outside parties. In this instance, perhaps, they were more than
ordinarily watchful, and had posted some of their keen-eyed
warriors on the high line of bluffs which ran almost parallel
to the trail over which the combatants moved. . . .

[Suddenly] what appeared to be a mere stationary dark line

drawn upon the green surface of the plain, developed itself to the searching eyes of the red man into a column of cavalry moving at a rapid gait toward the very point they were then occupying. . . .

Unwilling to incur this new risk, and seeing no prospect of overcoming their present adversaries by a sudden or combined dash, the chiefs decided to withdraw from the attack, and make their escape while the advantage was yet in their favor.

The surprise of the cavalrymen may be imagined at seeing the Indians, after pouring a shower of bullets and arrows into the train, withdraw to the bluffs, and immediately after continue their retreat until lost to view.

This victory for the troopers, although so unexpected, was none the less welcome. The Indians contrived to carry away with them their killed and wounded. Five of their bravest warriors were known to have been sent to the happy hunting-ground, while the list of their wounded was much larger.

After the Indians had withdrawn and left the cavalrymen masters of the field, our wounded, of whom there were comparatively few, received every possible care and attention. Those of the detachment who had escaped unharmed were busily engaged in exchanging congratulations and relating incidents of the fight. . . .

Among the other measures adopted for carrying the war to our enemy's doors, and in a manner "fight the devil with fire," was the employment of Indian allies. These were to be procured from the "reservation Indians," tribes who, from engaging in long and devastating wars with the whites and with other hostile bands, had become so reduced in power as to be glad to avail themselves of the protection and means of subsistence offered by the reservation plan. These tribes were most generally the objects of hatred in the eyes of their more powerful and independent neighbors of the Plains, and the latter, when making their raids and bloody incursions upon the white settlements of the frontiers, did not hesitate to visit their wrath equally upon whites and reservation Indians. To these smaller tribes it was a welcome opportunity to be permitted to ally themselves to the forces of the Government, and endeavor to obtain that satisfaction which acting alone they were powerless to secure. The tribes against which we proposed to operate during the approaching campaign had been particularly cruel and relentless in their wanton attacks upon the Osages and Kaws, two tribes living peaceably and contentedly on well-chosen reservations in southwestern Kansas and the northern portion of the Indian Territory. No assistance in fighting the hostile tribes was desired, but it was believed, and correctly too, that in finding the enemy and in discovering the location of his winter hiding-places, the experience and natural tact and cunning of the Indians would be a powerful auxiliary if we could enlist them in our cause. An officer was sent to the village of the Osages to negotiate with the head chiefs, and was successful in his mission, returning with a delegation consisting of the second chief in rank of the Osage tribe, named "Little Beaver," "Hard Rope," the counsellor or wise man of his people, and eleven warriors, with an interpreter. In addition to the monthly rate of compensation which the Government agreed to give them, they were also to be armed, clothed, and mounted at Government expense.

*   *   *

The United States made use of Indian allies in the Sioux War of 1875-1876, the conflict in which Custer lost his life. Though the Indians were forced to surrender late in October of 1876, they dealt the Americans a number of crippling blows in the course of the struggle. One of these was in the Battle of the Rosebud (June 17, 1876), in which the Dakota chieftain, Crazy Horse, administered General George Crook what Captain Anson Mills, one of his associates, called "a crashing defeat." The details of this engagement and the role of the Crow Indians, as allies of the Federal troops, were reported in War-Path and Bivouac *by John F. Finerty, an Irish-born member of the editorial staff of* The Chicago Times, *who accompanied Cook's men into battle.*

At six o'clock a picket galloped into camp to notify Crook that his allies were in sight.

Then we saw a grove of spears and a crowd of ponies

upon the northern heights, and there broke upon the air a fierce, savage whoop. The Crows had come in sight of our camp, and this was their mode of announcing their satisfaction. We went down to the creek to meet them, and a picturesque tribe they were. Their horses—nearly every man had an extra pony—were little beauties, and neighed shrilly at their American brethren, who, unused to Indians, kicked, plunged and reared in a manner that threatened a general stampede. "How! How!" the Crows shouted to us, one by one, as they filed past.

The head sachems were "Old Crow," "Medicine Crow," "Feather Head," and "Good Heart," all deadly enemies of the Sioux. Each man wore a gaily colored mantle, handsome leggings, eagle feathers, and elaborately worked moccasins. In addition to their carbines and spears, they carried the primeval bow and arrow. Their hair was long, but gracefully tied up and gorgeously plumed. . . .

Quick as lightning they gained the center of our camp, dismounted, watered and lariated their ponies, constructed their "tepees," or "lodges," and, like magic, the Indian village arose in our midst. Fires were lighted without delay, and the Crows were soon devouring their evening meal of dried bear's meat and black-tailed deer. . . .

That night an immense fire was kindled near Crook's tents, and there all the chiefs of both tribes, together with our commanding officers, held "a big talk." Louis Richard acted as interpreter, and had a hard time of it, having to translate in three or four languages. A quarter of an hour intervened between each sentence. The chiefs squatted on their heels according to their ancient custom, and passed the long pipe from man to man. Crook stood in the circle, with his hands in his pockets, looking half bored, half happy. . . .

"Old Crow," the greatest chief of the Crow nation, made the only consecutive speech of the night, and it was a short one. Translated, it was as follows: "The great white chief will hear his Indian brother. These are our lands by inheritance. The Great Spirit gave them to our fathers, but the Sioux stole them from us. They hunt upon our mountains. They fish in our streams. They have stolen our horses. They have mur-

dered our squaws, our children. What white man has done
these things to us? The face of the Sioux is red, but his
heart is black. But the heart of the pale face has ever been
red to the Crow. ['Ugh!' 'Ugh!' 'Hey!'] The scalp of no
white man hangs in our lodges. They are thick as grass in the
wigwams of the Sioux. ['Ugh!'] The great white chief will
lead us against no other tribe of red men. Our war is with
the Sioux and only them. We want back our lands. We want
their women for our slaves—to work for us as our women
have had to work for them. We want their horses for our
young men, and their mules for our squaws. The Sioux have
trampled upon our hearts. We shall spit upon their scalps.
['Ugh!' 'Hey!' and terrific yelling.] The great white chief
sees that my young men have come to fight. No Sioux shall
see their backs. Where the white warrior goes there shall we
be also. It is good. Is my brother content?"

The chief and Crook shook hands amid a storm of "Ughs"
and yells.

All the red men then left the council fire and went to their
villages, where they put on their warpaint and made night
hideous with a war-dance and barbarous music. . . .

Crook was bristling for a fight. The Sioux were said to be
encamped on the Rosebud, near the Yellowstone river, holding Gibbon at bay. "They are numerous as grass," was the
definite Crow manner of stating the strength of the enemy. . . .

At about 8 o'clock, we halted in a valley, very similar in
formation to the one in which we had pitched our camp
the preceding night. Rosebud stream, indicated by the thick
growth of wild roses, or sweet brier, from which its name is
derived, flowed sluggishly through it, dividing it from south
to north into two almost equal parts. . . .

At 8:30 o'clock, without any warning, we heard a few shots
from behind the bluffs to the north. "They are shooting
buffalo over there," said the Captain. Very soon we began
to know, by the alternate rise and fall of the reports, that
the shots were not all fired in one direction. Hardly had we
reached this conclusion, . . . when the flying Crow and
Snake scouts, utterly panic stricken, came into camp shout-

ing at the top of their voices, "Heap Sioux! heap Sioux!" gesticulating wildly in the direction of the bluffs which they had abandoned in such haste. All looked in that direction, and there, sure enough, were the Sioux in goodly numbers, and in loose, but formidable, array. . . .

Mills immediately swung his fine battalion, consisting of Troops A, E, I and M, by the right into line, and, rising in his stirrups, shouted "Charge!" Forward we went at our best pace, to reach the crest occupied by the enemy, who, meanwhile, were not idle, for men and horses rolled over pretty rapidly as we began the ascent. Many horses, owing to the rugged nature of the ground, fell upon their riders without receiving a wound. We went like a storm, and the Indians waited for us until we were within fifty paces. We were going too rapidly to use our carbines, but several of the men fired their revolvers, with what effect I could neither then, nor afterward, determine, for all passed "like a flash of lightning, or a dream." I remember, though, that our men broke into a mad cheer as the Sioux, unable to face that impetuous line of the warriors of the superior race, broke and fled, with what white men would consider undignified speed. . . .

The Sioux, having rallied on the second line of heights, became bold and impudent again. They rode up and down rapidly, sometimes wheeling in circles, slapping an indelicate portion of their persons at us, and beckoning us to come on. One chief, probably the late lamented Crazy Horse, directed their movements by signals made with a pocket mirror or some other reflector. Under Crook's orders, our whole line remounted, and, after another rapid charge, we became masters of the second crest. When we got there, another just like it rose on the other side of the valley. There, too, were the savages, as fresh, apparently, as ever. We dismounted accordingly, and the firing began again. . . .

Just then a tremendous yell arose behind us, and along through the intervals of our battalions, came the tumultuous array of the Crow and Shoshone Indians, rallied and led back to action by Maj. George M. Randall and Lieut. John G. Bourke, of General Crook's staff. . . .

The two bodies of savages, all stripped to the breech-clout, moccasins and war bonnet, came together in the trough of the valley, the Sioux having descended to meet our allies with right good will. . . .

The wild foemen, covering themselves with their horses, while going at full speed, blazed away rapidly. Our regulars did not fire because it would have been sure death to some of the friendly Indians, who were barely distinguishable by a red badge which they carried. Horses fell dead by the score—they were heaped there when the fight closed—but, strange to relate, the casualties among the warriors, including both sides, did not certainly exceed five and twenty. . . .

Finally the Sioux on the right, hearing the yelping and firing of the rival tribes, came up in great numbers, and our Indians, carefully picking up their wounded, and making their uninjured horses carry double, began to draw off in good order. . . .

As the day advanced, General Crook became tired of the indecisiveness of the action, and resolved to bring matters to a crisis. He rode up to . . . the officers of Mills' battalion . . . and said, in effect, "It is time to stop this skirmishing. . . . You must take your battalion and go for their village away down the cañon." . . . It was originally his intention to fling his whole force on the Indian village, and win or lose all by a single blow. The fall of Guy V. Henry, early in the fight on the left, had a bad effect upon the soldiers, . . . and a temporary success raised the spirits of the Indians and enabled them to keep our left wing in check sufficiently long to allow the savages to effect the safe retreat of their village to the valley of the Little Big Horn. Had Crook's original plan been carried out to the letter, our whole force—about 1,100 men—would have been in the hostile village at noon, and, in the light of after events, it is not improbable that all of us would have settled there permanently. Five thousand able-bodied warriors, well armed, would have given Crook all the trouble he wanted, if he had struck their village. . . . (General Custer, . . . with a force nearly equal to ours, suffered annihilation at the hands of the same enemy, about eighteen miles further westward, only eight days afterward.)

General Crook decided that evening to retire on his base of supplies—the wagon train—with his wounded, in view of the fact that his rations were almost used up, and that his ammunition had run pretty low. He was also convinced that all chance of surprising the Sioux camp was over for the present, and perhaps he felt that even if it could be surprised, his small force would be unequal to the task of carrying it by storm. The Indians had shown themselves good fighters, and he shrewdly calculated that his men had been opposed to only a part of the well-armed warriors actually in the field.

* * *

A major cause of Indian alarm, in the 1860's and 1870's, was their realization that they were being squeezed between a farmer frontier now advancing by rail from the east and a mining frontier encroaching erratically from the opposite direction. Between 1858 and 1875, miners, stimulated by the experience in California, pushed their corrosive way into the mountainous regions of Nevada and Colorado, the Pacific Northwest, Idaho, Montana, and the Black Hills of South Dakota. Everywhere mining communities, patterned on California precedent, sprang into prosperity overnight and waned as rapidly, leaving a residue of farmer settlement behind. One community which endured was Denver, founded in 1858, when a major rush was touched off in the Pike's Peak area. The cosmopolitanism of its population, like that of most mining towns, impressed Horace Greeley when he visited the new gold region in the Summer of 1859.

The first circumstance that strikes a stranger traversing this wild country is the vagrant instincts and habits of the great majority of its denizens—perhaps I should say, of the American people generally, as exhibited here. Among any ten whom you successively meet, there will be natives of New England, New York, Pennsylvania, Virginia or Georgia, Ohio or Indiana, Kentucky or Missouri, France, Germany, and perhaps Ireland. But, worse than this; you cannot enter a circle of a dozen persons of whom at least three will not have spent some years in California, two or three have made claims and built cabins in Kansas or Nebraska, and at least one spent a year or so in Texas. Boston, New York, Philadelphia, New Orleans, St. Louis, Cincinnati, have all contributed their quota toward peopling the new gold region. The next man you meet driving an ox-team, and white as a miller with dust, is probably an ex-banker or doctor, a broken merchant or manufacturer from the old states, who has scraped together the candle-ends charitably or contemptuously allowed him by his creditors on settlement, and risked them on a last desperate cast of the dice by coming hither. Ex-editors, ex-printers, ex-clerks, ex-steamboat men, are here in abundance—all on the keen hunt of the gold which only a few will secure. One of the stations at which we slept on our way up—a rough tent with a cheering hope (since blasted) of a log house in the near future—was kept by an ex-lawyer of Cincinnati and his wife, an ex-actress from our New York Bowery—she being cook. Omnibus-drivers from Broadway repeatedly handled the ribbons; ex-border ruffians from civilized Kansas—some of them of unblessed memory —were encountered on our way, at intervals none too long. All these, blended with veteran Mountain men, Indians of all grades from the tamest to the wildest, half-breeds, French trappers and *voyageurs* (who have generally two or three Indian wives apiece) and an occasional negro, compose a medley such as hardly another region can parallel. . . .

The old mountaineers form a caste by themselves, and they prize the distinction. Some of them are Frenchmen, or Franco-Americans, who have been trapping or trading in and around these mountains for a quarter of a century, have wives and children here, and here expect to live and die. Some of these have accumulated property and cash to the value of two hundred thousand dollars, which amount will not easily be reduced, as they are frugal in everything (liquor sometimes excepted), spend but a pittance on the clothing of their families, trust little, keep small stocks of goods, and sell at large profits. Others came years ago from the states, some of them on account each of a "difficulty" wherein they severally killed or savagely maimed their respective antagonists under circumstances on which the law refuses to look leniently;

whence their pilgrimage to and prolonged sojourn here, despite enticing placards offering five hundred dollars or perhaps one thousand dollars for their safe return to the places that knew them once, but shall know them no more. This class is not numerous, but is more influential than it should be in giving tone to the society of which its members form a part. Prone to deep drinking, soured in temper, always armed, bristling at a word, ready with the rifle, revolver or bowie-knife, they give law and set fashions which, in a country where the regular administration of justice is yet a matter of prophecy, it seems difficult to overrule or disregard. I apprehend that there have been during my two weeks sojourn, more brawls, more fights, more pistol-shots with criminal intent in this log city of one hundred and fifty dwellings, not three-fourths completed nor two-thirds inhabited, nor one-third fit to be, than in any community of no greater numbers on earth. This will be changed in time— I trust within a year, for the empty houses are steadily finding tenants from the two streams of emigration rolling in daily up the Platte on the one hand, down Cherry Creek on the other, including some scores of women and children, who generally stop here, as all of them should; for life in the mountains is yet horribly rough. Public religious worship, a regular mail and other civilizing influences, are being established; there is a gleam of hope that the Arapahoes—who have made the last two or three nights indescribably hideous by their infernal war-whoops, songs and dances—will at last clear out on the foray against the Utes they have so long threatened, diminishing largely the aggregate of drunkenness and riot, and justifying expectations of comparative peace.

*　　*　　*

Virginia City, one of the West's most notorious mining centers, was threatening to become "respectable" when it was visited by Charles W. Dilke, a young Englishman who had embarked on a trip around the world upon graduating from Cambridge University in 1866. Virginia City came into being in 1859, when prospectors discovered the Comstock Lode in the Washoe District of western Nevada. Precious metal valued at more than $15,000,000 was taken from the area in

the next four years. Dilke described his sojourn there in his
Greater Britain, *published in 1869.*

"Guess the governor's consid'rable skeert."

"You bet, he's mad."

My sitting down to breakfast at the same small table seemed
to end the talk; but I had not been out West for nothing,
so explaining that I was only four hours in Virginia City, I
inquired what had occurred to fill the governor of Nevada
with vexation and alarm.

"D'you tell now! only four hours in this great young city.
Wall, guess it's a bully business. You see, some time back
the governor pardoned a road agent after the citizens had
voted him a rope. Yes, sir! But that ain't all: yesterday, cuss
me if he didn't refuse ter pardon one of the boys who had
jess shot another in play like. Guess he thinks hisself some
pumpkins." I duly expressed my horror, and my informant
went on: "Wall, guess the citizens paid him off purty slick.
They jess sent him a short thick bit of rope with a label
'For his Excellency.' You bet ef he ain't mad—you bet! . . .

To see Virginia City and Carson, since I first heard their
fame in New York, had been with me a passion, but the
deed thus told me in the dining-room of the "Empire"
Hotel was worthy a place in the annals of "Washoe." Under
its former name, the chief town of Nevada was ranked . . .
the "cussedest" town in the States, its citizens expecting a
"dead man for breakfast" every day. . . . All the talk of
Nevada reformation applies only to the surface signs: when
a miner tells you that Washoe is turning pious, and that he
intends shortly to "vamose," he means that . . . Virginia
City has passed through the second period—that of "vigilance
committees" and "historic trees"—and is entering the third,
the stage of churches and "city officers," or police.

The population is still a shifting one. A by-law of the
municipality tells us that the "permanent population" con-
sists of those who reside more than a month within the city.
At this moment the miners are pouring into Washoe from
north and south and east, from Montana, from Arizona, and
from Utah, coming to the gayeties of the largest mining city

to spend their money during the fierce short winter. . . .

Every other house is a restaurant, a drinking-shop, a gaming-hell, or worse. With no one to make beds, to mend clothes, to cook food—with no house, no home—men are almost certain to drink and gamble. The Washoe bar-rooms are the most brilliant in the States: as we drove in . . . at 3 A.M., there was blaze enough for us to see from the frozen street the portrait of Lola Montez, Ada Menken, Heenan, and the other Californian celebrities with which the bar-rooms were adorned.

Although "petticoats," even Chinese, are scarce, dancing was going on in every house; but there is a rule in miners' balls that prevents all difficulties arising from an over-supply of men: every one who has a patch on the rear portion of his breeches does duty for a lady in the dance, and as gentlemen are forced by the custom of the place to treat their partners at the bar, patches are popular.

As I sat at dinner in a miner's restaurant, my opposite neighbor, finding that I was not long from England, informed me he was "the independent editor of the Nevada Union Gazette.". . . When we parted, he gave me a copy of his paper, in which I found that he called a rival editor "a walking whisky-bottle" and "a Fenian imp.". . . As for the . . . assertion in the "editorial," it was not a wild one, seeing that Virginia City has five hundred whisky-shops for a population of ten thousand. Artemus Ward said of Virginia City, in a farewell speech to the inhabitants that should have been published in his works: "I never, gentlemen, was in a city where I was treated so *well*, nor, I will add, so *often*." Through every open door the diggers can be seen tossing the whisky down their throats with a scowl of resolve, as though they were committing suicide—which, indeed, except in the point of speed, is probably the case.

*   *   *

The railroads, pushing westward from the Missouri, made possible the use of the West as a free highway and pasture for the Cattle Kingdom, which exploited the grassy plains of the public domain between 1867 and 1885. By the late

1860's, cheap Texas cattle were being driven to rail heads in Kansas and shipped from there to urban markets farther east. As the railroads built westward, bringing farmers in their wake, the great cattle trails also moved west; and cow towns like Abilene gave way to Dodge City, Ogallala, and Cheyenne. In the twenty years between 1865 and 1885, some five and a half million cattle were driven north from Texas, many of them to ranches on the northern plains where they were pastured and fattened before shipment to market. The drive of Texas long-horns northward up the trails became one of the storied features of the frontier and made the cowboy the most traditional, if not the most prevalent, personality of the American West. Life on the cattle trail was recalled by E. C. Abbott, who, as a young man, participated in the long drives of the early 1880's.

About '74-'75 the trail quit [Abilene] and moved west, on account of the country getting settled up; and after that the big cowtowns were Caldwell and Ellsworth and Dodge City, Kansas, and Ogallala, Nebraska. By 1880 Texas cattle had got as far north as Miles City, Montana, and Texas cowboys with them. The name cowpuncher came in about this time, when they got to shipping a lot of cattle on the railroad. Men would go along the train with a prod pole and punch up cattle that got down in the cars, and that was how it began. It caught on, and we were all cowpunchers on the northern range, till the close of range work. . . .

There were worlds of cattle in Texas after the Civil War. . . . By the time the war was over they was down to four dollars a head—when you could find a buyer. Here was all these cheap long-horned steers overrunning Texas; here was the rest of the country crying for beef—and no railroads to get them out. So they trailed them out, across hundreds of miles of wild country that was thick with Indians. In 1866 the first Texas herds crossed Red River. In 1867 the town of Abilene was founded at the end of the Kansas Pacific Railroad and that was when the trail really started. From that time on, big drives were made every year, and the cowboy was born. . . .

Those first trail outfits in the seventies were sure tough. . . .

They had very little grub and they usually run out of that and lived on straight beef; they had only three or four horses to the man, mostly with sore backs, because old time saddle eat both ways, the horse's back and the cowboy's pistol pocket; they had no tents, no tarps, and damn few slickers. They never kicked, because those boys was raised under just the same conditions as there was on the trail— corn meal and bacon for grub, dirt floors in the houses, and no luxuries. In the early days in Texas, in the sixties, when they gathered their cattle, they used to pack what they needed on a horse and go out for weeks, on a cow-hunt, they called it then. That was before the name roundup was invented, and before they had anything so civilized as mess wagons. . . .

Most all of them were Southerners, and they were a wild, reckless bunch. For dress they wore wide-brimmed beaver hats, black or brown with a low crown, fancy shirts, high-heeled boots, and sometimes a vest. Their clothes and saddles were all homemade. Most of them had an army coat with cape which was slicker and blanket too. Lay on your saddle blanket and cover up with a coat was about the only bed used on the Texas trail at first. . . .

As the business grew, great changes took place in their style of dress. . . . In place of the low-crowned hat of the seventies we had a high-crowned white Stetson hat, fancy shirts with pockets, and striped or checkered California pants made in Oregon City, the best pants ever made to ride in. Slickers came in too. In winter we had nice cloth overcoats with beaver collars and cuffs. The old twelve-inch-barrel Colt pistol was cut down to a six- and seven-and-a-half-inch barrel, with black rubber, ivory, or pearl handle. The old big roweled spurs with bells give place to hand-forged silver inlaid spurs with droop shanks and small rowels, and with that you had the cowpuncher of the eighties when he was in his glory.

In person the cowboys were mostly medium-sized men, as a heavy man was hard on horses, quick and wiry, and as a rule very good-natured; in fact it did not pay to be anything else. In character their like never was or will be again. They were intensely loyal to the outfit they were working for and

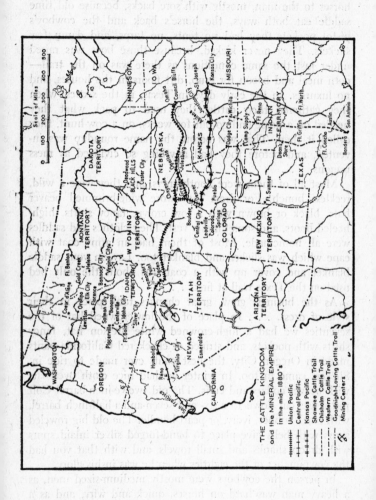

THE CATTLE KINGDOM and the MINERAL EMPIRE
in the mid–1880's

++++++ Union Pacific
+++++ Central Pacific
++++ Kansas Pacific
····· Shawnee Cattle Trail
- - - Chisholm Cattle Trail
-·-·- Western Cattle Trail
---·--- Goodnight-Loving Cattle Trail
✦ Mining Centers

would fight to the death for it. They would follow their wagon boss through hell and never complain. I have seen them ride into camp after two days and nights on herd, lay down on their saddle blankets in the rain, and sleep like dead men, then get up laughing and joking about some good time they had had in Ogallala or Dodge City. Living that kind of a life, they were bound to be wild and brave. . . .

[In 1883] I hired out in Texas to the FUF outfit, that was run by some people from New England, to take another herd up the trail. And that was the time I went all the way up to the Yellowstone River in Montana, which was the goal of every cowpuncher's ambition in the eighties. They all wanted to get to the Yellowstone.

We started out the tenth day of April, 1883, and we turned them loose on Armell's Creek, near Forsyth, Montana, in October. We put up that herd near San Antone. The trail outfit was hired there, and the different ranches was bringing the cattle in to us in little bunches, and we received them and road-branded them. . . .

One night at sundown, after we had been working the cattle in the brush all day, we came to a little open prairie just about big enough to bed down the herd. I tied my night horse to the wagon, took off my chaps and laid down on them, pulled my slicker over me, and went to sleep. About nine o'clock a clap of thunder woke me up, and somebody hollered: "They're running." I grabbed my hat and jumped for my horse, forgetting to put on my chaps, and I spent half the night chasing the cattle through that thorny brush. When daylight come and we got them all together, we hadn't lost a head. But I was a bloody sight. I had a big hole in my forehead, and my face was all over blood, my hands was cut to pieces—because I'd left my gloves in my chaps pocket— and my knees was the worst of all. I was picking thorns out of them all the way to Kansas. . . .

In the eighties, conditions on the trail were a whole lot better than they were in the seventies. Someone had invented mess boxes to set up in the hind end of the wagon; they had four-horse teams to pull it, lots of grub, and from six to eight horses for each man to ride; and the saddles had improved.

When I was on the trail in '83, we didn't have hardly a sore-backed horse all the way up to Montana, and the trail bosses had got the handling of a herd down to a science.

After some experience in the business, they found that about 2,000 head on an average was the best number in a herd. After you crossed Red River and got out on the open plains, it was sure a pretty sight to see them strung our [out] for almost a mile, the sun flashing on their horns. At noon you would see the men throw them off the trail, and half the crew would go to dinner while the other half would graze them onto water. No orders were given; every man knew his place and what to do. The left point, right swing, left flank, and right drag would go into dinner together. The first men off would eat in a hurry, catch up fresh horses, and go out on a lope to the herd. It sure looks good, when you are on herd and hungry, to see the relief come out on a lope.

Eleven men made the average crew with a trail herd. The two men in the lead were called the point men, and then as the herd strung out there would be two men behind them on the swing, two on the flank, and the two drag drivers in the rear. With the cook and horse wrangler and boss, that made eleven. The poorest men always worked with the drags, because a good hand wouldn't stand for it. I have seen them come off herd with the dust half an inch deep on their hats and thick as fur in their eyebrows and mustaches, and if they shook their head or you tapped their cheek, it would fall off them in showers. That dust was the reason a good man wouldn't work back there, and if they hired out to a trail outfit and were put with the drags, they would go to the boss and ask for their time. But the rest of them were pretty nearly as bad off when they were on the side away from the wind. They would go to the water barrel at the end of the day and rinse their mouths and cough and spit and bring up that black stuff out of their throats. But you couldn't get it up out of your lungs.

Going into a new country, the trail boss had to ride his tail off hunting for water. But he would come back to the wagon at night. Lots of times he would ride up on a little knoll and signal to the point—water this way, or water that way. And that is when you will see some trail work, when they are going to turn the herd. If they're going to turn to the right the man on the right point will drop back, and the man on left point will go ahead and start pushing them over, and the men behind can tell from their movements what they want to do. By watching and cutting the curve, you can save the drags two or three hundred yards. It's the drags you have to protect—they are the weak and sore-footed cattle—and that's what counts in the management of a herd.

There is quite an art, too, to watering a herd. You bring them up and spread them out along the bank, with the lead cattle headed downstream. The leads get there first, and of course they drink clear water, and as the drags keep coming in they get clear water, too, because they are upstream. . . .

They used to have some terrible storms on the North and South Platte. The year before this, in '82, I was in one that killed fourteen head of cattle and six or seven horses and two men, on the different herds. . . .

But . . . I believe the worst hardship we had on the trail was loss of sleep. . . . Our day wouldn't end till about nine o'clock, when we grazed the herd onto the bed ground. And after that every man in the outfit except the boss and horse wrangler and cook would have to stand two hours' night guard. Suppose my guard was twelve to two. I would stake my night horse, unroll my bed, pull off my boots, and crawl in at nine, get about three hours sleep, and then ride two hours. Then I would come off guard and get to sleep another hour and a half, till the cook yelled, "Roll out," at half past three. So I would get maybe five hours' sleep when the weather was nice and everything smooth and pretty, with cowboys singing under the stars. If it wasn't so nice, you'd be lucky to sleep an hour. But the wagon rolled on in the morning just the same.

That night guard got to be part of our lives. They never had to call me. I would hear the fellow coming off herd—because laying with your ear to the ground you could hear that horse trotting a mile off—and I would jump up and put my hat and boots on and go out to meet him. We were all just the same. I remember when we got up to the mouth of the Musselshell in '84 we turned them loose, and Johnny Burgess, the trail boss, said: "We won't stand no guard tonight, boys," and it sounded good. But every man in that outfit woke when his time to go on guard came, and looked around and wanted to know why they didn't call him.

* * *

Even before farmer settlement and state quarantine laws curtailed the "long drive," cattlemen were grazing large herds on the free grass of the Plains. Cattle were cheap, land was abundant, and profits were high, as ranchers appropriated broad tracts of open range, their boundaries defined and respected only by traditional "cow custom." A ranch headquarters was built near the center of such tracts; and riders, stationed in "cow camps" at its borders, kept the cattle within the limits of their own range. Men and capital, sometimes mobilized in large corporations, poured in, both from the East and from Europe, to take advantage of this new-found bonanza of the American West. Theodore Roosevelt, then in his mid-twenties, invested in ranch lands in Dakota late in 1883. In his opinion, the availability of the open range and the nature of ranch life on it fostered a kind of freedom that was peculiarly American. He described life on the cattleman's frontier in articles written for The Century Magazine *in 1888.*

The great grazing lands of the West lie in what is known as the arid belt, which stretches from British America on the north to Mexico on the south, through the middle of the United States. It includes New Mexico, part of Arizona, Colorado, Wyoming, Montana, and the western portion of Texas, Kansas, Nebraska, and Dakota. . . . The whole region is one vast stretch of grazing country, with only here and there spots of farm-land. . . . This is especially true of the northern portion of the region, which comprises the basin of the Upper Missouri and with which alone I am familiar. Here there are no fences to speak of, and all the land north of the Black Hills and the Big Horn Mountains and between the Rockies and the Dakota wheat-fields might be spoken of as one gigantic, unbroken pasture, where cowboys and branding-irons take the place of fences. . . .

The high plains of the Upper Missouri and its tributary rivers were first opened, and are still held, by the stockmen, and the whole civilization of the region has received the stamp of their marked and individual characteristics. They were from the South, not from the East, although many men from the latter region came out along the great transcontinental railway lines and joined them in their northern migration. . . .

When the northern plains began to be settled, . . . a ranch would at first be absolutely alone in the wilderness, but others of the same sort were sure soon to be established within twenty or thirty miles on one side or the other. . . .

By degrees the country becomes what in a stock-raising region passes for well settled. In addition to the great ranches smaller ones are established, with a few hundred, or even a few score, head of cattle apiece; and now and then miserable farmers straggle in to fight a losing and desperate battle with drought, cold, and grasshoppers. . . .

Cattle-ranching can only be carried on in its present form while the population is scanty; and so in stock-raising regions, pure and simple, there are usually few towns, and these are almost always at the shipping points for cattle. . . .

A town in the cattle country, when for some cause it is thronged with men from the neighborhood round about, always presents a picturesque sight on the wooden sidewalks of the broad, dusty streets. . . . Singly, or in twos or threes, . . . [cowboys] gallop their wiry little horses down the street, their lithe, supple figures erect or swaying slightly as they sit loosely in the saddle. . . . Their appearance is striking . . . and picturesque too, with their jingling spurs, the big revolvers stuck in their belts, and bright silk handkerchiefs knotted loosely round their necks over the open collars of the flannel shirts. When drunk on the villainous whisky of the frontier towns, they cut mad antics, riding their horses into the saloons, firing their pistols right and left, from boisterous lightheartedness rather than from any viciousness, and indulging too often in deadly shooting affrays, brought on either by the accidental contact of the moment or on account of some long-standing grudge, or perhaps because of bad blood between two ranches or localities; but except while on such sprees they are quiet, rather self-contained men. . . .

A stranger in the North-western cattle country is especially
struck by the resemblance the settlers show in their pursuits
and habits to the Southern people. Nebraska and Dakota, east
of the Missouri, resemble Minnesota and Iowa and the States
farther east, but Montana and the Dakota cow country show
more kinship with Texas; for while elsewhere in America settlement has advanced along the parallels of latitude, on the
great plains it has followed the meridians of longitude and
has gone northerly rather than westerly. The business is carried
on as it is in the South. The rough-rider of the plains, the hero
of rope and revolver, is first cousin to the backwoodsman of
the southern Alleghanies, the man of the ax and the rifle; he is
only a unique offshoot of the frontier stock of the Southwest. . . .

The rope, whether leather lariat or made of grass, is the one
essential feature of every cowboy's equipment. Loosely coiled,
it hangs from the horn or is tied to one side of the saddle in
front of the thigh, and is used for every conceivable emer-
gency, a twist being taken round the stout saddle-horn the
second the noose settles over the neck or around the legs of a
chased animal. In helping pull a wagon up a steep pitch, in
dragging an animal by the horns out of a bog-hole, in hauling
up logs for the fire, and in a hundred other ways aside from its
legitimate purpose, the rope is of invaluable service, and
dexterity with it is prized almost or quite as highly as good
horsemanship, and is much rarer. Once a cowboy is a good
roper and rider, the only other accomplishment he values is
skill with his great army revolver, it being taken for granted
that he is already a thorough plainsman and has long mas-
tered the details of cattle-work; for the best roper and rider
alive is of little use unless he is hardworking, honest, keenly
alive to his employer's interest, and very careful in the management of the cattle. . . .

All cattle are branded, usually on the hip, shoulder, and
side, or on any one of them, with letters, numbers, or figures,
in every combination, the outfit being known by its brand.
Near me, for instance, are the Three Sevens, the Thistle, the
Bellows, the OX, the VI., the Seventy-six Bar ($\underline{76}$), and the
Quarter Circle Diamond ($\Diamond$) outfits. The dew-lap and the

ears may also be cut, notched, or slit. All brands are registered, and are thus protected against imitators, any man tampering with them being punished as severely as possible. Unbranded animals are called *mavericks*. . . .

In our northern country we have "free grass"; that is, the stockmen rarely own more than small portions of the land over which their cattle range, the bulk of it being unsurveyed and still the property of the National Government—for the latter refuses to sell the soil except in small lots, acting on the wise principle of distributing it among as many owners as possible. Here and there some ranchman has acquired title to narrow strips of territory peculiarly valuable as giving water-right; but the amount of land thus occupied is small with us,—although the reverse is the case farther south,—and there is practically no fencing to speak of. As a consequence, the land is one vast pasture, and the man who overstocks his own range damages his neighbors as much as himself. These huge northern pastures are too dry and the soil too poor to be used for agriculture until the rich, wet lands to the east and west are occupied; and at present we have little fear from grangers. Of course, in the end much of the ground will be taken up for small farms, but the farmers that so far have come in have absolutely failed to make even a living, except now and then by raising a few vegetables for the use of the stockmen; and we are inclined to welcome the incoming of an occasional settler, if he is a decent man, especially as, by the laws of the Territories in which the great grazing plains lie, he is obliged to fence in his own patch of cleared ground, and we do not have to keep our cattle out of it. . . .

The great free ranches, with their barbarous, picturesque, and curiously fascinating surroundings, mark a primitive stage of existence as surely as do the great tracts of primeval forests, and like the latter must pass away before the onward march of our people; and we who have felt the charm of the life, and have exulted in its abounding vigor and its bold, restless freedom, will not only regret its passing for our own sakes only, but must also feel real sorrow that those who come after us are not to see, as we have seen, what is perhaps the pleasantest, healthiest, and most exciting phase of American existence.

* * *

*The advent of homesteaders on the Plains precipitated con-
flict between farmer and cattleman. The inevitable antagonism
between settlers and ranchers is poignantly described in Mari
Sandoz's biography of her father, Jules Ami Sandoz, who migrated from Switzerland to Nebraska at the turn of the 1880's.
In 1884 he took up land, under the homestead privilege, in
western Nebraska. Like many another small settler whose
fences cut into a range, he soon felt the hostility of the
ranch interests. The ranchers' agents often tried to run the
farmers off the land; and ranch-controlled courts frequently
made it difficult for the homesteader to get a hearing.*

July was brittle with sun. Through the noon hours grouse
squatted behind the ragged sunflowers along the soldier trail,
mouths open, wings out, tame as chickens under a Slav's table.

The drouth sucked up the water holes south of the river and
the Hunter ranch stock came in droves to the Niobrara. Any
night the wild steers might drift up on Mirage and eat out the
settlers. Shotguns boomed along the river. Jules filled several
shells with salt and laughed as the cattleman's stock retreated.

One afternoon, when he had worked a furious half hour
chopping the sod about his whips of trees and cleaning out
the tough weeds, two homeseekers stopped for their last filing
instructions. Glad of the respite, Jules squatted on the
shady side of the wagon with them and filed his gleaming hoe.

A cowboy, headed west for the upper Hunter ranch, reined
off towards the loafing settlers. His wildeyed dun side-jumped
at Jules's pile of bleaching buffalo skulls and broke away in a
run. The rider jerked the horse to his haunches, bloody froth
flying from the spade bit. Back before the settlers, he shifted
his heavy Colt, tossed a leg around the saddle horn, and rolled
a cigarette. He had been up to the tent town of Gordon, about
thirty miles away. It was going strong as a sheepman's socks.
Everything wide open; draw played in the dust of the street.
So?

Yeh, even had a resident sky pilot who organized a church
along in May, with seventy-five people scattered around his

tent, sitting on the woodpile, wagon tongues, empty whiskey
kegs, and the ground making a noise fit to stampede a herd of
longhorns clear down on the Cimarron. But the collection was
a mite disappointing, and after the praying the new congregation milled into the nearest saloon to wet their gullets and
celebrate the organization of the First Methodist Church west
of Valentine, much to the consternation of the rustling,
straight-shooting parson.

"Rustling—shooting?" Jules inquired. "Preachers steal cattle too?"

The horseman grabbed for his cigarette and laughed.

"Naw, you got the wind wrong. The parson ain't a rustler,
he's a *rustler*—works hard scratching souls together for Kingdom Come. He wouldn't chaw slow elk, starving. But he's bit
off a tough chunk—saving souls up there. They's liquor
enough running in the street of Gordon to lay anything excepting Nebraska dust."

It might be worth going up.

"Yeh, but better not tie your Sunday-school money in your
shirt tail."

"What you mean?"

The horsebacker slapped his worn chaps. "You'll lose it
when they steals your shirt, you greenhorn." Suddenly the man
leaned forward, his arms crossed on the saddle horn, his light,
sun-squinted eyes cold upon them. "But you grangers'll never
have no money. It don't never rain in this damned country
and you'll stop lead or stretch rope if you keeps shootin' cattle."

The two newcomers dropped back. Jules stood his ground
and pushed his cap away from eyes hard as the file in his
hands. Deliberately he spit upon the ground at the man's
stirrup.

"You don't run me off! I see the cattle business in hell first."

The ranch hand caressed the worn butt of his Colt absently.
"Fighting words, hoe man," he said. "But it'll be a different
tune—and you better roll up this snag of fence you got
strung around here or it won't be healthy for you."

With that he pinched the fire from his cigarette butt,
flipped it into the breaking, and sank his spurs. The clean-

limbed half mustang dropped into a short, easy lope, stringing
a trail of dust across the Flats.

Jules had no heart for more weed chopping.

After supper several neighbors came across the curled, dead
grass to sit on the piles of dirt. They talked and looked at a
newcomer's pamphlet on railroad land sales. "The New
Canaan," one called the Panhandle.

Big Andrew, who could lay twice as much sod in a day as
any other on the Flats, lifted his buffalo shoulders a little and
pulled his pipestem from his red beard. "Canaan—Promised
Land they call it?" He looked off over Jules's corn, dark,
rattling a little in the wind of dusk. "Yah, a panhandle, to the
Promised Land."

"I ain't seen much milk and honey," a truck gardener from
Missouri complained.

Jules stirred from his preoccupation. "It will come," he said.

They laughed comfortably, as men who had known each
other for a long time instead of weeks and days.

Off to the west lightning winked almost continuously, but
no one said anything about rain. "You can see the flash three
hundred miles," Jules had told them earlier in the summer.

"Three hundred miles? Who in hell you stringing now?"
they scoffed.

"Stringing—fooling? I don't fool when I talk business."

So they smoked in silence now, or picked their teeth with
grass. Before night settled they walked out to Jules's sod corn,
dark figures plodding through the late dusk. The corn was still
good, would make thirty bushels to the acre, maybe, with a
little rain. Chewing the drying leaves, they talked of the coming railroad, with markets for their produce. Then there would
be law, with probably a new county cut off from Sioux as
Cherry had been, with county officials.

"It will be important to get good ones, in sympathy with
the settlers," Jules pointed out, and told about the cowboy
that afternoon.

"Hell, no cattleman'll bother us much on the Flats. Grass
here's too short for nothing but sheep or horses."

Jules did not answer. They could not see that the Flats were almost settled. They knew nothing of the world's hunger for land. . . .

[*Increasingly, Jules became the spokesman for the settlers, and in 1890 he was arrested on charges brought by a vindictive neighbor who was supported by the cattle interests.*]

At the fall term of court, Jules faced a strange judge, entirely unprepared, a suicidal procedure, his friends and his attorneys insisted.

The trial dragged on, with the customary crowd, the customary hedging, evasion, and perjury, the customary attempts to confuse the witnesses who could not understand English well. The judge looked weary, bored, with distaste for his task sitting clearly at the corners of his lean mouth. The spectators from the Flats and the Running Water began to move their feet uneasily. Things looked bad for Jules, sitting with his fingers pressed along his nose, his rifle locked up in the sheriff's office.

When the evidence was in he asked permission to make a plea as he had always done before, and been refused. But this judge was a stranger. He looked down into the far-focused eyes of the early settler and nodded permission. The next second he was compelled to pound down the buzz of remonstrance and anticipation that swept the room like puffs of a coming storm over ripe wheat.

Jules rose to speak, his old hunting coat hanging in loose folds of buff duck about him. He opened his mouth and an eloquent flow of impassioned German, held back for two years, broke over the jury, the courtroom. From far back twitters arose, then laughs, boot stampings; even a juror or two grinned. John Maher, court reporter and newspaper correspondent, scribbled like mad.

In a minute the entire court was up, the gavel pounding before the defendant stopped. How was the court to know what was being said? He must speak English.

Jules scratched his beard. He was sorry, but he was only a poor foreigner, come to find a home in America, the land of the free. He could not express himself well in English. Was there any law forbidding his use of German?

He bowed like a pine tree and let the battle of the attorneys pass over him, waiting with a patience strange and unnatural in him. At last an interpreter was brought in and once more, Jules started, slowly, clearly, the interpreter wrinkling his brow and struggling with his words. Gradually Jules gathered speed. Suddenly he switched into French and despite the pounding gavel, and two men jerking at his sleeves, he ended in a fine bit of oratory, a plea for the settler, for protection against the cattlemen and their outside money, a plea for the little fellow in a world of powerful, selfish privilege, of gross corruption and graft, while the reporter scribbled on and the interpreter pawed his hair and sweat.

Long before Jules was through, the courtroom was in such an uproar of laughter, clapping, and cheers at the discomfiture of the officials that no one heard the end. His attorney had the good sense to ask for dismissal. The chuckling judge consented, and the doors were almost rushed from their hinges as the crowd poured out and down the street to celebrate.

The judge beckoned to Jules and spoke very sternly over his clasped hands. "See that you keep out of trouble in the future. You will never get to make another plea in this court."

Then his eyes twinkled; he gripped the early settler's hand. "Man, I never heard anything like it. Learn to do that in English and the sky's your limit."

Jules was halfway home before he remembered that he had left Henriette in town.

* * *

By the turn of the 1870's, homesteaders had begun to farm the grassy table lands that stretched from mid-Nebraska, Kansas, and the Dakotas to the first range of the Rockies. This treeless, often arid, wind-swept expanse had originally been by-passed by farmers, as an unfertile desert, fit only for the hostile, nomadic Indians of the Plains. In time, technology came to the aid of pioneers unaccustomed to a treeless frontier. Barbed wire, first sold in 1874, made up for the lack of wood, for fences; and windmills provided a means of drawing water from deep beneath the matted turf. Heavy farm machinery was now available to break the stubborn sod and to harvest the potentially abundant crops of these broad, uninterrupted acres. Migration was encouraged by the homestead legislation of the Federal Government which, as passed in 1862, offered a quarter-section free of charge, except for a small filing fee, to settlers who would live on the land for five years and meet certain conditions with respect to cultivation. Even more influential, in inducing settlement, were the promotional activities of the land-grant railroads, with lands to sell and transportation to offer. As a result, the occupation of the Plains swelled to avalanche proportions, between 1870 and 1890, as farms and cities sprang into being under the same expansive impulse that had generated the settlement of previous Wests. The letters of Howard Ruede, a young Moravian who left Bethlehem, Pennsylvania, for Kansas, in 1877, supply the details of homesteading on this sod-house frontier.

We took out homesteads directly. We might have 'filed' on the land [established a preemption claim], and that filing would have been good for 30 months, at the end of which time (or before) we could have bought the land or put a homestead on it. As it is, we must live on it five years. The first two years we live "off and on"—that is, we must sleep on it once in a while and make some improvements on it within 6 months, or it will be forfeited. It is to be our home, but we can hire out by the day or month as we like. A man here has three rights—homestead, filing and timber filing. By taking land under the first he must live on it five years, and at the end of five years of actual residence can "prove up" and get a deed. . . . The timber filing requires a man to break 10 acres the first year, which he must plant with trees 12 feet apart the second year, besides breaking an additional 10 acres. The third year he must plant these 10, and break 20, which must be planted the fourth year. Then he is entitled to an additional 160 acres. . . .

Snyder thought he could make room for us until we had a place to sleep in, so here we are fixed for a few days. This is a sod house, plastered inside. The sod wall is about 2 feet thick at the ground, and slopes off on the outside to about 14 inches at the top. The roof is composed of a ridge pole and rafters of rough split logs, on which is laid corn stalks, and on top of those are two layers of sod. The roof has a very slight pitch, for if it had more, the sod would wash off when there is a heavy rain.

Perhaps you will be interested in the way a sod house is built. Sod is the most available material, in fact, the only material the homesteader has at hand, unless he happens to be one of the fortunates who secured a creek claim with timber suitable for house logs.

Occasionally a new comer has a "bee," and the neighbors for miles around gather at his claim and put up his house in a day. Of course there is no charge for labor in such cases. The women come too, and while the men lay up the sod walls, they prepare dinner for the crowd, and have a very sociable hour at noon. A house put up in this way is very likely to settle and get out of shape, but it is seldom deserted for that reason.

The builder usually "cords up" the sods, though sometimes he crosses the layers, making the walls about two feet thick, but a little experience shows that the extra thick walls are of no real advantage. When the prairie is thoroughly soaked by rain or snow is the best time for breaking sod for building. The regulation thickness is 2½ inches, buffalo sod preferred on account of its superior toughness. The furrow slices are laid flat and as straight as a steady-walking team can be driven. These furrow slices, 12 inches wide, are cut with a sharp spade into 18-inch lengths, and carefully handled as they are laid in the wall, one length reaching across the wall, which rises rapidly even when the builders are green hands. Care must be taken to break joints and bind the corners of the house. "Seven feet to the square" is the rule, as the wall is likely to settle a good deal, especially if the sod is very wet when laid. The door and window frames are set in place first and the wall built around them. Building such a house is hard work.

When the square is reached, the crotches (forks of a tree) are set at the ends and in the middle of the house and the ridge pole—usually a single tree trunk the length of the building, but sometimes spliced—is raised to its place by sheer strength of arm, it being impossible to use any other power. Then rails are laid from the ridge log to the walls and covered with any available material—straight sorghum stalks, willow switches and straw, or any thing that will prevent the sod on the roof from falling between the rafters. From the comb of the roof to the earthen floor is usually about nine feet.

The gables are finished before the roof is put on, as in roofing the layer of sod is started at the outer edge of the wall. If the builder is able, he has sawed cottonwood rafters and a pine or cottonwood board roof covered with sod. Occasionally a sod house with a shingle roof is seen, but of course this costs more money.

At first these sod houses are unplastered, and this is thought perfectly all right, but such a house is somewhat cold in the winter, as the crevices between the sods admit some cold air; so some of the houses are plastered with a kind of "native lime," made of sand and a very sticky native clay. This plaster is very good unless it happens to get wet. In a few of the houses this plaster is whitewashed, and this helps the looks very much. Some sod houses are mighty comfortable places to go into in cold weather, and it don't take much fire to keep them warm. I will have to be contented with a very modest affair for a while, but perhaps I can improve it later. . . .

I made out an estimate of the cost of our house. This does not include what was paid for in work: Ridgepole and hauling (including two loads of firewood) $1.50; rafters and straw, 50¢; 2 lb. nails, 15¢; hinges 20¢; window 75¢; total cash paid, $4.05. Then there was $4 worth of lumber, which was paid for in work, and $1.50 for hauling it over, which, together with hauling the firewood, 50¢, makes $10.05 for a place to live in and firewood enough to last all summer. . . .

The people who live in sod houses, and, in fact, all who live under a dirt roof, are pestered with swarms of bed bugs. . . . The vermin were not brought here by the immigrants; they grew on the trees along the river and creeks before the first settlers arrived. The bugs infest the log and sod chicken coops, too, in countless thousands, or, if you wish to measure them in a spoon, you can gather them up in that way from between the sods in the wall. I have heard chicken raisers complain that their fowls are killed by the bugs getting into their ears. Whether or not that is the cause of the fowls dying, the bugs are blamed. Where the sod houses are plastered the bed bugs are not such a nuisance.

You don't have to keep a dog in order to have plenty of fleas, for they are natives too and do their best to drive out the intruding settlers. Just have a dirt floor and you have fleas, sure. They seem to spring from the dust of the earth. Coal oil and water are sometimes used to sprinkle the floor, but that abates the pest only for a short time, and oil costs 35 cents a gallon. People who have board floors are not bothered so much with these fleas.

Another nuisance here is what people call "Kansas itch," which attacks nearly everybody within a short time after arrival here; few are immune. Not all are affected alike; some scratch a few days, other are affected for months. It is not contagious—at least not all who come in contact with those suffering with it take the disease. There is only one way in which a sufferer can get relief—scratching; and that aggravates the itching and sometimes produces raw sore spots. But those are easier to heal than it is to get the disease out of your system. Change of water is sometimes given as the cause; bed bugs and fleas are sometimes blamed, but it seems as if the itch has to run its course in every case. It disappears as mysteriously as it came. . . .

The event of today was the killing of a two foot rattlesnake. . . . I heard a buzz, and, looking round, I saw a snake within six inches of my foot, and it was mad too. . . . I . . . brought the fork down with force enough to break the handle, but did not kill the snake. Then Will stuck his fork through the squirming reptile and Bub chopped its head off.

*   *   *

Prophetically, city-making was a major goal in the spectacular rush of homeseekers who stormed the Indian Territory when lands were opened to white settlement there in 1889. On the morning of April 22, tens of thousands of potential settlers lined up on the borders, awaiting the signal to advance. At the shot of a pistol, the throng poured in: on horseback, by fast driven wagons, and in railroad cars overflowing with prospective residents. When the dust had cleared away, it appeared that some 60,000 pioneers had cast their lot with

Oklahoma. It was consistent with the nation's growing urbanization in the 1880's that the settlers of Oklahoma should be as interested in founding cities as in finding farms. The details of this phenomenon of western settlement were reported by William W. Howard in Harper's Weekly *for May 18, 1889.*

In some respects the recent settlement of Oklahoma was the most remarkable thing of the present century. Unlike Rome, the city of Guthrie was built in a day. To be strictly accurate in the matter, it might be said that it was built in an afternoon. At twelve o'clock on Monday, April 22d, the resident population of Guthrie was nothing; before sundown it was at least ten thousand. In that time streets had been laid out, town lots staked off, and steps taken toward the formation of a municipal government. At twilight the camp-fires of ten thousand people gleamed on the grassy slopes of the Cimarron Valley, where, the night before, the coyote, the gray wolf, and the deer had roamed undisturbed. Never before in the history of the West has so large a number of people been concentrated in one place in so short a time. To the conservative Eastern man, who is wont to see cities grow by decades, the settlement of Guthrie was magical beyond belief; to the quick-acting resident of the West, it was merely a particularly lively townsite speculation.

The preparations for the settlement of Oklahoma had been complete, even to the slightest detail, for weeks before the opening day. The Santa Fe Railway, which runs through Oklahoma north and south, was prepared to take any number of people from its handsome station at Arkansas City, Kansas, and to deposit them in almost any part of Oklahoma as soon as the law allowed; thousands of covered wagons were gathered in camps on all sides of the new Territory waiting for the embargo to be lifted. In its picturesque aspects the rush across the border at noon on the opening day must go down in history as one of the most noteworthy events of Western civilization. At the time fixed, thousands of hungry home-seekers, who had gathered from all parts of the country, and particularly from Kansas and Missouri, were arranged in line along the border, ready to lash their horses into furious speed in the race for fertile spots in the beautiful land before them.

As the expectant home-seekers waited with restless patience, the clear, sweet notes of a cavalry bugle rose and hung a moment upon the startled air. It was noon. The last barrier of savagery in the United States was broken down. Moved by the same impulse, each driver lashed his horses furiously; each rider dug his spurs into his willing steed, and each man on foot caught his breath hard and darted forward. A cloud of dust rose where the home-seekers had stood in line, and when it had drifted away before the gentle breeze, the horses and wagons and men were tearing across the open country like fiends. The horsemen had the best of it from the start. It was a fine race for a few minutes, but soon the riders began to spread out like a fan, and by the time they had reached the horizon they were scattered about as far as eye could see. Even the fleetest of the horsemen found upon reaching their chosen localities that men in wagons and men on foot were there before them. As it was clearly impossible for a man on foot to outrun a horseman, the inference is plain that Oklahoma had been entered hours before the appointed time. Notwithstanding the assertions of the soldiers that every boomer had been driven out of Oklahoma, the fact remains that the woods along the various streams within Oklahoma were literally full of people Sunday night. Nine-tenths of these people made settlement upon the land illegally. The other tenth would have done so had there been any desirable land left to settle upon. This action on the part of the first claim-holders will cause a great deal of land litigation in the future, as it is not to be expected that the man who ran his horse at its utmost speed for ten miles only to find a settler with an ox team in quiet possession of his chosen farm will tamely submit to this plain infringement of the law.

Some of the men who started from the line on foot were quite as successful in securing desirable claims as many who rode fleet horses. They had the advantage of knowing just where their land was located. One man left the line with the others, carrying on his back a tent, a blanket, some camp dishes, an axe, and provisions for two days. He ran down the railway track for six miles, and reached his claim in just sixty minutes. Upon arriving on his land he fell down under a tree, unable to speak or see. I am glad to be able to say that his claim is one of the best in Oklahoma. The rush from the line was so impetuous that by the time the first railway train arrived from the north at twenty-five minutes past twelve o'clock, only a few of the hundreds of boomers were anywhere to be seen. The journey of this first train was well-nigh as interesting as the rush of the men in wagons. The train left Arkansas City at 8:45 o'clock in the forenoon. It consisted of an empty baggage car, which was set apart for the use of the newspaper correspondents, eight passenger coaches, and the caboose of a freight train. The coaches were so densely packed with men that not another human being could get on board. So uncomfortably crowded were they that some of the younger boomers climbed to the roofs of the cars and clung perilously to the ventilators. An adventurous person secured at great risk a seat on the forward truck of the baggage car.

In this way the train was loaded to its utmost capacity. . . .

Hardly had the train slackened its speed when the impatient boomers began to leap from the cars and run up the slope. Men jumped from the roofs of the moving cars at the risk of their lives. Some were so stunned by the fall that they could not get up for some minutes. The coaches were so crowded that many men were compelled to squeeze through the windows in order to get a fair start at the head of the crowd. Almost before the train had come to a standstill the cars were emptied. In their haste and eagerness, men fell over each other in heaps, others stumbled and fell headlong, while many ran forward so blindly and impetuously that it was not until they had passed the best of the town lots that they came to a realization of their actions. . . .

It is estimated that between six and seven thousand persons reached Guthrie by train from the north the first afternoon, and that fully three thousand came in by wagon from the north and east, and by train from Purcell on the south, thus making a total population for the first day of about ten thousand. By taking thought in the matter, three-fourths of these people had provided themselves with tents and blankets, so that even on the first night they had ample shelter from the weather. The rest of them slept the first night as best they could, with only the red earth for a pillow and the starry arch of heaven for a blanket. At dawn of Tuesday the unrefreshed home-seekers and town-site speculators arose, and began anew the location of disputed claims. The tents multiplied like mushrooms in a rain that day, and by night the building of frame houses had been begun in earnest in the new streets. The buildings were by no means elaborate, yet they were as good as the average frontier structure, and they served their purpose, which was all that was required.

On that day the trains going north were filled with returning boomers, disgusted beyond expression with the dismal outlook of the new country. Their places were taken by others who came in to see the fun, and perhaps pick up a bargain in the way of town lots or commercial speculation. . . .

During the first three days food was nearly as hard to get as water. Dusty ham sandwiches sold on the streets as high as twenty-five cents each, while in the restaurants a plate of pork and beans was valued at seventy-five cents. Few men were well enough provided with funds to buy themselves a hearty meal. One disgusted home-seeker estimated that if he ate as much as he was accustomed to eat back in Missouri his board would cost him $7.75 per day. Not being able to spend that amount of money every day, he contented himself with such stray sandwiches as were within his means. In this manner he contrived to subsist until Wednesday afternoon, when he was forced to return to civilization in southern Kansas in order to keep from starving to death.

*　　*　　*

By the time of the Oklahoma rush, the boom in Western lands had passed its peak. By 1887, capital had been invested in the area far beyond the figure on which a return could be expected. And in that year a decade of drought set in to aggravate the discomforts—hot winds, grasshoppers, and chinch bugs—which normally prevailed on the Plains. Now mortgages were foreclosed and loans curtailed. Farmers lost the equipment purchased so optimistically on credit. Farms were abandoned, as settlers back-tracked to the East; and once flourishing towns melted away. Kansas lost 180,000 people between 1887 and 1891; and 18,000 eastward-bound prairie schooners crossed the Missouri River bridge at Omaha in 1891 alone. An indigenous ballad, entitled "The Lane County Bachelor," portrayed with grim humor the plight of the homesteader in western Kansas in these distressed times.

1.

My name is Frank Bolar, 'nole bachelor I am,
I'm keepin' old bach on an elegant plan.
You'll find me out West in the County of Lane
Starving to death on a government claim;
My house it is built of the national soil,
The walls are erected according to Hoyle,
The roof has no pitch but is level and plain
And I always get wet when it happens to rain.

Chorus

But hurrah for Lane County, the land of the free,
The home of the grasshopper, bedbug, and flea,
I'll sing loud her praises and boast of her fame
While starving to death on my government claim.

2.

My clothes they are ragged, my language is rough,
My head is case-hardened, both solid and tough;
The dough it is scattered all over the room
And the floor would get scared at the sight of a broom;
My dishes are dirty and some in the bed
Covered with sorghum and government bread;
But I have a good time, and live at my ease
On common sop-sorghum, old bacon and grease.

Chorus

But hurrah for Lane County, the land of the West,
Where the farmers and laborers are always at rest,
Where you've nothing to do but sweetly remain,
And starve like a man on your government claim.

3.

How happy am I when I crawl into bed,
And a rattlesnake rattles his tail at my head,
And the gay little centipede, void of all fear,
Crawls over my pillow and into my ear,
And the nice little bedbug, so cheerful and bright,
Keeps me a scratching full half of the night,
And the gay little flea, with toes sharp as a tack,
Plays 'Why don't you catch me?' all over my back.

Chorus

But hurrah for Lane County, where blizzards arise,
Where the winds never cease and the flea never dies,
Where the sun is so hot if in it you remain
'T will burn you quite black on your government claim.

4.

How happy am I on my government claim,
Where I've nothing to lose and nothing to gain,
Nothing to eat and nothing to wear,
Nothing from nothing is honest and square.
But here I am stuck, and here I must stay,
My money's all gone and I can't get away;
There's nothing will make a man hard and profane
Like starving to death on a government claim.

Chorus

Then come to Lane County, there's room for you all,
Where the winds never cease and the rains never fall,
Come join in the chorus and boast of her fame,
While starving to death on your government claim.

5.

Now don't get discouraged, ye poor hungry men,
We're all here as free as a pig in a pen;
Just stick to your homestead and battle your fleas,
And pray to your Maker to send you a breeze.

Now a word to claim-holders who are bound for to stay:
You may chew your hard-tack 'till you're toothless and gray,
But as for me, I'll no longer remain
And starve like a dog on my government claim.

Chorus

Farewell to Lane County, farewell to the West,
I'll travel back East to the girl I love best;
I'll stop in Missouri and get me a wife,
And live on corn dodgers the rest of my life.

* * *

When the farmers looked around for the source of their difficulties, the railroads and the money interests appeared to be the culprits—the railroads for exacting monopolistic freight rates and for holding choice lands at high prices, the money interests for alleged financial manipulation which forced farmers to pay debts, incurred when prices were high, at a time when returns for farm produce were low. "There are three great crops raised in Nebraska," an agricultural editor asserted. "One is a crop of corn, one a crop of freight rates, and one a crop of interest. One is produced by farmers who by sweat and toil farm the land. The other two are produced by men who sit in their offices and behind their bank counters and farm the farmers." As Kansan William A. Peffer put it, the railroad builder "took possession of the land"; and the money changer "took possession of the farmer." Peffer was a spokesman, in the United States Senate, for the Populist Party, which like the Patrons of Husbandry (the Grangers) and the Farmers' Alliance, in earlier crises, championed the farmer's cause. Peffer formulated the farmer's argument in his book, The Farmer's Side: His Troubles and Their Remedy, *published in 1891.*

In 1862 a large area of the public land was granted by Congress to the Union Pacific Railroad Company and auxiliaries, in all amounting to some twenty-eight million acres, and the next year to other roads as much more. With these grants began a system of disposing of the public lands in immense quantities to railroad companies by name. The extent of territory given to each road was measured by a limit extending out from ten to twenty miles on either side of the line as it should be finally located, the company receiving alternate sections, leaving the other half as public lands belonging to the Government. The railroad companies at once undertook the settlement of the new region by bringing in immigrants from other parts of the world. Europe was flooded with advertising literature, portraying in glowing colors the wonderful fertility of this new unsettled region and the marvelous facilities there for acquiring wealth by early settlers. . . .

. . . Large numbers of people were attracted by the inducements offered, and in the course of a few years after the war an area . . . larger than the original thirteen States was settled and large portions of it brought under cultivation. Farms were opened, towns were built, churches and schoolhouses dotted the plains and hills, and a post-office was established within easy reach of every man's door. But in doing this it became necessary to make extended investments, both of credit and of money. The settlers were generally poor; they were offered the railroad lands at an average of about $3 an acre upon the payment of a small portion cash—10 per cent or thereabouts—the rest in ten annual payments with interest at 7 to 10 per cent, giving a mortgage to the company as security for deferred payments. In connection with this sort of railroad extension and settlement, feeding roads were projected in all directions, and the people who settled upon the lands to be supplied with the new roads were asked to assist in the projects by voting municipal bonds. This resulted in a large bonded indebtedness of the townships, counties, and cities all through the West. The price which the railroad companies fixed upon the lands had the effect in law and in fact to raise the price of the reserved Government sections to two dollars and a half an acre. The homestead law did not apply anywhere within the limits of a railroad grant. Upon the public lands outside of the railroad limits any person authorized to make a homestead entry was entitled to locate, and for a few dollars (to pay fees and necessary expenses) he could obtain a quarter section of land and make a home upon it; but it required money to buy the lands within the railroad limits either from the company or from the Government, and a good deal of money for a poor man. The only way to obtain the money was to borrow it, and as a part of this scheme of settlement a vast system of money lending had been established, with agents in every town along the lines of the new roads engaged in the business of negotiating loans, advertising their work far and wide, so that the purchasers of lands from either the railroad company or from the Government within the limits of the grants need only apply to these money lenders, and for a commission to the "middle man" could obtain money from Eastern owners in any conceivable amount. It was not long until the whole country in the region of these new roads was mortgaged. While the lands were fertile they did not produce any more than other lands of equal fertility, and they were so far away from the markets of the country that transportation ate up from 60 to 75 per cent of the value of the crops. While a good deal could be produced upon these rich acres, still the profit margin was so small that there was really but little left in the end. Where a person took up a homestead claim and raised one good crop of wheat, he was considerably ahead in the world; but where he had to pay from two and a half to three dollars an acre, borrow the money, and pay 50 per cent interest upon it, renewed every year, he had a hard road to travel; it was with difficulty that even the best of the new farmers and the most economical among them were enabled to meet their engagements and save their homes. In a large majority of cases it became necessary to borrow more money in order to meet maturing obligations. Rates of interest were exorbitant, rates of transportation on the railroads were unreasonably high, taxes were excessive, salaries of officers were established by law and were uniformly high, while there was [sic] but little property and comparatively few tax payers at that early period in the settlement, so that the burdens of taxation fell heavily upon the few who were ready to be caught by the tax gatherer. . . .

While the burdens just mentioned were increasing other forces were operating to add to the difficulties in the farmers' way. The people were rapidly taking upon themselves new obligations, while, by reason of the contraction of currency, prices of farm products fell to a very low figure—in many cases below the cost line—and in a proportionate degree taxes and debts of all kinds increased relatively. While one hundred dollars were the same on paper in 1889 that they were in 1869, yet by reason of the fall in values of products out of which debts were to be paid the dollars grew just that much larger. It required twice as many bushels of wheat or of corn or of oats, twice as many pounds of cotton or tobacco or wool to pay a debt in 1887 as it did to pay a debt of the same amount in 1867. While dollars remained the same in name, they increased 100 per cent in value when compared with the property of the farmer out of which debts were to be paid; and while a bushel of wheat or of oats or of corn was the same in weight and in measure in 1887 that it was in 1867, yet it required twice as many bushels to pay the same amount of debt. The same principle holds good in all of the different obligations for which the farmers were liable, and is applicable to the only property with which they were supplied to pay their indebtedness. It became necessary under those conditions to renew loans, pay additional commissions, contract new obligations, until today we find that fully one third of the farms of the country, especially of the western part of the country, are under mortgage. In some counties from three fourths to seven eighths of the homes of the farmers are mortgaged for more than they would sell for under the hammer.

It is said frequently that the farmer himself is to blame for all of these misfortunes. If that were true it would afford no relief, but it is not true. The farmer has been the victim of a gigantic scheme of spoliation. Never before was such a vast aggregation of brains and money brought to bear to force men into labor for the benefit of a few. The railroad companies, after obtaining grants of land with which to build their roads, not only sold the lands to settlers and took mortgages for deferred payments, but, after beginning the work of building their roads, they issued bonds and put them upon the market, doubled their capital upon paper, compelling the people who patronized the roads to pay in enhanced cost of transportation all these additional burdens.

The roads were built without any considerable amount of money upon the part of the original stockholders, and where any money had been invested in the first place, shrewd managers soon obtained control of the business and the property. So large a proportion of the public lands was taken up by these grants to corporations that there was practically very little land left for the homestead settler. It appears from an examination of the records that from the time our first land laws went into operation until the present time the amount of money received from sales of public lands does not exceed the amount of money received from customs duties on foreign goods imported into this country during the last year, while the lands granted to railroad companies directly, and to States for the purpose of building railroads indirectly, if sold at the Government price of $1.25 an acre, would be equal to three times as much as was received from sales of the public lands directly to actual settlers. The farmer was virtually compelled to do just what he has done. The railroad builder took the initiative. Close by his side was the money changer. The first took possession of the land, the other took possession of the farmer. One compelled the settler to pay the price fixed upon the railroad lands by the railroad company; the other compelled the settler on the public lands within the grant to pay the increased price, and to borrow money through him to make the payments on both. This system continued until the farmer, accommodating himself to prevailing conditions, was in the hands of his destroyers. Now we find the railroad companies capitalized for from five to eight times their assessed value, the farmer's home is mortgaged, the city lot is mortgaged, the city itself is mortgaged, the county is mortgaged, the township is mortgaged, and all to satisfy this over-reaching, soulless, merciless, conscienceless grasping of avarice. In the beginning of our history nearly all the people were farmers, and they made our laws; but as the national wealth increased they gradually dropped out and became hewers of wood and drawers of water to those that own or control large aggregations of wealth. They toiled while others took the increase; they sowed, but others reaped the harvest. It is avarice that

despoiled the farmer. Usury absorbed his substance. He
sweat gold, and the money changers coined it. And now,
when misfortunes gather about and calamity overtakes him,
he appeals to those he has enriched only to learn how poor
and helpless he is alone.

*   *   *

*Hamlin Garland participated in the farmer trek that carried
the frontier out of the Mississippi Valley and into the upper
plains in the 1870's and 1880's; and at the turn of the
nineties, he observed the conditions that caused the tide of
migrating America to reverse itself in unprecedented retreat.
Born on a Wisconsin coulee in 1860, he came of a family
whose removal from Maine typified the zest with which New
Englanders moved westward in the 1840's. In the sixties, he
left Wisconsin, as his family succumbed first to the lure of
Iowa and then to the "Dakota fever." In his autobiographical
work,* A Son of the Middle Border, *written after he had
committed himself to a literary career in the East, Garland
suggests not only the alluring dream but the frustrating reality
associated with the American West at a time when dis-
illusionment characterized the attitude of many who had
once yielded to its lure.*

[Wisconsin, 1868] "Well, Dick," Grandad began, "so
ye're plannin' to go west, air ye?"

"Yes, as soon as I get all my grain and hogs marketed I'm
going to pull out for my new farm over in Iowa."

"Ye'd better stick to the old coulee," warned my grandfather, a touch of sadness in his voice. "Ye'll find none
better."

My father was disposed to resent this. "That's all very well
for the few who have the level land in the middle of the
valley," he retorted, "but how about those of us who are
crowded against the hills? You should see the farm I have
in Winneshiek! Not a hill on it big enough for a boy to
coast on. It's right on the edge of Looking Glass Prairie, and
I have a spring of water, and a fine grove of trees just where
I want them, not where they have to be grubbed out."

"But ye belong here," repeated Grandfather. "You were

married here, your children were born here. Ye'll find no
such friends in the west as you have here in Neshonoc. And
Belle will miss the family."

My father laughed. "Oh, you'll all come along. Dave has
the fever already. Even William is likely to catch it."

Old Hugh sighed deeply. "I hope ye're wrong," he said.
"I'd like to spend me last days here with me sons and
daughters around me, sich as are left to me," here his voice
became sterner. "It's the curse of our country,—this constant
moving, moving. I'd have been better off had I stayed in
Ohio, though this valley seemed very beautiful to me the
first time I saw it.". . .

Slowly, one by one, the men drew back and returned to
the sitting room, leaving the women to wash up the dishes
and put the kitchen to rights. David seized the opportunity
to ask my father to tell once again of the trip he had made, of
the lands he had seen, and the farm he had purchased, for his
young heart was also fired with desire of exploration. The
level lands toward the sunset allured him. In his visions the
wild meadows were filled with game, and the free lands needed
only to be tickled with a hoe to laugh into harvest.

He said, "As soon as Dad and Frank are settled on a farm
here, I'm going west also. I'm as tired of climbing these hills
as you are. I want a place of my own—and besides, from all
you say of that wheat country out there, a threshing machine
would pay wonderfully well." As the women came in, my
father called out, "Come, Belle, sing 'O'er the Hills in Legions
Boys!'—Dave get out your fiddle—and tune us all up."

David tuned up his fiddle and while he twanged on the
strings mother lifted her voice in our fine old marching song.

> Cheer up, brothers, as we go,
> O'er the mountains, westward ho—

and we all joined in the jubilant chorus—

> Then o'er the hills in legions, boys,
> Fair freedom's star
> Points to the sunset regions, boys,
> Ha, ha, ha-ha!—

My father's face shone with the light of the explorer, the pioneer. The words of this song appealed to him as the finest poetry. It meant all that was fine and hopeful and buoyant in American life, to him—but on my mother's sweet face a wistful expression deepened and in her fine eyes a reflective shadow lay. To her this song meant not so much the acquisition of a new home as the loss of all her friends and relatives. She sang it submissively, not exultantly, and I think the other women were of the same mood though their faces were less expressive to me. To all of the pioneer wives of the past that song had meant deprivation, suffering, loneliness, heartache. . . .

[Iowa, 1874] As I look back over my life on that Iowa farm the song of the reaper fills large place in my mind. We were all worshippers of wheat in those days. The men thought and talked of little else between seeding and harvest, and you will not wonder at this if you have known and bowed down before such abundance as we then enjoyed. . . .

We trembled when the storm lay hard upon the wheat, we exulted as the lilac shadows of noon-day drifted over it! We went out into it at noon when all was still—so still we could hear the pulse of the transforming sap as it crept from cool root to swaying plume. We stood before it at evening when the setting sun flooded it with crimson, the bearded heads lazily swirling under the wings of the wind, the mousing hawk dipping into its green deeps like the eagle into the sea, and our hearts expanded with the beauty and the mystery of it,—and back of all this was the knowledge that its abundance meant a new carriage, an addition to the house or a new suit of clothes.

Many of our social affairs were now connected with "the Grange." During these years on the new farm while we were busied with breaking and fencing and raising wheat, there had been growing up among the farmers of the west a social organization officially known as The Patrons of Husbandry. The places of meeting were called "Granges" and very naturally the members were at once called "Grangers."

My father was an early and enthusiastic member of the order, and during the early seventies its meetings became very important dates on our calendar. In winter "oyster suppers," with debates, songs and essays, drew us all to the Burr Oak Grove school-house, and each spring, on the twelfth of June, the Grange Picnic was a grand "turn-out." It was almost as well attended as the circus.

We all looked forward to it for weeks and every young man who owned a top-buggy got it out and washed and polished it for the use of his best girl, and those who were not so fortunate as to own "a rig" paid high tribute to the livery stable of the nearest town. Others, less able or less extravagant, doubled teams with a comrade and built a "bowery wagon" out of a wagon-box, and with hampers heaped with food rode away in state, drawn by a four or six-horse team. It seemed a splendid and daring thing to do, and some day I hoped to drive a six-horse bowery wagon myself.

The central place of meeting was usually in some grove along the Big Cedar to the west and south of us, and early on the appointed day the various lodges of our region came together one by one at convenient places, each one moving in procession and led by great banners on which the women had blazoned the motto of their home lodge. Some of the columns had bands and came preceded by far faint strains of music, with marshals in red sashes galloping to and fro in fine assumption of military command.

It was grand, it was inspiring—to us, to see those long lines of carriages winding down the lanes, joining one to another at the cross roads till at last all the granges from the northern end of the county were united in one mighty column advancing on the picnic ground, where orators awaited our approach with calm dignity and high resolve. Nothing more picturesque, more delightful, more helpful has ever risen out of American rural life. Each of these assemblies was a most grateful relief from the sordid loneliness of the farm. . . .

The movement of settlers toward Dakota had now become an exodus, a stampede. Hardly anything else was talked about as neighbors met one another on the road or at the Burr Oak school-house on Sundays. Every man who could sell out had gone west or was going. In vain did the county papers and Farmer's Institute lecturers advise cattle raising and plead for diversified tillage, predicting wealth for those who held on; farmer after farmer joined the march to Kansas, Nebraska, and Dakota. "We are wheat raisers," they said, "and we intend to keep in the wheat belt."

Our own family group was breaking up. My uncle David of pioneer spirit had already gone to the far Missouri Valley. Rachel had moved to Georgia, and Grandad McClintock was with his daughters, Samantha and Deborah, in western Minnesota. My mother, thus widely separated from her kin, resigned herself once more to the thought of founding a new home. Once more she sang, "O'er the hills in legions, boys," with such spirit as she could command, her clear voice a little touched with the huskiness of regret. . . .

[Dakota, 1881] I did not see the actual packing up and moving of the household goods, for I had determined to set forth in advance. . . . I bought a ticket for Aberdeen, and entered the train crammed with movers who had found the "prairie schooner" all too slow. The epoch of the canvas-covered wagon had passed. The era of the locomotive, the day of the chartered car, had arrived. Free land was receding at railroad speed. . . .

All that day we rumbled and rattled into a strange country, feeding our little engine with logs of wood, which we stopped occasionally to secure from long ricks which lined the banks of the river. . . . All around me . . . the talk was all of land, land! Nearly every man I met was bound for the "Jim River valley," and each voice was aquiver with hope, each eye alight with anticipation of certain success. . . .

Aberdeen was the end of the line, and when we came into it . . . it seemed a near neighbor to Sitting Bull. . . . It was twelve miles from here to where my father had set his stakes for his new home. . . . I remember . . . my walk across the dead-level plain. . . . For the first time I set foot upon a landscape without a tree to break its sere expanse. . . . There was beauty in this plain, delicate beauty and a weird charm, despite its lack of undulation. Its lonely unplowed sweep gave me the satisfying sensation of being at last among the men who held the outposts,—sentinels for the marching millions who were approaching from the east. . . .

[Dakota, 1883] . . . an ominous change had crept over the plain. The winds were hot and dry and the grass, baked on the stem, had become as inflammable as hay. The birds were silent. The sky, absolutely cloudless, began to scare us with its light. The sun rose through the dusty air, sinister with flare of horizontal heat. The little gardens on the breaking withered, and many of the women began to complain bitterly of the loneliness, and lack of shade. The tiny cabins were like ovens at midday.

Smiling faces were less frequent. Timid souls began to inquire, "Are all summers like this?" and those with greatest penetration reasoned, from the quality of the grass which was curly and fine as hair, that they had unwittingly settled upon an arid soil.

And so, week by week the holiday spirit faded from the colony and men in feverish unrest uttered words of bitterness. Eyes ached with light and hearts sickened with loneliness. Defeat seemed facing every man.

By the first of September many of those who were in greatest need of land were ready to abandon their advanced position on the border and fall back into the ranks behind. . . .

Then winter came.

Winter! No man knows what winter means until he has lived through one in a pine-board shanty on a Dakota plain with only buffalo bones for fuel. . . . Many . . . would have starved and frozen had it not been for the buffalo skeletons which lay scattered over the sod, and for which a sudden market developed. Upon the proceeds of this singular harvest they almost literally lived. Thus "the herds of deer and buffalo" did indeed strangely "furnish the cheer.". . .

February and March were of pitiless severity. One blizzard followed another with ever-increasing fury. . . . The timbers of the house creaked as the blast lay hard upon it, and now and again the faint fine crystals came sifting down upon my face,—driven beneath the shingles by the tempest. . . .

This may be taken as a turning point in my career, for this experience . . . permanently chilled my enthusiasm for pioneering the plain. Never again did I sing "Sunset Regions" with the same exultant spirit. "O'er the hills in legions, boys," no longer meant sunlit savannahs, flower meadows and deer-filled glades. The mingled "wood and prairie land" of the song was gone and Uncle Sam's domain, bleak, semi-arid, and wind-swept, offered little charm to my imagination. . . .

[Iowa and Dakota, 1887] I set forth at the close of school, on a vacation tour which was planned to include the old home in the Coulee, the Iowa farm, and my father's house in Dakota. . . . Every house I visited had its individual message of sordid struggle and half-hidden despair. . . . Leaving the village of Osage, with my mind still in a tumult of revolt, I took the train for the Northwest. . . . Not only were my senses exceedingly alert and impressionable, my eyes saw nothing but the loneliness and the lack of beauty in the landscape, and the farther west I went, the lonelier became the boxlike habitations of the plain. . . .

[Dakota, 1889] Another dry year was upon the land and the settlers were deeply disheartened. The holiday spirit of eight years before had entirely vanished. In its place was a sullen rebellion against government and against God. The stress of misfortune had not only destroyed hope, it had brought out the evil side of many men. Dissensions had grown common. Two of my father's neighbors had gone insane over the failure of their crops. . . .

The trees which my father had planted, the flowers which my mother had so faithfully watered, had withered in the heat. The lawn was burned brown. . . . On every side stretched scanty yellowing fields of grain. . . .

"Think of it!" I wrote to my brother. "After eight years of cultivation, father's farm possesses neither tree nor vine. Mother's head has no protection from the burning rays of the sun, except the shadow which the house casts on the dry, hard door-yard. . . . Doesn't the whole migration of the Garlands and McClintocks seem a madness?" . . .

All my schooling had been to migrate, to keep moving. "If your crop fails, go west and try a new soil. If disagreeable

neighbors surround you, sell out and move,—always toward
the open country. To remain quietly in your native place is a
sign of weakness, of irresolution. Happiness dwells afar.
Wealth and fame are to be found by journeying toward the
sunset star!" Such had been the spirit, the message of all the
songs and stories of my youth. Now suddenly I perceived the
futility of our quest.

After nearly a third of a century of migration, the Garlands
were about to double on their trail, and their decision was
deeply significant. It meant that a certain phase of American
pioneering had ended, that "the woods and prairie lands" having all been taken up, nothing remained but the semi-arid
valleys of the Rocky Mountains. "Irrigation" was a new word
and a vague word in the ears of my father's generation, and
had little of the charm which lay in the "flowery savannahs"
of the Mississippi valley. In the years between 1865 and 1892
the nation had swiftly passed through the buoyant era of free
land settlement, and now the day of reckoning had come.

Gregory Gold Diggings, Colorado (1859)

Part VIII

A MEANING FOR THE WESTWARD MARCH

> "The existence of an area of free land, its continuous
> recession, and the advance of American settlement west-
> ward, explain American development." (*Frederick Jackson
> Turner*)

*From the beginning of nationhood, the existence of the West
was seen to have significance for the American economy. Men
like Benjamin Franklin and George Washington were alert
to the opportunities for individual profit through speculation
in western lands; but they sensed also that the vast and un-
exploited resources to the westward could underwrite a
society capable of standing on its own, with qualities that
would recommend it over the older nations of the world.
Poets and statesmen invoked the abundance of "virgin land"
as embodying the promise of a prosperous and democratic
America. As early as 1755, Franklin contended that the
American West encouraged an increase in population beyond
what was possible in Europe. He implied that the West was
a "safety valve" for labor in asserting that the attraction of
western lands would for many years reduce the labor force
and keep its wages high. He expressed these views in his*
Observations Concerning the Increase of Mankind, Peopling
of Countries, &c.

. . . People increase in Proportion to the Number of Marriages, and that is greater in Proportion to the Ease and Convenience of supporting a Family. . . .

In Cities, where all Trades, Occupations and Offices are full,
many delay marrying, till they can see how to bear the Charges
of a Family; . . . many live single during Life, and continue
Servants to Families, Journeymen to Trades, &c. hence Cities
do not by natural Generation supply themselves with Inhabitants; the Deaths are more than the Births.

In Countries full settled, the Case must be nearly the same;
all Lands being occupied and improved to the Heighth; those

who cannot get Land, must Labour for others that have it; when Labourers are plenty, their Wages will be low; by low Wages a Family is supported with Difficulty; this Difficulty deters many from Marriage, who therefore long continue Servants and single. . . .

Land being thus plenty in *America*, and so cheap as that a labouring Man that understands Husbandry, can in a short Time save Money enough to purchase a Piece of new Land sufficient for a Plantation, whereon he may subsist a Family; such are not afraid to marry; for if they even look far enough forward to consider how their Children when grown up are to be provided for, they see that more Land is to be had at Rates equally easy, all Circumstances considered.

Hence Marriages in *America* are more general, and more generally early, than in *Europe*. And if it is reckoned there, that there is but one Marriage per Annum among 100 Persons, perhaps we may here reckon two; and if in *Europe* they have but 4 Births to a Marriage (many of their Marriages being late) we may here reckon 8, of which if one half grow up, and our Marriages are made, reckoning one with another at 20 Years of Age our People must at least be doubled every 20 Years.

But not withstanding this Increase, so vast is the Territory of *North-America*, that it will require many Ages to settle it fully; and till it is fully settled, Labour will never be cheap here, where no Man continues long a Labourer for others, but gets a Plantation of his own, no Man continues long a Journey-man to a Trade, but goes among those new Settlers, and sets up for himself, &c. Hence Labour is no cheaper now in *Pennsylvania*, than it was 30 Years ago, tho' so many Thousand labouring People have been imported.

* * *

Travelers from Europe, observing young America of the 1830's, concluded that the success of the democratic experiment could be laid to "the vast extent and boundless resources of the territory in which it was established." This was the contention of the English novelist, Frederick Marryat, who visited the United States in 1837. "Among the advantages of democracy, the greatest is, perhaps that all start fair," *he wrote in his* Diary in America, with Remarks on its Institutions; *"and the boy who holds the traveller's horse, as Van Buren is said to have done, may become the president of the United States. But it is the* country, *and not the government, which has been productive of such rapid strides. . . . Let the American direct his career to any goal he pleases, his energies are unshackled. . . . There is room for all, and millions more."* An even more famous European visitor, Alexis de Tocqueville, had already put a similar interpretation on the force of the West and the pioneer experience, after his visit in 1831. This liberal French aristocrat seemed to be intent on showing that democracy was succeeding in the United States because of the nature of the environment, and that it would be less likely to succeed in France, which, in territory, was not similarly endowed. In his Democracy in America, *he foresaw the development in the United States of a society whose manners and habits would be conditioned above all else by the experience of occupying a relatively "empty continent" awaiting development by the pioneer.*

At the end of the last century a few bold adventurers began to penetrate into the valleys of the Mississippi, and the mass of the population very soon began to move in that direction: communities unheard of till then were seen to emerge from the wilds: States whose names were not in existence a few years before claimed their place in the American Union; and in the Western settlements we may behold democracy arrived at its utmost extreme. In these States, . . . the inhabitants are but of yesterday. Scarcely known to one another, the nearest neighbours are ignorant of each other's history. In this part of the American continent, therefore, the population has not experienced the influence of great names and great wealth, nor even that of the natural aristocracy of knowledge and virtue. . . .

America, then, exhibits in her social state a most extraordinary phenomenon. Men are there seen on a greater equality in point of fortune and intellect, or, in other words, more equal in their strength, than in any other country of the world, or in any age of which history has preserved the remembrance. . . .

The chief circumstance which has favoured the establishment and the maintenance of a democratic republic in the United States is the nature of the territory which the Americans inhabit. Their ancestors gave them the love of equality and of freedom, but God himself gave them the means of remaining equal and free, by placing them upon a boundless continent, which is open to their exertions. . . .

In what part of human tradition can be found anything at all similar to that which is occurring under our eyes in North America? The celebrated communities of antiquity were all founded in the midst of hostile nations, which they were obliged to subjugate before they could flourish in their place. . . . But North America was only inhabited by wandering tribes, who took no thought of the natural riches of the soil, and that vast country was still, properly speaking, an empty continent, a desert land awaiting its inhabitants. . . .

At this very time thirteen millions of civilized Europeans are peaceably spreading over those fertile plains, with whose resources and whose extent they are not yet themselves accurately acquainted. Three or four thousand soldiers drive the wandering races of the aborigines before them; these are followed by the pioneers, who pierce the woods, scare off the beasts of prey, explore the courses of the inland streams, and make ready the triumphal procession of civilization across the waste. . . .

It is difficult to describe the rapacity with which the American rushes forward to secure the immense booty which fortune proffers to him. In the pursuit he fearlessly braves the arrow of the Indian and the distempers of the forest; he is unimpressed by the silence of the woods; the approach of beasts of prey does not disturb him; for he is goaded onward by a passion more intense than the love of life. Before him lies a boundless continent, and he urges onward as if time pressed, and he was afraid of finding no room for his exertions. . . . Fifty years have scarcely elapsed since . . . Ohio was founded; the greater part of its inhabitants were not born within its confines; its capital has only been built thirty years, and its territory is still covered by an immense extent of uncultivated fields; nevertheless, the population of Ohio is already proceed-

ing westward, and most of the settlers who descend to the fertile savannas of Illinois are citizens of Ohio. These men left
their first country to improve their condition; they quit their
resting-place to ameliorate it still more; fortune awaits them
everywhere, but happiness they can not attain. The desire of
prosperity is become an ardent and restless passion in their
minds which grows by what it gains. They early broke the ties
which bound them to their natal earth, and they have contracted no fresh ones on their way. Emigration was at first
necessary to them as a means of subsistence; and it soon becomes a sort of game of chance, which they pursue for the
emotions it excites as much as for the gain it procures. . . .

Everything . . . [around the pioneer] is primitive and un-
formed, but he is himself the result of the labour and the
experience of eighteen centuries. He wears the dress and he
speaks the language of cities; he is acquainted with the past,
curious of the future, and ready for argument upon the present; he is, in short, a highly civilized being, who consents, for
a time, to inhabit the backwoods, and who penetrates into the
wilds of the New World with the Bible, an axe, and a file of
newspapers. . . .

The time will . . . come when one hundred and fifty millions of men will be living in North America, equal in condition, the progeny of one race, owing their origin to the same
cause, and preserving the same civilization, the same language,
the same religion, the same habits, the same manners, and
imbued with the same opinions, propagated under the same
forms. The rest is uncertain, but this is certain; and it is a fact
new to the world—a fact fraught with such portentous consequences as to baffle the efforts even of the imagination.

*   *   *

*The mingling of peoples to form a new amalgam—American
in character—was one of the consequences of the westward
march which impressed the author of an anonymous article
published in the July, 1840 issue of* The Merchants' Magazine
and Commercial Review, *a periodical founded in 1839 by
Freeman Hunt, with the claims of commerce in mind. The
writer of this early and quite remarkable commentary on the
westward movement alluded also to the sense of individualism,*

equality, and opportunity, and to the open-mindedness as
well as materialism, which he saw as products of life on the
American frontier.

The great bulk of the western population is constituted of
various . . . elements, . . . from almost every trade, profes-
sion, and condition in life. The greater portion is comprised
of recent emigrants, for the original pioneers of the west are
nearly lost in the crowd of new-comers. Substantial house-
holders who have sold out their domains at the east, have here
made their clearings and erected their comfortable mansions
on the soil; but the great mass of the emigrants is composed of
men of limited means and large enterprise, who have adven-
tured into this country to improve their condition, amid its
great resources and expanding growth. . . .

The poor man at the east, with a large family, laboring,
for example, upon the ungenerous soil of New England, finding that there is a country westward, where labor is dear and
broad acres yielding an abundance of the necessaries of life are
cheap, is induced to migrate with his household goods and all
his effects, to this "land of promise," where provision may be
made for his children. Houses must be built for the population. They require, as they advance, all the appliances which
belong to a civilized form of society; and, to supply this demand, the mechanics in the various trades follow in his track,
who are succeeded by the merchants, and he in his turn is followed by the members of the different professions, who find
that the avenues to wealth and distinction at the east are more
crowded than in the broad and growing region of a new
country. To these are added, settlers, Dutch, Irish, English,
Swiss, and immigrants from almost every part of Europe; and
they all settle upon the soil from the same general motives.
The discordant elements of society thus become strangely
mingled. Here may be found the ruddy-faced Yankee farmer,
with his axe on his shoulder, or the New York merchant;
there the volatile Canadian Frenchman. Here the scholar, ripe
from the eastern schools; there the original backwoodsman,
who may be classed among the early pioneers of the country.
Here the English peasant, fresh from the markets of London,

mixed with pale-faced Virginians from the banks of the Mississippi, whose fathers, perhaps, followed Daniel Boone through
the gap of the Alleghany Mountains; the most of them without large wealth, the most of them intelligent, and all anxious
to advance their fortunes. The various forms of character thus
thrown in contact, while they prevent any general and permanent moral traits, also exclude those settled prejudices always
springing from the prescribed habitudes of a long-established
and local population; and the necessary consequence of this
condition of things is to cause the general frame of society to
appear somewhat crude, rough, and in some portions, even
lawless. . . .

If the settler has once cleared his farm, and placed it under
a vigorous cultivation, it produces in abundance. He is impressed with a spirit of independence, always arising in the
mind of every freeholder, for he looks down upon his own rich
domain. . . .

The people of the west are generous, though crude, unmind-
ful from habit of the luxuries of life, endowed with great
boldness and originality of mind, from the circumstances under which they are placed. They are, from the various elements
of which they are composed, in a state of amalgamation, and
from this amalgamation a new and valuable form of American
character will spring up. If they do not, in all cases, appreciate
the refinements of polished life, this is in favor of their con-
tentment, for the new condition of the country does not at
present warrant them. Luxury and taste are, in general, the offspring of refinement and of ripened age; and he who should
look back a few years in our oldest states, would find a marked
advance in these qualities, even here, within that time. The
great body of the people of the west are employed, not in
trailing vines, but in acquiring their support. A wheat field is
more pleasing to their taste than a flower garden. A well-
ploughed lot is more satisfactory to their eye than the most ex-
quisite painting of a Raphael or a Claude. They would prefer
seeing a gristmill working on their own stream to the sight of
the sculptured marble of the Venus or the Apollo! A widely-
diffused, deeply-stamped spirit of equality and republicanism
extends throughout the whole social frame of the northwest;

and over all is thrown an openness and candor, as well as a benevolence, which arises from their common interests as emigrants, co-workers engaged in the common cause of carrying forward the enterprises of a new country, without sympathy from any source but the mutual sympathy which exists between themselves.

*   *   *

Critics of American society in the years following the Civil War attributed its shortcomings, more than its virtues, to the frontier experience. Whereas Alexis de Tocqueville had argued that democracy worked in America because of the existence of an open West, the American editor and reformer E. L. Godkin took the view in 1865 that it was the frontier which had engendered the traits of character that were giving democracy a bad name. Godkin contended that most of the "phenomena of American society which . . . distinguish it from that of older countries . . . may be attributed to . . . 'the frontier life' led by a large proportion of its inhabitants." These he catalogued as strong individualism, contempt for experience, eagerness in pursuit of material gain, want of respect for training, the absence of a strong sense of social or national continuity, and the lack of taste in art, literature, and oratory. In his opinion, these qualities reflected, not the inadequacies of democracy in the United States, but rather the consequences of the "enormous extent of unoccupied land," in the exploitation of which the "self-made man" had become the American ideal. The distinguished English commentator, Lord Bryce, took a middle of the road position in assessing the impact of the West upon the American way of life. To him, the occupation of the West was the source of both the dynamism and the materialism which he observed in American society in the 1880's. He included a chapter on "The Temper of the West" in the original edition of The American Commonwealth, *published in 1888.*

Western America is one of the most interesting subjects of study the modern world has seen. There has been nothing in the past resembling its growth, and probably there will be nothing in the future. A vast territory, wonderfully rich in natural resources of many kinds; a temperate and healthy climate, fit for European labour; a soil generally, and in many places marvellously, fertile; in some regions mountains full of minerals, in others trackless forests where every tree is over two hundred feet high; and the whole of this virtually unoccupied territory thrown open to an energetic race, with all the appliances and contrivances of modern science at its command,—these are phenomena absolutely without precedent in history, and which cannot recur elsewhere, because our planet contains no such other favoured tract of country. . . .

. . . the West is the most American part of America . . . the part where those features which distinguish America from Europe come out in the strongest relief. . . . In the West . . . all is bustle, motion, and struggle, most so of course among the native Americans, yet even the immigrant from the secluded valleys of Thuringia, or the shores of some Norwegian fjord, learns the ways almost as readily as the tongue of the country, and is soon swept into the whirlpool.

It is the most enterprising and unsettled Americans that come West; and when they have left their old homes, broken their old ties, resigned the comforts and pleasures of their former homes, they are resolved to obtain the wealth and success for which they come. They throw themselves into work with a feverish yet sustained intensity. They rise early, they work all day, they have few pleasures, few opportunities for relaxation. I remember in the young city of Seattle on Puget Sound to have found business in full swing at seven o'clock A. M.: the shops open, the streets full of people. Everything is speculative, land . . . most so. . . . No one has any fixed occupation; he is a storekeeper to-day, a ranchman to-morrow, a miner next week. I found the waiters in the chief hotel at Denver . . . saving their autumn and winter wages to start off in the spring "prospecting" for silver "claims" in the mountains. Few men stay in one of the newer cities more than a few weeks or months; to have been there a whole year is to be an old inhabitant, an oracle if you have succeeded, a by-word if you have not, for to prosper in the West you must be able to turn your hand to anything. . . . This venturesome and shifting life strengthens the reckless and heedless habits of the people. . . .

These people are intoxicated by the majestic scale of the nature in which their lot is cast, enormous mineral deposits, boundless prairies, forests which, even squandered—wickedly squandered—as they now are, will supply timber to the United States for centuries; a soil which, with the rudest cultivation, yields the most abundant crops, a populous continent for their market. They see all round them railways being built, telegraph wires laid, steamboat lines across the Pacific projected, cities springing up in the solitudes, and settlers making the wilderness to blossom like the rose. . . .

This constant reaching forward to and grasping at the future does not so much express itself in words . . . as in the air of ceaseless haste and stress which pervades the West. . . . Time seems too short for what they have to do, and result always to come short of their desire. . . .

Politically, and perhaps socially also, this haste and excitement, this absorption in the development of the material resources of the country, are unfortunate. As a town built in a hurry is seldom well built, so a society will be the sounder in health for not having grown too swiftly. Doubtless much of the scum will be cleared away from the surface when the liquid settles and cools down. Lawlessness and lynch law will disappear; saloons and gambling-houses will not prosper in a well-conducted population; schools will improve and universities grow out of the raw colleges which one already finds even in the newer Territories.   Nevertheless the bad habits of professional politics, as one sees them on the Atlantic coast, are not unknown in these communities; and the unrestfulness, the passion for speculation, the feverish eagerness for quick and showy results, may so soak into the texture of the popular mind as to colour it for centuries to come. These are the shadows which to the eye of the traveller seem to fall across the glowing landscape of the Great West.

*   *   *

It was left for a college professor to formulate the meaning of the westward movement in such a way as greatly to expand the recognition of the influence of an ever present West in the American experience. This was the accomplishment of

Professor Frederick Jackson Turner, of the University of Wisconsin, in the now famous paper entitled "The Significance of the Frontier in American History," which he read at a session of the American Historical Association in Chicago, in 1893. The essay was in many ways a product of the times; for Turner, like many scholars and publicists of his generation, saw a danger to American institutions should the public domain be exhausted and this supposed "safety valve" for Americanization and social and economic regeneration no longer be available. He viewed the continuous settlement of an unoccupied West as the force most responsible for the social fluidity of American society, the creation of a composite American nationality, the development of a strong national government, the promotion of democratic institutions, and the pervasive sense of opportunity for the individual which characterized the United States of his day. In the years since Turner expressed these views, historians have debated and to some extent qualified his interpretation. None, however, will deny the significance of his contribution in setting the sweep of settlement across the Continent in an historical perspective in which it had not previously been seen, and in emphasizing the relationship of the unoccupied West, and its progressive exploitation, to American history and the development of the American way of life.

In a recent bulletin of the Superintendent of the Census for 1890 appear these significant words: "Up to and including 1880 the country had a frontier of settlement, but at present the unsettled area has been so broken into by isolated bodies of settlement that there can hardly be said to be a frontier line.". . . This brief official statement marks the closing of a great historic movement. Up to our own day American history has been in a large degree the history of the colonization of the Great West. The existence of an area of free land, its continuous recession, and the advance of American settlement westward, explain American development. . . .

The peculiarity of American institutions is, the fact that they have been compelled to adapt themselves to the changes of an expanding people—to the changes involved in crossing a continent, in winning a wilderness, and in developing at each area of this progress out of the primitive economic and political conditions of the frontier into the complexity of city life. . . . American social development has been continually beginning over again on the frontier. This perennial rebirth, this fluidity of American life, this expansion westward with its new opportunities, its continuous touch with the simplicity of primitive society, furnish the forces dominating American character. . . .

First, we note that the frontier promoted the formation of a composite nationality for the American people. The coast was preponderantly English, but the later tides of continental immigration flowed across to the free lands. . . . In the crucible of the frontier the immigrants were Americanized, liberated, and fused into a mixed race, English in neither nationality nor characteristics. The process has gone on from the early days to our own. . . .

. . . the advance of the frontier decreased our dependence on England. The coast, particularly of the South, lacked diversified industries, and was dependent on England for the bulk of its supplies. In the South there was even a dependence on the Northern colonies for articles of food. . . . Before long the frontier created a demand for merchants. As it retreated from the coast it became less and less possible for England to bring her supplies directly to the consumer's wharfs, and carry away staple crops, and staple crops began to give way to diversified agriculture for a time. The effect of this phase of the frontier action upon the northern section is perceived when we realize how the advance of the frontier aroused seaboard cities like Boston, New York, and Baltimore to engage in rivalry for what Washington called "the extensive and valuable trade of a rising empire.". . .

The growth of nationalism and the evolution of American political institutions were dependent on the advance of the frontier. . . . Administratively the frontier called out some of the highest and most vitalizing activities of the General Government. The purchase of Louisiana was perhaps the constitutional turning point in the history of the Republic, inasmuch as it afforded both a new area for national legislation and the occasion of the downfall of the policy of strict construction. But the purchase of Louisiana was called out by frontier needs and demands. As frontier States accrued to the Union the national power grew. In a speech on the dedication of the Calhoun monument Mr. Lamar explained: "In 1789 the States were the creators of the Federal Government; in 1861 the Federal Government was the creator of a large majority of the States.". . .

It is safe to say that the legislation with regard to land, tariff, and internal improvements—the American system of the nationalizing Whig party—was conditioned on frontier ideas and needs. But it was not merely in legislative action that the frontier worked against the sectionalism of the coast. . . .

It was this nationalizing tendency of the West that transformed the democracy of Jefferson into the national republicanism of Monroe and the democracy of Andrew Jackson. The West of the war of 1812, the West of Clay, and Benton, and Harrison, and Andrew Jackson, shut off by the Middle States and the mountains from the coast sections, had a solidarity of its own with national tendencies. On the tide of the Father of Waters, North and South met and mingled into a nation. Interstate migration went steadily on—a process of cross-fertilization of ideas and institutions. . . . Slavery was a sectional trait that would not down, but in the West it could not remain sectional. It was the greatest of frontiersmen who declared: "I believe this Government can not endure permanently half slave and half free. It will become all of one thing or all of the other." Nothing works for nationalism like intercourse within the nation. Mobility of population is death to localism, and the western frontier worked irresistibly in unsettling population. The effects reached back from the frontier and affected profoundly the Atlantic coast and even the Old World.

But the most important effect of the frontier has been in the promotion of democracy here and in Europe. As has been indicated, the frontier is productive of individualism. Complex society is precipitated by the wilderness into a kind of primitive organization based on the family. The tendency is antisocial. It produces antipathy to control, and particularly to any direct control. . . . The frontier individualism has from the beginning promoted democracy.

The frontier States that came into the Union in the first quarter of a century of its existence came in with democratic suffrage provisions, and had reactive effects of the highest importance upon the older States whose peoples were being attracted there. An extension of the franchise became essential. It was *western* New York that forced an extension of suffrage in the constitutional convention of that State in 1821; and it was *western* Virginia that compelled the tide-water region to put a more liberal suffrage provision in the constitution framed in 1830, and to give to the frontier region a more nearly proportionate representation with the tide-water aristocracy. The rise of democracy as an effective force in the nation came in with western preponderance under Jackson and William Henry Harrison, and it meant the triumph of the frontier— with all of its good and with all of its evil elements. . . .

So long as free land exists, the opportunity for a competency exists, and economic power secures political power. But the democracy born of free land, strong in selfishness and individualism, intolerant of administrative experience and education, and pressing individual liberty beyond its proper bounds, has its dangers as well as its benefits. Individualism in America has allowed a laxity in regard to governmental affairs which has rendered possible the spoils system and all the manifest evils that follow from the lack of a highly developed civic spirit. In this connection may be noted also the influence of frontier conditions in permitting lax business honor, inflated paper currency and wild-cat banking. . . .

But the attempts to limit the boundaries, to restrict land sales and settlement, and to deprive the West of its share of political power were all in vain. Steadily the frontier of settlement advanced and carried with it individualism, democracy, and nationalism, and powerfully affected the East and the Old World. . . .

From the conditions of frontier life came intellectual traits of profound importance. . . . The result is that to the frontier the American intellect owes its striking characteristics. That coarseness and strength combined with acuteness and inquisitiveness; that practical, inventive turn of mind, quick to find expedients; that masterful grasp of material things, lacking in the artistic but powerful to effect great ends; that restless, nervous energy; that dominant individualism, working for good and for evil, and withal that buoyancy and exuberance which comes with freedom—these are traits of the frontier, or traits called out elsewhere because of the existence of the frontier. Since the days when the fleet of Columbus sailed into the waters of the New World, America has been another name for opportunity, and the people of the United States have taken their tone from the incessant expansion which has not only been open but has even been forced upon them. He would be a rash prophet who should assert that the expansive character of American life has now entirely ceased. Movement has been its dominant fact, and, unless this training has no effect upon a people, the American energy will continually demand a wider field for its exercise. But never again will such gifts of free land offer themselves. For a moment, at the frontier, the bonds of custom are broken and unrestraint is triumphant. There is not *tabula rasa*. The stubborn American environment is there with its imperious summons to accept its conditions; the inherited ways of doing things are also there; and yet, in spite of environment, and in spite of custom, each frontier did indeed furnish a new field of opportunity, a gate of escape from the bondage of the past; and freshness, and confidence, and scorn of older society, impatience of its restraints and its ideas, and indifference to its lessons, have accompanied the frontier. What the Mediterranean Sea was to the Greeks, breaking the bond of custom, offering new experiences, calling out new institutions and activities, that, and more, the ever retreating frontier has been to the United States directly, and to the nations of Europe more remotely. And now, four centuries from the discovery of America, at the end of a hundred years of life under the Constitution, the frontier has gone, and with its going has closed the first period of American history.

ACKNOWLEDGMENTS

Thanks are due to the following persons and publishers for permission to reprint material for which they hold the copyrights: to The Bobbs-Merrill Company for a passage from Milo M. Quaife, *The Capture of Old Vincennes*; to G. P. Putnam's Sons for a passage from John M. Oskison, *Tecumseh and His Times*; to the University of Minnesota Press for a passage from Nils W. Olsson, ed., *A Pioneer in Northwest America 1841-1858, The Memoirs of Gustaf Unonius*, translated by Jonas O. Backlund; to the editors of *The Wisconsin Magazine of History* for a passage from "Letters of Joseph V. Quarles, 1837-40"; to the American Historical Association for a passage from "The Austin Papers," in its *Annual Report, 1919*; to Alice E. Smith and the editors of *The Wisconsin Magazine of History* for a passage from "Wisconsin's First Railroad: Linsley Letters, 1852," edited by Miss Smith; to the Harvard University Press for a passage from Paul W. Gates, *The Illinois Central Railroad and Its Colonization Work*; to Houghton Mifflin Company for a passage from Bernard DeVoto, ed., *The Journals of Lewis and Clark*; to Alfred A. Knopf, Incorporated, for a passage from Louise A. Clappe, *The Shirley Letters from the California Mines, 1851-1852*, ed. by Carl I. Wheat; to the University of Oklahoma Press for a passage from E. C. Abbott ("Teddy Blue") and Helena Huntington Smith, *We Pointed Them North*; to Hastings House, Publishers, Incorporated, for a passage from Mari Sandoz, *Old Jules*; to the Columbia University Press for a passage from Howard Ruede, *Sod-House Days: Letters from a Kansas Homesteader, 1877-78*, ed. by John Ise; to Henry Holt and Company, Incorporated, for a passage from Robert E. Riegel, *America Moves West*; to the Macmillan Company for a passage from Hamlin Garland, *A Son of the Middle Border*.

NOTE ON SOURCES

PART I. EUROPE'S FRONTIER IN THE NEW WORLD:

[Robert Beverley], *The History and Present State of Virginia . . . , By a Native and Inhabitant of the Place* (London: R. Parker, 1705), pp. 1-3. Daniel Denton, *A Brief Description of New-York: Formerly Called New-Netherlands. With the Places thereunto Adjoyning. Together with the Manner of its Scituation, Fertility of the Soyle, Healthfulness of the Climate, and the Commodities thence produced. Also Some Directions and Advice to such as shall go thither: an Account of what Commodities they shall take with them; The Profit and Pleasure that may accrew to them thereby. . . .* (London: 1670), pp. 17-19. William Bradford, *Of Plimoth Plantation* (Boston: Wright and Potter Printing Company, 1901), pp. 94-97. Spelling of text has been modernized. Jacques de La Metairie, "Narrative of the Expedition of M. Cavalier [*sic*] de la Salle," pp. 17-27, in *Historical Collections of Louisiana and Florida . . . ,* ed. by B. F. French (New York: Albert Mason, 1875), pp. 18-19, 22-27.

PART II. BREACHING THE APPALACHIAN BARRIER:

John Fontaine, "Journal," pp. 245-310, in Ann Maury, *Memoirs of a Huguenot Family: translated and compiled from the original autobiography of the Rev. James Fontaine, and other family manuscripts; comprising an original journal of travels in Virginia, New York, etc., in 1715 and 1716* (New York: George P. Putnam & Co., 1853), pp. 283-89. The first recorded crossing of the Appalachians by Englishmen was made in 1671 by a party led by Thomas Batts and Robert Fallam. "Conrad Weiser's Journal of a Tour to the Ohio, August 11—October 2, 1748," pp. 15-44, in *Early Western Travels, 1748-1846,* ed. by R. G. Thwaites (Cleveland: Arthur H. Clark Co., 1904), pp. 24, 28-30, 38-41. "The Adventures of Col. Daniel Boon . . . ," Appendix to John Filson, *The Discovery, Settlement And present State of Kentucke . . .* (Wilmington: Printed by James Adams, 1784), pp. 50-58. Joseph Doddridge, *Notes on the Settlement and Indian Wars of the Western Parts of Virginia and Pennsylvania from 1763 to 1783, Inclusive, together with a View of the State of Society, and Manners of the First Settlers of the Western Country*, ed. by Alfred Williams (Albany: Joel Munsell, 1876), pp. 129-30, 137-38, 140-42, 144-45, 160. George Rogers Clark, *Original Narrative*, as rendered and edited by Milo M. Quaife, in *The Capture of Old Vincennes* (Indianapolis: The Bobbs-Merrill Company, 1927), pp. 57-58, 67-68, 80-86.

PART III. THE OHIO VALLEY THRUST:

Northwest Ordinance from *Select Documents Illustrative of the History of the United States, 1776-1861*, ed. by William Mac Donald (New York: Macmillan Co., 1903), pp. 23-28. C. F. Volney, *A View of the Soil and Climate of the United States of America . . .* , tr. by C. B. Brown (Philadelphia: J. Conrad & Co., 1804), pp. 322-28. John M. Oskison, *Tecumseh and His Times* (New York: G. P. Putnam's Sons, 1938), pp. 129-33. Morris Birkbeck, *Notes on a Journey in America from the Coast of Virginia to the Territory of Illinois* (2nd edition, Philadelphia, 1818), pp. 34-36, 48-49. Timothy Flint, *The History and Geography of the Mississippi Valley* (2nd edition, 2 vols. in one, Cincinnati: E. H. Flint and L. R. Lincoln, 1832), pp. 184-87. George Flower, *History of the English Settlement in Edwards County, Illinois, founded in 1817 and 1818 by Morris Birkbeck and George Flower*, with preface and footnotes by E. B. Washburne, in Chicago Historical Society, *Collections*, I (1882), 94, 99, 189-90, 287-88. *Important Extracts from Original and Recent Letters, written by Englishmen, in the United States of America, Second Series*, ed. by J. Knight (Manchester: Thomas Wilkinson, 1818), pp. 36-38. [Henry Trumbull], *Western Emigration: Journal of Dr. Jeremiah Smipleton's [Simpleton's] Tour to Ohio, Containing an account of the numerous difficulties, Hair-breadth Escapes, Mortifications and Privations, which the Doctor and his family experienced on their Journey from Maine, to the 'Land of Promise,' and during a residence of three years in that highly extolled country*. By H. Trumbull. (Boston: S. Sewall [1819?]), pp. 35-36.

PART IV. FRONTIER SOCIETY:

Flint, *The History and Geography of the Mississippi Valley*, pp. 190-93. John Knight, *The Emigrants Best Instructor, or, the most Recent and Important Information respecting the United States of America, Selected from the Works of the latest Travellers in that Country. . . .* (Manchester: M. Wilson, 1818), p. 24. Gottfried Duden, *Bericht über eine Reise nach den westlichen Staaten Nordamerika's und einen mehrjahrigen Aufenthalt am Missouri (in den Jahren 1824, 25, 26 und 27), in Bezug auf Auswanderung und*

Uebervölkerung (St. Gallen, 1832), pp. 69-73, 75. Flower, pp. 126-29, 313. Frances M. Trollope, *Domestic Manners of the Americans* (New York: Howard Wilford Bell, 1904), pp. 37-38, 41, 58-61, 65. Timothy Flint, *Recollections of the Last Ten Years, passed in occasional residences and journeyings in the Valley of the Mississippi . . . in a series of letters to the Rev. James Flint, of Salem, Massachusetts* (Boston: Cummings, Hilliard, and Co., 1826), pp. 13-15, 103-107. Robert Baird, *View of the Valley of the Mississippi: or the Emigrants' and Travellers' Guide to the West* (Philadelphia: H. S. Tanner, 1832), pp. 321-23. *Autobiography of Peter Cartwright, the Backwoods Preacher*, ed. by W. P. Strickland (New York: Phillips and Hunt, 1856), pp. 45-46, 48-49, 175-76. Baird, pp. 89-91. A. B., "Sketches of Kentucky. By a Yankee," pp. 479-82, in *Western Monthly Magazine* (July-Dec., 1834), 481-82. John M. Peck, *A New Guide for Emigrants to the West, containing sketches of Michigan, Ohio, Indiana, Illinois, Missouri, Arkansas, with the Territory of Wisconsin and the Adjacent Parts* (2nd edition, Boston: Gould, Kendall, & Lincoln, 1837), pp. 119-21.

PART V. WIDENING THE PERIMETER OF THE "GREAT WEST":

A Pioneer in Northwest America 1841-1858: The Memoirs of Gustaf Unonius, tr. from the Swedish by Jonas O. Backlund, ed. by Nils W. Olsson (Minneapolis: University of Minnesota Press, 1950), pp. 55, 58-60, 63, 79-80, 89-91, 111. "Letters of Joseph V. Quarles, 1837-40," pp. 297-320, in *Wisconsin Magazine of History*, XVI (1932-33), 300-301, 305-306, 315. Edward W. Barber, "The Vermontville Colony: Its Genesis and History, with Personal Sketches of the Colonists," pp. 197-265, in Michigan Pioneer and Historical Society, *Collections*, XXVIII (1897), 203-206. Frederick Law Olmsted, *A Journey Through Texas; or a Saddle-Trip on the Southwestern Frontier* (New York: Mason Brothers, 1860), pp. 140-47. "The Austin Papers," ed. by Eugene C. Barker, in American Historical Association, *Annual Report, 1919*, II (Washington, D. C., 1924), 385-86, 400, 679-81. *The Life of David Crockett, the Original Humorist and Irrepressible Backwoodsman: An Autobiography to which is added An Account of his Glorious Death at the Alamo while Fighting in Defense of Texan Independence* (New York: A. L. Burt Co., 1902), pp. 386, 391-94, 401-403. James D. Richardson, compiler, *Messages and Papers of the Presidents, 1789-1897* (Washington, 1897), IV, 379-81. Charles I. Linsley to Charles Linsley in "Wisconsin's First Railroad: Linsley Letters, 1852," ed. by Alice E. Smith, pp. 335-52, in *Wisconsin Magazine of History*, XXX (March, 1947), 336-40, 342, 347, 349, 351. "Homes for the Industrious in the Garden State of the West," quoted from advertising cut used by the Illinois Central Railroad in 1860 and 1861, as reproduced in Paul Wallace Gates, *The Illinois Central Railroad and Its Colonization Work* (Cambridge: Harvard University Press, 1934), p. 187. Henry Ward Beecher, *Eyes and Ears* (Boston: Ticknor and Fields, 1862), pp. 99-100. Edward Everett Hale, *Memories of a Hundred Years* (2 vols., New York: Macmillan Company, 1902), II, 153-60, 165. "Kansas Matters—Appeal to the South," in *DeBow's Review*, XX (May, 1856), 635-37.

PART VI. "ACROSS THE WIDE MISSOURI":

The Journals of Lewis and Clark, ed. by Bernard DeVoto (Boston: Houghton Mifflin Company, 1953), pp. 92, 181-82, 186-89. George Frederick Ruxton, *Life in the Far West* (Edinburgh and London: William Blackwood and Sons, 1849), pp. 73-76, 105-106, 133-35. Josiah Gregg, *Commerce of the Prairies or the Journal of a Santa Fé Trader during Eight Expeditions across the Great Western Prairies . . .* (New York: J. & H. G. Langley, 1845), pp. 34-40, 43, 45-48, 111-12. Ruxton, pp. 248-51. Jesse Applegate, "A Day with the Cow Column in 1843," pp. 57-65, in *Transactions of the Fourth Annual Re-union of the Oregon Pioneer Association for 1876* (Salem, 1877), pp. 57-65. Francis Parkman, *The Oregon Trail: Sketches of Prairie and Rocky-Mountain Life* (Boston: Little Brown and Co., 1894), pp. 51-53, 58-59, 80-82, 86-90. Benjamin G. Ferris, *Utah and the Mormons* (New York: Harper and Brothers, 1854), pp. 41-44. Jules Remy and Julius Brenchley, *A Journey to Great Salt-Lake City* (London: W. Jeffs, 1861), pp. 164, 196-201, 213-15. [R. H. Dana], *Two Years before the Mast: a Personal Narrative of Life at Sea* (New York: Harper & Brothers, [c. 1840]), pp. 98-103. Rev. Walter Colton, *Three Years in California* (New York: S. A. Rollo & Co., 1859), pp. 242-44, 246-48, 251-53. Bayard Taylor, *Eldorado or Adventures in the Path of Empire* (New York: G. P. Putnam and Son, 1868), pp. 54-60, 87-89, 92. Louise A. Clappe, *The Shirley Letters from the California Mines, 1851-1852*, ed. by Carl I. Wheat (New York: Alfred A. Knopf, 1949), pp. 131-37. William Gilpin, "Speech of Col. William Gilpin on the subject of the Pacific Railway delivered at Independence, Mo., at a mass meeting of citizens of Jackson County, Nov. 5, 1849," in appendix to William Gilpin, *The Central Gold Region* (Philadelphia: Sower, Barnes & Co., 1860), pp. v, 146-49; William Gilpin, "The Great Basin of the Mississippi," in *DeBow's Review*, XXIV (February, 1858), 159, 161, 164-65.

Part VII. Filling in the Last West:

Mark Twain, *Roughing It* (2 vols., New York: Harper and Brothers, 1871, 1899), I, 18, 21-22, 35-36, 39-40, 44-45, 70-71, 100-101. Grenville M. Dodge, *How We Built the Union Pacific Railway and Other Railway Papers and Addresses* (New York? Publisher? 1910?), pp. 15-16, 18, 28-30. J. H. Beadle, *The Undeveloped West; or Five Years in the Territories* . . . (Philadelphia: National Publishing Company, 1873), pp. 87-90, 92, 99-100, 131. [William F. Cody], *The Life of Hon. William F. Cody Known as Buffalo Bill, the Famous Hunter, Scout and Guide: an Autobiography* (Hartford, Conn.: Frank E. Bliss, 1879), pp. 161-67. Horace Greeley, *An Overland Journey from New York to San Francisco, in the Summer of 1859* (New York: C. M. Saxton, Barker & Co., 1860), pp. 81-82, 86-88, 90. General G. A. Custer, *My Life on the Plains, or Personal Experiences with Indians* (New York: Sheldon & Co., 1876), pp. 22-23, 24-27, 64-68, 142. John F. Finerty, *War-Path and Bivouac, or The Conquest of the Sioux* (Chicago: Donohue Brothers, [1890?]), pp. 101-105, 122-28, 130, 132, 135, 137. Greeley, pp. 157-60. Charles Wentworth Dilke, *Greater Britain* (2 vols., Philadelphia: T. B. Lippincott and Co., 1869), I, 166-69. E. C. Abbott ("Teddy Blue") and Helena Huntington Smith, *We Pointed Them North* (Norman: University of Oklahoma Press, 1955), pp. 5-8, 60-64, 67. Theodore Roosevelt, "Ranch Life in the Far West: In the Cattle Country," pp. 495-510, in *The Century Magazine*, XXXV (February, 1888), 495-96, 500-502, 505-507, 510. Mari Sandoz, *Old Jules* (Boston: Little, Brown, and Co., 1946), pp. 36-39, 142-44. Howard Ruede, *Sod-House Days: Letters from a Kansas Homesteader, 1877-78*, ed. by John Ise (New York: Columbia University Press, 1937), pp. 19-20, 27-29, 43, 91-92, 156. William W. Howard, "The Rush to Oklahoma," pp. 391-94, in *Harper's Weekly* (May 18, 1889), 391-92. "The Lane County Bachelor," quoted in Robert E. Riegel, *America Moves West* (New York: Henry Holt and Co., 1930), pp. 395-97. William A. Peffer, *The Farmer's Side: His Troubles and Their Remedy* (New York: D. Appleton and Co., 1891), pp. 68-74. Hamlin Garland, *A Son of the Middle Border* (New York: Macmillan Company, 1925), pp. 61-63, 147, 164-66, 234, 238, 244, 246, 308-310, 312, 353, 364, 367, 398-99, 403-404, 437-39.

Part VIII. A Meaning for the Westward March:

[Benjamin Franklin], *Observations concerning the Increase of Mankind, Peopling of Countries, &c.*, in [William Clarke], *Observations*

On the late and present Conduct of the French . . . (Boston: S. Kneeland, 1755), pp. 1-4.   Alexis de Tocqueville, *Democracy in America*, tr. by Henry Reeve (2 vols., New York: D. Appleton and Company, 1899), I, 38-41, 312, 316-17, 341-42; II, 482.   Anon., "The Progress of the Northwest," in *The Merchants' Magazine and Commercial Review*, III (July, 1840), 37, 39.   [E. L. Godkin], "Aristocratic Opinions of Democracy," in *The North American Review*, CCVI (January, 1865), 209, 217-19, 222-23, 232.   James Bryce, *The American Commonwealth* (3 vols., London: Macmillan and Co., 1888), III, 634-37, 640, 645, 647.   Frederick J. Turner, "The Significance of the Frontier in American History," in American Historical Association, *Annual Report, 1893* (Washington, D. C.: Government Printing Office, 1894), pp. 199-200, 215-23, 226-27.

BAYRD STILL writes with authority about the American West. He is a native of the Middle West and a graduate of the University of Wisconsin, which, because of the identification of Frederick Jackson Turner, Frederic L. Paxson, John D. Hicks, and Merle Curti with its faculty, has been traditionally the center for the study of the American West. Professor Still received his doctorate from Wisconsin in 1933. Since then he has been a member of the faculties of Ohio Wesleyan University, the University of Wisconsin-Milwaukee, Duke University, and New York University, where he is now Professor of History and Head of the History Department. Professor Still is the author, also, of *Milwaukee, the History of a City* (1948) and *Mirror for Gotham: New York as Seen by Contemporaries from Dutch Days to the Present* (1956).